WITHDRAWN

What Every Engineer Should Know
About Artificial Intelligence

What Every Engineer Should Know About Artificial Intelligence

William A. Taylor

The MIT Press
Cambridge, Massachusetts
London, England

PUBLISHER'S NOTE

This format is intended to reduce the cost of publishing certain works in book form and to shorten the gap between editorial preparation and final publication. Detailed editing and composition have been avoided by photographing the pages of this book directly from the author's prepared copy.

Library of Congress Cataloging-in-Publication Data

Taylor, William A.

   What every engineer should know about artificial intelligence/William A. Taylor

   p.   cm.
   Bibliography: p.
   Includes index.
   ISBN 0-262-20069-4
   1. Artificial intelligence. 2. Artificial intelligence--Data processing. I. Title.
Q335.T39   1988
006.3--dc19   87-35343

This book is dedicated to my parents, Arch and Margaret Taylor, who taught me the skills to write a book, and to my family, Roberta, Kenneth, Ronald, and Benjamin, who made the effort worthwhile.

Contents

Acknowledgments

I had a great deal of help from many people. Dick Morley provided a suitable environment. Bob Morley drew the pictures and demanded clarity. Art Habel passed a superbly experienced editorial eye over the text. Other people offered suggestions and, best of all, frank criticism.

Debugging text is harder than debugging programs—a computer is willing to read and criticize a program after each change as if it had never seen it before, whereas finding human text critics is difficult. Steve Rowley is a premier AI practitioner who was kind enough to read the manuscript and mark it up. His critical pen improved the book immeasurably. Thanks, Steve.

Harold Abelson of MIT made helpful comments.

I also received help from AI vendors. Gold Hill, Symbolics, and Texas Instruments all gave me experience with different Lisp systems at their facilities and told me about their customers. Eloquent Systems provided AI combat stories, and Flavors Technology let me use their computers and typesetting equipment.

Worchester Polytechnic and Frost & Sullivan forced me to broaden my experience by signing me up to lecture about AI, and Gould sponsored my first effort at writing an expert system.

What Every Engineer Should Know
About Artificial Intelligence

1
What Is Artificial Intelligence?

Artificial intelligence (AI) will have profound effects on engineering practice, but it is sometimes hard to see why. The popular definition of artificial intelligence research means designing computers that think as people do, and who needs that? There is no commercial reason to duplicate human thought because there is no market for electronic people, although it might be nice if everyone could have a maid and butler. There are plenty of organic people, and computer vendors can't compete with the modern low-cost technology used in making people.

Computers that think like people are far enough in the future that we can safely ignore them. From that point of view, AI research has failed because there are no computer programs anywhere that imitate human thought.

To be fair, AI is still very young. Atoms were thought to be indivisible for millennia after Aristotle invented atomic physics, and AI has moved faster than that. Research into how the human mind works forced the development of many new software tools and techniques that can greatly benefit the engineering profession.

For engineering purposes artificial intelligence is a few software ideas that work well enough for commercial use. These accidental offshoots of AI research are slowly but surely changing the ground rules of engineering practice. In this book I explain AI so that engineers can understand what is happening and prepare for it.

Engineering Opportunity in AI

People buy computers because they are useful, not just for the thrill of owning an electronic gadget. Engineers should care deeply about artificial intelligence because it makes computers more useful. A computer without software is like a newborn infant. Human hardware is available at the moment of birth, but it cannot be used without knowledge and experience.[1] Humans become more useful as they mature and learn; computers become more useful as new programs are written. AI tools and techniques help write new and useful programs.

Limitations of Computers in Engineering
Computer-aided design (CAD) systems are really electronic drafting boards. They bear the same relationship to T-squares, pencils, and drafting tables that word processors bear to typewriters. A CAD system erases and redraws lines as needed to describe a design. The computer serves as a high-cost replacement for a sketch pad, a pencil, and an eraser. Especially the eraser—computers are superb at erasing.

CAD systems are misnamed because they do not aid the *design* process at all. Design requires understanding a problem, imagining a solution, trying it, then changing the solution until it works. Computers reduce the effort required for documentation. This helps designers to focus their thoughts and convey the design to others who have to implement it, but generating documentation is not design.[2]

The associations between seemingly unrelated facts that constitute the core of creative design happen between the

---

[1] The brain grows larger as a child grows, but most of the growth seems to occur in the synapses, which wire neurons together. That would be like shipping a personal computer with all the ICs piled in the bottom of the case and adding circuit board traces to establish connections over time. This idea is explained in *The Amazing Brain*, by R. Ornstein and R. Thompson (Boston, Mass.: Houghton Mifflin, 1984), p. 69. However, Ornstein and Thompson later assert that there are more connections in infant brains than in adult brains and that development consists of pruning unneeded connections rather than growing new ones (p. 166).

[2] There are a few software packages which help with the design process. The ICAD package is discussed in chapter 4. Symbolics, Inc. uses the NS software package to design custom integrated circuits.

engineers' ears, not on paper or on a computer terminal.   Except for some aid in redrafting, computers are of little help in design. Computers cannot suggest changes because they understand neither the problem nor the solution.   Without understanding of goals and means, there can be no design.

This is not to say that computers have no place in engineering. Engineers abandoned slide rules for pocket calculators and personal computers, and mainframe computers carry out tedious calculations to verify designs. The difficulty is that the engineer supplies all of the design knowledge. The computer grinds out numbers but has no idea what they mean. Only humans possess the insight to attach meaning to the numbers, so only humans can tell whether the numbers are correct.

This is true even when the computer seems to be helping with the design.   Computer-aided engineering (CAE) workstations simulate electronic circuits to find errors. Electronic simulation programs are good enough that many products go directly from schematic to printed circuit boards, but calculating numbers according to a formula is not engineering. Circuit simulation serves essentially the same design verification function as stress analysis—the computer cranks out numbers showing voltage at any point in the circuit, but the engineer decides if the voltages are correct. The computer's task is purely clerical, albeit quite useful.

The Promise of Artificial Intelligence

AI promises that computers will be able to provide design help instead of being limited to clerical and numerical tasks. Researchers are beginning to put design rules into computers to help with the design process. Computers are beginning to ask, "Is that wire too long?" "Why not drill the hole bigger?" or "Are you sure the building won't sway during a hurricane?"

Computers that understand design rules will serve as electronic apprentices by taking over the simpler design tasks. Just as Michelangelo had his students paint backgrounds while he concentrated on major figures, computers will make suggestions and handle the simpler parts of the design.

Today's computers make many silly suggestions just like human novices, but as computers gain experience, computer programs will take over more and more of the mundane parts of engineering. Computers already check circuit design rules and verify manufacturability of printed circuit boards. They will soon calculate part routing in machine shops and devise assembly procedures.

Computers that know when to calculate stresses and that can make simple design changes will come with time.   Once computers take over some of the clerical parts of engineering, humans will have more time for creative work. We will be able to spend more time proposing new solutions and less time checking old ones.

Practical Impact of Artificial Intelligence

The practical fruits of AI research help to make computers more useful and to make it possible to apply computers to new fields. Opportunities to use computers in engineering are multiplying. Just as computers called "engineering workstations" altered the draftsman's job, using computers to help with design will change the engineering profession.[1]

Whenever computers are applied to a new problem, great changes occur. Anyone involved in computerizing accounting and financial management remembers that it was an unholy mess. The balance sheet did not balance. Paychecks were not distributed on time. Invoices were not sent out. After much hair pulling, computers were taught to keep accounts and things settled down. *But nobody saved any money!*   Accounting departments replaced armies of low-paid ledger clerks with platoons of high-paid programmers dwelling in air-conditioned splendor.[2] After accounting software matured, computerized accounting became cheaper than manual bookkeeping, but getting there took time.

Using computers in the design process will cause anguish and pain at first, but once the dues are paid, engineers will emerge from the fray with a whole new bag of tricks. The profession will improve beyond recognition.

The Intellectual Revolution

Artificial intelligence techniques are bringing about a revolution in the way people handle information. Engineers are essentially information processors. We wrinkle paper and make telephone lines hot; we do not shovel sand. We are paid for telling others

---

[1] Architects still argue about when it is best to use a pencil and when to use a computer. There are engine plants in Detroit where engineers redraw any computer-generated prints they receive because computers do not follow their notation conventions and the shop floor people prefer familiar drawings.

[2] *Fortune* magazine states that employment in the accounting departments of the 1,000 largest firms stayed constant in terms of bodies per dollar of annual sales throughout the computer revolution.

what we know, not for what we do. Computers will help us know more so we can be paid more.

Today's ditch diggers move more dirt than their ancestors not because they are stronger but because they have better tools. We will create better designs than earlier engineers not because we are necessarily smarter but because we have tools to help us think. Computer technology is bringing about a revolution in thinking. Engineers must participate in the intellectual revolution or be left behind, just as slide rule users were left behind when pocket calculators arrived.

Artificial intelligence has already begun to affect careers. This book explains the effects of the AI revolution on technical professions so that you can prepare.

Driving Forces behind AI

The major reason for the current interest in AI is the precipitous and sustained drop in computer costs. Figure 1.1 shows how computer costs fell and labor costs rose throughout the 1970s.

This figure holds the key to the current interest in artificial intelligence. It is not that AI research has produced any sudden breakthroughs—it is reasonable to claim that there have been no significant new ideas in AI since the late 1970s. Rather, interest in AI has blossomed because computers became cheap enough to permit wide use of AI and AI ideas.

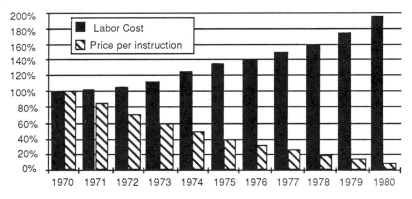

Figure 1.1
Graph comparing increases in labor costs with decreases in computing costs. Costs are normalized at 100% in 1970. Labor costs rose to almost 200% of the 1970 level by 1980, and computation costs dropped to about 10% by the same year. This continued after 1980, and it seems as if the trend will continue at least until the end of the century.

Adoption of any new technology depends on the relative cost of the new technology and of old ways of doing the same thing.

Computers long ago replaced humans for clerical tasks such as accounting. By the mid-1970s, computers could have replaced humans at some engineering tasks but were too expensive to make it worthwhile. Now that costs have dropped, entrepreneurs see new opportunities and are developing new engineering support tools based on AI.

Technologies for Human Emulation

Emulating human behavior requires many different technologies. Being human is a complex task,[1] so researchers divided their efforts into specialties: vision, speech recognition, natural language processing, locomotion, expert systems, planning, and automatic learning.

Vision is required for humanoid robots and would be helpful in factories because visual gauges do not touch the workpiece and do not wear. Vision systems have begun to creep into factories but are still very difficult for factory people to use.

Speech recognition is hearing a stream of human speech and identifying all the words. People do not really hear all the words during conversation. We deduce many words by understanding their context.

Natural language processing (NLP) means analyzing a string of words to decide what they mean. Conversation requires speech recognition to identify the words being said, NLP to understand what they mean, and speech synthesis to formulate replies. Speech synthesis is too simple to be a core part of AI.

Robotics researchers are trying to design machines that walk around like C3PO in *Star Wars*. Studying locomotion is not strictly part of the research into how the human mind works; it grew out of efforts to understand the parts of the brain that control motion. Two-legged walking has turned out to be extremely difficult to duplicate.

Expert systems encode knowledge in if/then rules. Computer programs embody human knowledge. All programs are the result of a human telling a computer how to do a task. Rules provide a new way of coding knowledge that saves time and money in some situations.

Planning is necessary for intelligent behavior. Building a successful robot requires computerized planning because the

---

[1] The more I study artificial intelligence, the more I appreciate the genuine article. Psalm 139:14 sums it up — "I will praise thee; for I am fearfully and wonderfully made: marvellous are thy works, and that my soul knoweth right well." It has been said that artificial intelligence is better than none. This is true, but only barely.

computer controlling the robot has to figure out how to move the robot's limbs in order to accomplish tasks. Planning research tries to find out how to solve such problems as screwing a nut on a bolt, maneuvering a machine through a crowded aisle, or opening a child-proof medicine container.

Automatic learning is the Holy Grail of AI research. Children are born with the ability to learn new ways of learning. If computers could learn by themselves, they would become intelligent over time. Although some game-playing programs record situations and moves that lead to defeat and try to avoid them, there are no computer programs that learn in the human sense.

Derivative Results of Artificial Intelligence

AI problems require extremely large computer programs that manipulate knowledge instead of numbers. Researchers invented new programming languages and new kinds of software development tools in order to attack these problems. These languages and tools have commercial applications. Using AI programming languages and software development tools seems to increase programming productivity by a factor of 3 to 10.[1] Because a lack of programs is limiting computer sales, anything that promises to increase software development productivity gets a lot of attention.

Lisp

Computers were originally invented to calculate artillery aiming tables more rapidly. Because of the need to express arithmetic equations, most programming languages are designed to deal with arithmetic expressions. They are designed to add, subtract, multiply, and divide. Conventional programming languages can tell the computer how to do anything that a pocket calculator can do.

Pocket calculators are all right so far as they go, but most expertise is not expressed in numbers. Human knowledge consists of abstract associations between symbols and ideas. Wisdom consists of rules, such as "Plant corn when the oak leaves are as

---

[1] The question of software development productivity is perplexing and controversial. Programmers believe that they get more done using AI techniques instead of other methods, but it is hard to prove this from objective evidence. Perhaps the best study of programmer productivity available was reported by Antonio Elias (*An Ad-Hoc Method for Estimating the Unit Cost of Aerospace Software*, FTL Memorandum M82-3, Cambridge, Mass.: Flight Transportation Laboratory, MIT, 1982). He presents evidence that Lisp is a significantly more productive programming language than any other.

big as mouse ears," or "Wine is a mocker, and strong drink a raging, and he who is deceived by them is not wise," or "Anything that can go wrong, will go wrong," or even "$F = ma$."

Such concepts are almost impossible to handle with conventional programming languages. Before AI research could really get underway, researchers needed a language that could manipulate symbols and the associations between them.

"Lisp" stands for "List processing," and is the name of a programming language invented in the early 1960s by John McCarthy at MIT. McCarthy designed Lisp to keep track of relationships between different kinds of information. Information is represented by symbols that stand for ideas, just as the symbols "dog" and "cat" stand for the idea of friendly furry domestic animals. Programming in terms of relationships between symbols is called "symbolic programming" and has been the key to efforts to understand human thought.

Purely by accident Lisp turned out to be commercially useful as well as academically interesting.

Software Development Tools

AI researchers developed special computer programs to help write other programs. Software developers produce far more function per unit of effort in the AI programming environment than in any other environment.

Powerful tools were desperately needed because early AI programs were the largest that had been written at the time. Researchers quickly saturated the biggest computers MIT could buy. Some computers had as many as 256,000 words, but programs outgrew memories that small by the mid-1960s.[1] Keeping track of all the parts of such large programs is a clerical task for which computers are well suited.

Commercial firms that adopt the software development tools and procedures pioneered in AI research centers eventually find that their software costs drop. When products such as microwave ovens, toasters, and washing machines are controlled by computers, software becomes important to more and more products. Firms that write software in less time or with fewer people than their competitors will have a significant advantage in the era of electronic appliances and software-based products.

The cost of the software in a microwave oven is not particularly high, especially when spread over thousands of units.

---

[1] Patrick Winston, director of the MIT AI Lab, said at a press conference at AAAI '87 that his portable personal computer has enough memory to have cost $3 million in 1967, when he began his AI work.

The advantage of having better software tools is that new software can be developed more quickly. The faster a company can develop new software and produce newer models, the easier it is to keep ahead.

One factor that contributed to the Japanese victory in the American electronics market was their ability to produce new models quickly. Sony introduces new models of the Walkman cassette player several times per year. Developing products this rapidly is not possible without superb engineering tools.

A Definition of Artificial Intelligence

Donald Knuth once said, "The difference between art and science is that science is what we can program into a computer. All else is art." Artificial intelligence covers so much intellectual ground that it can be difficult to define it much more precisely than that.

To me, AI is two unrelated things—human emulation that does not work and a few software techniques that are ready for use. I define AI as a programming style, where programs operate on data according to rules in order to accomplish goals.[1] To a chess-playing program, the data are the positions of the men on the board. Rules are the moves permitted in the game of chess and other rules that define strategy. The goal is to win the game.

This programming style corresponds to engineering practice. Data are supplied in the statement of the problem. Rules are the properties of materials, engineering lore, design experience, contents of technical manuals, the accumulated wisdom of the profession. The goal is to solve a problem—build a dam, bridge a river, make a circuit do something a customer wants badly enough to allocate resources to acquire it.

Upward and Onward

As AI technology matures, it will become easier and easier to encode rules of engineering practice in computers. Watching computers take over more and more engineering tasks will be absolutely fascinating to those who stay on top of the new techniques and extremely threatening to those who fall behind.

AI has moved out of the academic and intellectual stage and is showing signs of commercial worth. Welcome to the world of the artificial intelligentsia.

---

[1] This is a narrow definition of AI because it excludes everything AI researchers are doing except building bigger and better expert systems. This part of AI seems likely to have commercial potential sooner than other areas.

2
Humans and Computers,
Silicon Life and Carbon Life

Computers are not "thinking machines" or "giant brains" or any of the other terms commonly used to describe them in the early days. In this chapter I discuss some of the reasons why it is so difficult to program computers to exhibit intelligent behavior.

Life based on carbon compounds is made in both intelligent and unintelligent varieties, but the entire product line is built out of cells. Cells are made of a membrane wrapped around a bit of organic goo wrapped around a nucleus. The membrane collects raw materials from the environment and passes waste products out of the cell, the goo manufactures chemicals the cell needs to survive, and the nucleus contains the information needed to make more cells.

Silicon life is not manufactured in as many models as carbon life, and none of them is intelligent. Silicon life is based on transistors, which were invented in 1948. All that a transistor in a computer can do is switch current on and off. Transistors have no metabolism, cannot manufacture chemicals, and cannot reproduce themselves.

On a purely functional basis, cells seem to be much better components with which to build intelligence, but transistors have a major advantage. A transistor processes information much faster than a cell. If we knew how to connect up transistors to emulate human thought, silicon life would think *fast*.

Theory and Practice

In theory, the thinking performance of silicon life ought to be comparable to carbon life. A human brain has about 10^{10} neurons, and they seem to be able to change state by switching from on to off at peak rates of about 1,000 times per second. If all the neurons in a brain switch at once, the maximum compute power is about 10^{13} state changes per second.

The fastest supercomputer made has about 10^9 transistors, but transistors can change state 10^6 times as fast as neurons—about 10^9 times per second. If all the transistors are switching at once, the supercomputer has a compute capacity of 10^{18} transitions per second, or 5 orders of magnitude faster than a human brain.[1]

It should be possible to build computers that think faster than human minds, but computers cannot be made to think at all. Part of the reason is that only a small fraction of 1% of the transistors in a computer are switching at a time. This is because most computers are organized to do only one thing at a time, unlike the human brain, which does many things at once.

New computers incorporating many processors are being developed to do many different things at once. Although it is too early to tell, there is hope that these research efforts will lead to computers that are more intelligent and more useful than the computers of today.[2]

---

[1] Saying that a neuron switches 1,000 times per second may overestimate the switching capacity of the brain. Only the fastest neurons in the eye switch at 1,000 times per second, and most are much slower. The real rate does not matter much for the purposes of this comparison.

Neurons may transmit information using frequency modulation rather than amplitude modulation. That is, the rate at which a neuron switches is the signal, not the individual pulses themselves. If this is so, 1,000 transitions per second is the carrier frequency and not the data rate, and neurons generate information far slower than 1,000 transitions per second. The overall human neural system seems to be able to make a simple decision, such as jumping away from danger, in about 0.2 second, or five urgent decisions per second.

No one is sure what a neuron really does. Bernard Woodrow of Stanford University proposed a neuron model in 1964 in which a neuron could learn to play blackjack. If playing blackjack really takes only one neuron, it is not surprising that humans can work marvels given that we have so many.

[2] Putting many small computers in the same box and having them work on the same problem has been a research area for more than twenty years. It has always been much cheaper to buy many small computers than to buy one big one. A microprocessor costing about $10,000 executes 4 or 5 million instructions per

Status Report on AI Research

Setting the goal of emulating human thought was all very well, but researchers needed to know when the goal had been achieved. "Intelligence" is difficult to define rigorously, so AI researchers accepted a standard for computer intelligence known as the *Turing test*.

The Turing test is simple. An untutored human interrogator is alone in a room with two computer terminals. One terminal is connected to a computer, and the other is linked to another terminal with a human operator. The interrogator may type *anything* on either terminal—questions, statements, discussions of any topic. The operator wins if the interrogator correctly identifies the human. If the interrogator cannot differentiate between the human and the computer, the computer passes the test and is intelligent *by definition*.[1]

There are some nonobvious difficulties in passing the test because the computer must introduce typing errors and type slowly in order to seem human. The computer must emulate both human intelligence and human fallibility in order to be mistaken for a human. The Turing test does not measure pure intelligence any more than human IQ tests do but demands a mixture of abilities, including imitating human typing patterns. This mixture of skills is defined as intelligence for the purposes of the test.

Like IQ tests, the Turing test has the virtue of not requiring a definition of intelligence. Humans behave intelligently, so any computer that mimics human behavior is intelligent by definition. This reminds me of the method once used to weigh hogs in the Appalachian mountains. Nobody had scales. Farmers put the hog on one end of a balance pole and piled rocks

---

second. The world's fastest supercomputers run only 100 times faster but cost 2,000 times as much. Economies of scale do not apply to large computers.

One solution is to put many microprocessors in a box and run them in parallel. Nearly 30 vendors offer parallel computers but they have not made significant commercial impact yet. Parallel processing is subject to difficult software problems and requires new computer architectures. One of the most unusual parallel computers is described in *The Connection Machine*, by W. Daniel Hillis (Cambridge, Mass.: MIT Press, 1985).

[1] There is another definition of the Turing test. The human is a man pretending to be a woman; the computer pretends to be a woman. The computer is intelligent if the computer is chosen as the "woman." The details of the definition do not matter because no computer could imitate either a man or a woman today.

on the other end. When the hog and the rocks were in balance, they guessed the weight of the rocks. The Turing test is an *indirect* measurement. When computer intelligence and human intelligence balance, computers are intelligent.

The question of whether the Turing test is valid is moot as of today because no computer could fool any human interrogator for more than a few minutes. By the Turing definition, artificial intelligence is an utter failure. In engineering terms, however, AI succeeded because researchers accidentally discovered unexpected commercial uses for computers.

How Computers Work

Just about all commercial computers are based on the von Neumann architecture designed in the 1940s. With few exceptions, all computers from the humblest 1-bit microprocessor to the mightiest supercomputer are structured in essentially the same way. A computer has a memory that stores information, a processor that manipulates information in the memory, and some way to get information into and out of the memory.

The processor is often abbreviated "CPU," which stands for central processing unit. The CPU is responsible for all changes that happen to information while it is in memory. The CPU also decides when to write old data out of memory and when to read new information in.

Data are transferred between memory and devices such as disks, magnetic tapes, terminals, printers, card readers and other peripheral devices which are collectively called "I/O." Whenever the CPU decides to move data, it sends commands to an I/O device, telling it which data to move and where to put it.

The CPU and memory in a computer are usually put close together because information must pass between them quickly. Having the CPU too far from the memory would slow the computer down. I/O devices can be located further away because data move more slowly between memory and I/O devices. Terminals hundreds of miles from the computer can transfer data over telephone lines, but telephone lines cannot transfer data as quickly as the connections inside the computer.

Humans Operate Differently from Computers

There is an attractive similarity between computers and humans. It is almost impossible to resist the temptation to compare a CPU and memory to the human brain and I/O devices to our senses. Information flows into our memory through sight, sound, touch, taste, and smell. Our brain remembers the information, decides to take action, and sends commands to our muscles so that we speak or move around. This analogy is the origin of the term "electronic brain."

Assuming that things are alike because they look alike is a common error. In this case, although there are similarities in structure, computers and humans operate in fundamentally different ways.

Computers Require Explicit Programming

Computers are sensitive to events such as an operator pressing a key on a terminal, a printer finishing a line of print, or an interrupt telling the computer that enough time has passed that it is time to update its clock. Whenever a computer notices an event, it interrupts what it was doing to handle the event.

The first step in handling interrupts is bringing information about the event into the computer's memory. This tells the computer what happened—the event processor finds out the name of the key the operator pressed, tells which printer has finished printing and needs more text to print, or that the clock needs to be changed.

Once the computer knows what happened, it carries out instructions that tell it how to process the event. The event rattles around inside the computer for a while, finally generating some output. Each step along the way is handled by explicit instructions previously entered by a human programmer. The instructions tell the computer exactly what to do under every conceivable set of circumstances. Computers are the ultimate bureaucrats—they have no choice except to handle events according to previously defined procedures because they cannot make up new procedures on their own.

Handling Independent Tasks

Explicit programming suffices for independent tasks such as airline reservations. Although hundreds of seat requests may be processed at the same time, each transaction is essentially independent. The fact that Jones wants to fly between Boston and New York on June 7 has little to do with the fact that Smith wants a seat on the same flight.

Computers are unbelievably literalminded. Tell them, "Give out seats," and that is what they do.

Each event can be handled pretty much as if nothing else was happening. There is some interaction in that if two people are trying to get on the same flight at the same time, the computer ought to at least *try* to assign them different seats. Keeping resources from being assigned to more than one user at once can be fairly complicated, but solutions to that problem were devised many years ago.

Only a small number of situations come up when assigning airline seats because seats are either available or they are not. If too many reservations are issued or if two people are given the same seat, well, the flight attendants can always straighten out the mess—that is what humans are for.

Handling Interdependent Tasks

There is a major difficulty in using explicit programs to handle all the interrelated tasks needed to run an automobile plant. An engine factory a mile long and half a mile wide has as many as 300 or 400 complex machines running at the same time. Eight or ten machines make pistons, thirty or forty work together to make engine blocks, and so on. When everything goes right, the plant pushes out a couple of thousand engines per day. An automobile assembly plant running at a car per minute cranks out about $50 million worth of product on a good day. When vital equipment is broken, the plant produces nothing. Plant management has heavy incentives to keep things running.

Factory tasks cannot be treated as if they were independent because they are not. It would be wonderful if automakers could manufacture pistons without worrying about drilling holes for them and drill piston holes without worrying about piston sizes, but pistons and engine blocks cannot be treated separately because the two parts must fit together. If factories could make all of the pistons and all of the holes exactly the right size, they could be made separately, but machines precise enough to do that cost too much for automobile factories.

Automobile companies use cheaper machines that tend to drift. In order to ensure that the pistons will fit into the piston holes, process engineers watch the piston machine and the hole machine at the same time. If holes are coming out a tad big, the plant needs bigger pistons. If the piston machine is making them small, smaller holes are required. *Everything is related to everything else!* There are so many combinations of circumstances that no one can write programs providing instructions to handle every possible event.

Process engineers would rather give computers general guidelines about manufacturing practice and let them figure out how to handle events as they arise. Factory automation people are interested in AI because computerized factories *must* be rulebased in order to work at all.

Humans Operate with General Rules
In contrast to computers, humans do not operate according to explicit programming. Human memory is not well suited to remembering detailed procedures. When details are important, humans use checklists to make sure nothing is omitted. When details are vital, one human reads the checklist and another makes sure the first does not skip anything. Humans are poor at details, but they are superb at remembering overall rules of behavior and adapting rules to new situations as they arise.

Humans managing complex activities such as space shuttle launches and manufacturing automobiles do not remember every single detail. They learn broad patterns of how the situation ought to operate and adapt to events as they occur.

It takes a great many rules to operate well in a complicated domain. Chess grandmasters memorize on the order of 50,000 rules of chess strategy such as "Keep the knights away from the edge of the board."[1] Computers can store 50,000 rules, but cannot search through them rapidly enough to plan chess moves fast enough to win.

Human inability to remember details leads to mistakes. Space shuttle engineers knew that cold weather could endanger the seals on the booster rockets, but political considerations kept this information from being presented to the launch directors who made the decision to lift off. Human frailty with respect to detail caused the accident.

If computers could accept a little more rule-based programming, the combination of human ability to recognize overall patterns and the computer's ability to keep track of details would be an unbeatable combination.

---

[1] *The Sciences of the Artificial*, by Herbert A. Simon (Cambridge Mass.: MIT Press 1982), p. 106. Given a brief glance at a chessboard, chess grandmasters can remember 100% of the board position, masters about 90%; novices remember only five or six pieces. If the positions of the pieces are random instead of drawn from a valid game, grandmasters do about as well as novices in remembering the board layout. Masters seem to break a board down into "standard" chunks containing only a few pieces. See also *Thought and Choice in Chess* by A. DeGroot (Hawthorne, N.Y.: Mouton, 1965).

Computers Use Divergent Logic

When a computer accepts an event and it starts rattling around inside, the computer usually produces much more data than it received. A terminal operator at John Hancock enters a policy number and the computer prints the entire insurance history. The billing operator at the telephone company types a telephone number and the computer displays the last six months' bills. Kids push a button on an arcade game to fire a missile and the entire screen changes. The IRS puts in a social security number and out comes a tax history. Computers produce more output than input—they are all mouth and no ears.

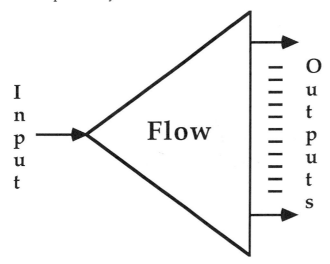

Information enters a computer, rattles around inside, and produces vast quantities of output.

This is partly because manufacturers know how to build better computer output devices than input devices. A television monitor that generates thirty pictures per second costs a few hundred dollars. Attaching a TV camera to a computer costs thousands of dollars, and the computer cannot make much sense of the picture anyway. Entry clerks type data at peak rates of ten characters per second, whereas line printers type data at twenty lines per second. Lack of good ways to get sensory information into computers has held back efforts to write programs that process real-world information effectively.

Humans Use Convergent Logic

Humans have much higher capacity input devices than output devices. Our eyes can resolve ten separate images per second. There are more than one million nerve fibers in the optic nerve running from the back of each eye to the brain, and each nerve transmits one point in the picture to the brain. Each eye sends the brain ten *million* picture elements per second, and the brain has no trouble processing this flood of information. Visual images are compared with memory, and decisions of what to do are made quickly enough to avoid threats.

When sending information out, the brain can call on only 600 muscles in the entire body. Some muscles are used for overhead functions such as breathing, digestion, and heartbeat. Some are really used for input because they move the ears and swivel the eyes. Having so few muscles for output, the brain can send out only a tiny fraction of the information it receives. Humans are all ears and no mouth.

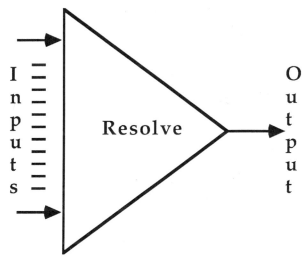

Humans have tremendous input bandwidth and limited output capability.

The earliest known human writing dates back to at least 3000 B.C. No one knows when speech was invented, but there are indications that people did not use speech very long before inventing writing. The fact that children can be taught to read within a year or two of learning to talk is supporting evidence for the idea that reading is a natural human activity in that it. uses neural pathways that occur naturally in the brain. Skills such as algebra, geometry, and solving differential equations, all of which are taught relatively late in the education process, seem not to be natural human activities.

AI Is Unlike Electronic Data Processing

Given these differences between computers and humans, it should not be surprising that AI research requires computers that are structured differently from those used for electronic data processing (EDP). Data processing installations handle many small transactions, such as reserving an airplane seat or hotel bed, adding or subtracting a payment from a customer's account balance, adjusting an insurance policy, or carrying out some other commercial activity.

Transaction processing usually requires an account number, a transaction type, and an amount, and generates a great deal of output. Most events observed by humans produce no output and are quickly forgotten. Events that justify the effort of a response are rare.

This is not to say that humans are lazy, only that most events do not affect us. Computers have the advantage of knowing that humans do not enter data unless the computer ought to be interested. Computers do not have to decide what is relevant and what is not because that decision is made by humans.

Computer hardware and human hardware are designed for different purposes and differ in many respects:

• Humans have more memory. The memory of a large computer holds at most 20-50 million characters, about as many as several sets of encyclopedia. Human memory holds *much* more information. Few people can remember large volumes of text, but we all remember thousands and thousands of detailed pictures of major events in our lives, with accompanying sound, smell, and emotional feelings.

• Computers can do more arithmetic. Arithmetic is of relatively little use to humans most of the time. If someone asks the cube root of 300, most people stall. If someone wants the cube root of 27, a few people can remember that it is 3. Very few can calculate it quickly.

• Humans retrieve information much more quickly than computers. If we are reminded of a long-ago event, we can recall a full-color picture of the event and run the picture forward and backward while we watch. We can retrieve the pictures without scanning through all our memories and somehow go directly to the right one. Computers deal with collections of information that are tiny by human memory standards. People think computers are fast because computers remember a different *kind* of information—people are not as skilled at remembering long, boring columns of numbers as computers are.

• Computers do one thing at a time, humans worry about many things at once. Software techniques called "multiprogramming" or "multitasking" make computers seem as if they are doing many things at once, but that is only a clever fake. The computer spends a little time on one task, then drops it for the next task. By switching between tasks quickly enough, the computer gives the illusion of working on all the tasks. Humans, in contrast, really do pay attention to many things at once. Engineers can get involved in a job and forget to eat, but no matter how hard we think, people react to sudden noises and know when to visit the toilet. Some people can read and converse at the same time, and Julius Caesar could dictate seven letters at once.

• Computers do things that are hard for humans; humans do things that are hard for computers. There seems to be a relationship between how young humans are when they learn a skill and how difficult it is to program a computer to do it. Infants learn to recognize their mothers early on. Despite a lot of research, no one has programmed a computer to recognize faces well. Toddlers can converse, but no computer comes close to their ability to understand speech. Children 10 or 12 years old can learn to drive cars, and a major research effort is slowly leading to an autonomous computerized vehicle that drives itself on highways. On the other hand, it takes a college education to do calculus or to learn accounting, and computers do both these tasks fairly well. The later humans learn a skill, the easier it is to teach computers.

Handling Life's Little Problems

Computers and humans are structured differently because they are designed to solve different problems. Suppose that I am bounding across the desert. I peek out from behind a rock and encounter an object. There is a question I must answer *very* quickly, and I had better answer it correctly: "Must I flee?" Get the wrong answer, and I probably never have to worry about anything else again, ever.

Most animals are biased toward flight. If a cat hears a sudden noise, it starts to run and looks back to see if it is safe to stop. Cats have been domesticated for a long time and are seldom threatened with dismemberment, but the flight reflex remains.

Assuming that I need not flee, I consider the question "Must I fight?" These two questions are so closely related that behavioral psychologists talk of the "fight or flight" reflex, but there is more to life than fleeing and fighting. Having decided not to fight, I ask, "May I feed?"

Having found an object that I need not flee or fight and on which I cannot feed, there is only one more possibility—"May I fondle?" If I need not flee or fight and cannot feed or fondle, I do the only sensible thing and forget it.

The human senses, nervous system, and memory are designed to answer these four questions quickly and accurately. Our eyes constantly flicker to and fro, scanning for threats. No matter how dull our lives, we listen continually for threatening noises.[1]

Human hardware is designed to answer these four vital questions quickly and accurately. All else is culture. Living creatures have no inherent interest in whether an engine has the right number of pistons, or whether airplane seats are assigned correctly, or if the balance sheet balances—these are cultural matters.

Who Needs Intelligent Computers?

These functional differences are the reason why we do not think there will be much demand for intelligent computers as long as computer intelligence is like human intelligence. People have

---

[1] Human male vision systems seem to have special cells that recognize women although women seem not to have special hardware to recognize men. See *The Amazing Brain*, by R. Ornstein and R. Thompson (Boston, Mass.: Houghton Mifflin 1984), pp. 170-171, for a discussion of some of the more obvious differences between male and female brains.

good pattern memories but have trouble remembering details. They have short attention spans and are subject to whim—in short, they are not suited for manufacturing or clerical work.

Computers, in contrast, are *almost* ideal. Their patience is limited only by how long people are willing to supply electricity. Their memory for detail is limited by the money spent for disk storage. Commercial uses demand computers that retain all these virtues and add just a *touch* of human ability to recognize patterns. A computer that said, "This design reminds me of the part you designed last year, and there were problems with early field failure," would be immensely valuable. A computer that said, "Things were a lot better around this place when we were making those parts last year," would not be as helpful.

A Robot's View   A Robot's Thoughts

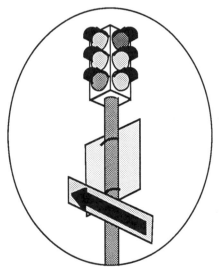

Query: Flee? No.
Fight? No.
Feed? No.
Attempt to Fondle!!
Result: Skinny, Big green
Eyes,
Nice Legs, Bright.
Decision: "Hey baby, I/O?"
Timeout.

Letting computers worry about details and recognize simple patterns while humans supply the imagination would lead to fruitful partnerships. We do not want intelligent computers competing with us. We want computers to complement our skills so we can do our jobs better. Computers should bring out the best in us, not make us feel inadequate. The ideal computer is like a spouse, not a competitor.

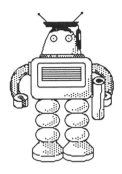

3
Results of AI Research

Ideas have flowed out of AI research labs in a steady stream since the field was founded. Some ideas found immediate application, some seem about to become useful, and many are unlikely to become valuable in the foreseeable future. In this chapter I discuss some results of AI research and explore their impact.

Human thought is such a complicated and mysterious process that even partial human emulation is a long way off. Despite this unfortunate delay, however, there are many results of AI research in commercial use.

Time Sharing

Early computers were so expensive that an entire university had to make do with only one, even with a government grant. Researchers tired of waiting for their turn on the computer and developed software to let many people share a computer at once. Most of the early work was done by project MAC at MIT. The name stood either for "multiple access computing" or for "machine-aided cognition" depending on whether professors were seeking grants for AI or for time sharing. Cynics stated that it stood for "man against computer."

Man-Machine Interfaces

One of the factors limiting computer use is difficult user interfaces. Hackers who appreciate computers for their own sake memorize arcane commands, but people who are more interested in getting the job done than in playing with the tool demand computers that can be used with little training.

People who do not use computers for a living usually ignore their computers except when they need them. If the commands are too complicated to remember between work sessions, the computer is essentially useless.

AI researchers are not always computer experts. They have backgrounds in biology, physiology, cognitive psychology, anthropology, and physics. Researchers are less tolerant of inconvenient computer tools than commercial users because they get paid for results, not for putting in their time. Not only that, programs to mimic human behavior were so large that even hackers could not cope unaided. In order to make progress, it was necessary to make research computers easy to use.

Making computers easy to use turned out to be so difficult that an entire subdiscipline grew up to address user convenience. Xerox's Palo Alto Research Center pioneered "windowing," a technique of dividing a computer screen among several tasks, as shown in figure 3.1.

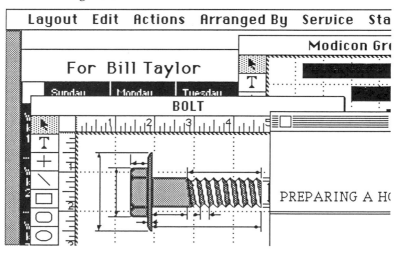

Figure 3.1
A portion of a window display. Output from many different programs can be viewed on the screen at the same time. Keyboard input goes to only one program at a time, of course.

Shared displays seem to be far too busy until users become accustomed to them, then most people wonder how they got along without them. Users edit programs in one part of the screen, look at input to their program in another, and see output from the program in a third. Displaying many tasks at once is like spreading many different sheets of paper on a desk—it helps people keep track of what they are doing.

Windowing spread from Xerox to Apple Computer, where it became the basis for the Apple Macintosh. Developing the software to manage overlapping windows smoothly is difficult and required many insights to get it right the first time. Even now, there are very few programming groups who can develop acceptable windowing systems.

Window systems are beginning to appear on engineering workstations and personal computers, but it has taken years of trial and error to get the software to work correctly. Even IBM fans concede that the Macintosh is easier to use. This ease of use is rooted in AI research.[1]

Natural Language Processing

Researchers have struggled to write programs that understand human languages since the late 1960s. It was originally thought that computers would soon translate freely from English into any other language. Software gurus spoke confidently of holding telephone conversations while a computer translated. Alas, computers *still* cannot translate human languages; translation evidently requires more knowledge about the meanings of words than anyone knows how to program into a computer.

Computers can understand human language *if the domain of discourse is simple enough*. The first program that demonstrated this was called ETAOIN SHRDLU[2], or SHRDLU for short, and was written by Terry Winograd in 1972.

---

[1] Even though Xerox did the fundamental research on how window systems ought to operate, Apple reaped the commercial rewards. The original idea was that the computer display should emulate a desk top. Papers hide one another on a real desk, so Xerox designed overlapping windows that hid one another. Now that Apple sells half a billion dollars worth of computers with overlapping windows every year, Xerox has decided that the fact that papers hide one another on a desk is a bug, not a feature. Instead of one window covering another so that the lower window is hidden, the lower window should shrink to make way for the upper window.

[2] "ETAOIN SHRDLU" is the alphabet ordered by letter frequency in English prose. The most common letter is "e" followed by "t" and so on. This order was the basis of the keyboard layout for the Linotype system. Typesetters would

SHRDLU understood commands about a fictional universe
called the "blocks world." The blocks world is a table, a pile of
children's blocks, and a robot arm. The human enters commands such as "Pick up the block which is taller than the one
you are holding, and put it into the box." SHRDLU figured out
what the commands meant and ordered the robot arm to move
the blocks as directed.

Blocks world is a very small universe. "Blue" is only a color,
not a mood or a kind of music. "Red" has no political over-
tones. "Pyramid" is a kind of block, not an Egyptian tomb or a
scheme for mail fraud. "Block" is not something that football
teams do on Sunday or a part of a city. Blocks world is simple
enough that most words have only one meaning. This made it
possible for Winograd to give the computer enough knowledge
to understand the words.

SHRDLU worked so well that many people assumed that the
problem of natural language processing had been solved. The
difficulty is that SHRDLU could not cope with ambiguity in word
meaning. Scaling it up did not enable computers to handle
realistically ambiguous problems. There will have to be many
insights into how people process natural language before computers will be able to understand natural language as readily as
humans do.[1]

Natural language processing can handle slightly more complex universes than blocks world. IBM offers a database retrieval
program called "Intellec™" which "understands" questions
about information in databases. When told to "List all the
salesmen in New York who are under quota," Intellec™ realizes
that the word "in" is usually followed by a place and that places
are found in the city or state columns in the database. It looks
for a match between whatever follows "in" and a city or state in
the file.

---

run their fingers over the keyboard whenever they wanted a temporary lead
slug to fill some space. References to "ETAOIN SHRDLU" appeared when
printers forgot to take the spacers out.

[1] Skeptics are invited to meditate on the knowledge required to understand
this conversation between a colleague and me as I passed his desk on my way to
the soda machine:

"Hey Bob, can you break a buck?"
"Don't bother, it's unlocked. Just push the button."

or this interchange between a 12-year-old girl and her mother:

"Mom, where can I find a needle?"
"Top right drawer of my dresser."
Three minute pause
"Mom, how old were you when you had your ears pierced?"

In this case, Intellec™ finds "New York" in both the city column and the state column and asks the user to resolve the ambiguity. When analyzing the query, "Which of the New York employees live in Buffalo?" Intellec™ knows that cities are located in states and that "New York" refers to the state.

Human languages are riddled with ambiguities. Children learn to deal with ambiguous statements over a period of years, but computer scientists have a great deal of work to do before computers can progress much beyond data retrieval.

Users find that Intellec™ increases the volume of database requests by a factor of 10 or more. This is not surprising. Whenever anything becomes easier, people do more of it whether it is worth doing or not. Increasing the volume of retrieval requests has a predictable result—the first $10 million in Intellec™ sales generated about $30 million worth of additional business for IBM. Artificial intelligence is a *great* way to sell more computers.

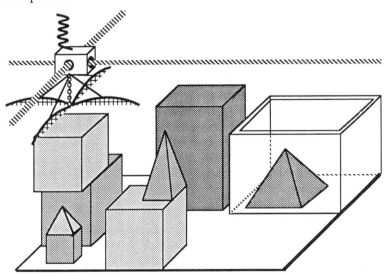

Drawings of the "blocks world" are common in AI publications. Writing a program to move a picture of a robot arm is much easier than writing a program for natural language processing.

Expert Systems

Expert systems get a disproportionate share of media attention. Reporters seem to feel there is something magical about knowledge-based systems, as if all prior efforts were based on ignorance. Reporters' interest in expert systems may be justified, because some expert systems are beginning to make money.

The central idea behind expert systems is expressing computer knowledge in the form of rules such as

if the AC light and the DC light on a power supply are both off
then check to make sure that the device is plugged in

Rules are a handy way to express certain kinds of human expertise, just as equations are suitable for expressing other kinds of information. In chapter 10 I explain that there is a great deal more to expert systems than rules.

Logic Programming

Expert systems are based on the rules of mathematical logic, just as conventional programs are based on the rules of arithmetic. Prolog, which stands for "programming in logic," was invented to express mathematical logic in computer notation. This is necessary in order to use rules in computer programs. The result is a style of computer usage called "logic programming" or "rule-based programming."[1]

Prolog is a primitive language just as Fortran was when first introduced, but the introduction of logic notation to computers was as important a development as the first use of algebraic programming in the late 1950s. Expert systems should become more intelligent and easier to use as logic languages develop.

In chapter 8 I explain the basics of rule-oriented programming in order to prepare for a discussion of expert systems in chapter 9. Logic programming is discussed in more detail in chapter 10 and Prolog in chapter 13.

Object-Oriented Programming

Object-oriented programming is a way of structuring programs so that a particular type of data and the parts of a program that process that type of data are combined. Data and the functions that process them are collectively called an "object." Objects are manipulated as a unit; code and data cannot be separated.[2]

---

[1] Prolog was not the first language to use rules. Planner seems to have been the first rule-based language. As with most innovations, the roots are difficult to unravel because so many people contributed to the idea.

[2] Xerox developed the first commercial object-oriented programming system. Their Smalltalk language reached a reasonably stable state by 1972. Smalltalk systems are available for the IBM PC, the Apple Macintosh, and for a line of AI workstations marketed by Tektronix Inc. No one has figured out

Thinking in terms of objects makes it easier to organize and maintain large computer programs. Once the interface to an object has been defined, programs that manipulate it do not care how any of the code associated with an object works. For example, a transportation management program might define objects of the type "ship." Each ship records its latitude and longitude, the cargo it can carry, the crew size, and other information. The scheduling program must be able to find out where a ship is. This requires a piece of code that looks up a ship's latitude and longitude and returns the position.

Structuring ships as objects makes it easy to change the way in which information about ships is stored. Suppose that it later turns out to be better to store ships' locations in polar coordinates instead of latitude and longitude. If the software were written using conventional programming methods, developers would have to examine every part of the program that used a ship's position and change it to reflect the new way of storing position information.

The definition of the ship object defines all data about ships and the code to manipulate the data. The only way other programs can find a ship is to ask the object for its location. A developer can change the part of the object that looks up the ship's position to convert polar coordinates to latitude and longitude. No other parts of the program are affected by the change because they receive latitude and longitude as before.

Object-oriented programming has little to do with emulating human thought. It was invented because AI programs are so big that conventional ways of organizing software systems did not work. There is nothing magical about object-oriented programming. It only formalizes good software design principles, but it is a worthwhile result of AI research. There is more information about object-oriented programming in chapter 8.

Spreadsheets

Spreadsheet programs such as Visi-Calc and Lotus 1,2,3 are based on an AI idea known as "constraint propagation." A spreadsheet is a collection of cells that are displayed on a computer screen. Input cells contain numbers, and output cells contain mathematical expressions that refer to numbers in other cells. The number displayed by an output cell is the result of applying the expression in the cell to numbers stored in other cells.

---

why Xerox has been unable to profit from this and other equally important discoveries made at their Palo Alto Research Center.

Whenever a user changes a number in an input cell, all output formulas that refer to that number are recalculated. When these calculations are completed, formulas that refer to the changed output cells are recalculated, and so on until all affected numbers have been updated. The formulas apply constraints on the values displayed in their cells. These constraints are propagated through the entire spreadsheet whenever an input is changed.

Constraint propagation was an old idea when two entrepreneurs, Dan Bricklin and Bob Frankston, introduced the first commercial spreadsheet program in 1979. Their innovation was to package the idea of constraint propagation behind a matrix of cells that looked like multicolumn accounting paper. Financial people who made their living manipulating sheets of numbers found that Visi-Calc saved considerable time and bought enough copies to found an industry.[1] There are probably many ideas of equal commercial merit[2] lurking in AI labs just waiting for someone to market them properly.

AI Technologies That Do Not Work Well Yet

There are many areas of AI research that seem to be about to produce profitable results. It makes business sense for a technical company to be ahead of the competition, but not too far ahead. If a product is too advanced, the market is not ready to accept it, and it costs too much to educate customers enough to get them to buy. Taking technical risks to enter new markets is

---

[1] After enough copies of Visi-Calc had been sold to demonstrate that there was a market for spreadsheet software, an employee of the inventors named Mitch Kapor suggested several improvements. The inventors were busy trying to control their explosive growth and told Mr. Kapor to get back to work. He quit, raised money, and founded Lotus Development Corp to sell a rival spreadsheet called Lotus 1,2,3 which came to dominate the spreadsheet market. It is common for technical innovators to be eclipsed by others who understand the market implications of the invention better than the original entrepreneurs.

[2] In the sense that a natural language is anything that many people know, spreadsheets can be thought of as natural language computer interfaces. There is nothing spreadsheet users do that cannot be done by writing a program in Basic or C or Lisp, but most people are unwilling to learn these languages. By turning computer programming from arcane mumbo-jumbo into the process of manipulating familiar columns of numbers, spreadsheets made computers accessible to millions of new users, earning millions of dollars in the process.

There are probably other opportunities to computerize "languages" that are already known to potential customers. The statement "knit one, purl two decreasing every row" is perfectly intelligible to millions of knitters. There may be a market for a computer that understands "knitting language."

often worthwhile. Most old products are difficult to sell except in special circumstances. Ivory Soap goes on forever, but technical products become obsolete rapidly.

The ideal position is *just slightly* ahead of the competition—advanced enough to command a premium price, yet not so far ahead as to make customers nervous or make life difficult for component suppliers. Using yesterday's technology to solve tomorrow's problems seems to pay off well.

Investors and entrepreneurs sift technology for commercial opportunities. Sometimes a company tries to develop a new product even if they think the project is likely to fail because the potential rewards are so great. That is why so many companies have developed industrial robots—the present market is small, but sales would be immense if robots could be made practical.

At other times, companies develop products even if they are not sure who will buy them because the technology is so fascinating. Once in a great while, a product developed for the sake of technology turns out to be successful, but technology-driven products often end in commercial failure.

Failure is more common than technical innovators like to admit. Engineers enjoy developing new features, but users only pay for benefits. Product developers often forget that users do not buy technology, they pay to have their problems solved. If technology is absolutely necessary to solve the problem, customers will tolerate it, but only until a less technical solution is available.

Robotics and the Factory of the Future

Robots are in the "barely viable" stage. Despite tremendous interest in robots and many experiments using robots, industrial robot sales are only a bit more than $300 million per year.[1] In economic terms, annual robot sales are about as important as the movie industry and come to about one month's computer sales for Digital Equipment Corporation.

The Japanese claim to have many more robots working in their factories than Americans do. This is partly a matter of definition. The Japanese define a robot as any machine that picks up parts and moves them around. Americans think of "pick-and-place" devices as machines, not robots, and argue that Americans have as many pick-and-place robots as the Japanese.

Regardless of which country is using robots more effectively, the fact remains that programmable controllers, which are an

---

[1] Industrial robot sales should reach $370 million in 1987 and $1 billion by the mid-1990s according to *Fortune* magazine (September 14, 1987, p. 82).

older form of factory automation, sell at least $500 million per year in the United States. For all the interest in robotics, robots have had a minimal impact on most factories.   The robot market is limited because robots are difficult to use under realistic factory conditions.

The popular idea behind factory robots is C3PO in a hard hat slaving away on the assembly line, but this is unrealistic. No one expects robots to have a major impact on high-volume manufacturing. Manufacturing more than 1,000 parts per day usually justifies the cost of custom-made machines. A machine designed to do just one job costs less than a robot that can do many different jobs. Machines used in high-volume production usually wear out before the part becomes obsolete, so it makes no sense to pay extra for a flexible robot.

Low-volume manufacturers would like to buy one machine and make many different parts with it. Most parts are produced in batches of fifty or fewer, and this is the natural market for robots. The problem is that factories are full of machines that were designed to be operated by humans, and parts designers are accustomed to designing parts to be made by such machines. A computer-operated machine has different capabilities from a human-operated machine. Before robotic machines can be used to full advantage, parts designers need to learn new techniques to design parts so that computers can make them easily.

Difficulties Controlling Robots   Computers which control robots are extremely difficult to program. Making each part requires a separate computer program to tell the robot how the part should be made.   Like human machinists, robot machinists need instructions which they can understand.

There simply are not enough part programs available to make robots useful. Just as personal computers could not achieve wide sales until there were enough programs to make people want to buy them, robots will find limited application until there is enough high-quality software available.

It costs so much to program a robot to make a part that unless a factory can spread the programming cost over many parts, it is usually cheaper to make them manually. Unfortunately for robot vendors, if a customer needs enough parts to justify the cost of programming a robot, engineers can often justify the cost of special tooling. If the order is too small for special tooling, it is usually cheaper to make the parts by hand.

Sensor Problems   The main difficulty in programming robots is that computer programs must be precise. Every possibility must be anticipated and special instructions have to be written to deal with every possible contingency. Unfortunately for robots, factories are not precise environments. Part dimensions vary, tools and jigs wear over time. Manufacturing staff must make precise parts in spite of these variations.

It is hard for computers controlling robots to cope with these variations because there are few sensors that work well with robot arms. The computer can usually determine the bending angle of each joint in the robot arm and tell how far apart the fingers are spread, but that is about all.

The computer is like a sightless person whose fingers have been deadened by Novocain. Blind people can screw nuts on bolts using their sense of touch. Sighted people can put nuts on bolts even if their fingers are numb. Controlling a robot is like being both blind *and* numb.

Sensors for Robots Researchers are developing touch sensors for robot fingers and hope that improved sensors will help robots adapt to changing circumstances. However, additional sensor information will not help unless computers can be programmed to know what to do with it.

There is evidence that touch sensors are not really necessary if the computer controlling the robot is smart enough. Watching backhoes at work reveals that a backhoe operator can encounter a large rock way down in the bottom of a ditch out of sight, and then feel around with the bucket to find out how big the rock is and where it is located.

Backhoe operators know what the arm has encountered by listening to the sound of the engine and getting the "feel" of the controls. They do not need sensors on the arm. Just knowing how the controls feel suffices. Maybe computers which control robots will not need sensors once they become smart enough.

Advantages of Organic Robots For all their defects, such as limited attention span and periodic tea breaks, organic robots have a tremendous advantage over mechanical robots. People can read blueprints, specifications, and assembly instructions. Experienced machinists resolve ambiguities and even fill in gaps in the instructions. This saves a great deal of design time.

Teaching a robot to read blueprints well enough so that it would no longer need to be programmed requires that computers be capable of natural language processing, process planning, and motion planning, all of which are extremely difficult.

Until mechanical robots are demonstrably more efficient, economical, flexible, and reliable than organic robots, factories will continue to use organic robots. Replacing human factory workers with machines is a gradual process that is not happening nearly as fast as pundits claim.

Speech Recognition

Devices that can recognize a few hundred spoken words have been on the market for several years. Most speech recognition systems are trained separately to recognize each user's voice. Limited vocabularies are useful in materials handling applications because a warehouse clerk can tell the computer what is in a box while moving the box. The operator can do the job and tell the computer about it at the same time.

The biggest problem is deciding where one word stops and the next begins because people do not pause between words when speaking. Some researchers speculate that the speech recognition problem cannot be solved until computers understand what they are hearing. Humans seem to recognize words from context as much as from hearing then precisely.

There would be an immense market for a reasonably priced device that could recognize 2,000 to 3,000 words—executives could tell the computer to "take a letter."[1]

Computer Vision

It is easy to describe how computer vision should work: Attach a TV camera to a computer, point the camera at a scene, and have the computer list the objects in the camera's field of view. Vision is far easier done than said. People see without difficulty, but no one can say how vision works. There is a saying: "There is more to vision than meets the eye."

The earliest efforts were directed at "feature extraction," which finds significant parts of a scene and tries to make sense of them. Researchers are not exactly sure what features our eyes extract from a visual image but have shown that the eye is sensitive to edges, color contrast, texture, and certain kinds of shading.

Having located features in a visual scene, the problem is to match the features with objects in memory to see what is going on. Even though a Nobel prize was awarded for research in how simple creatures such as snails store information, we do not

---

[1] There are many speech recognition systems on the market. Most of them have vocabularies limited to less than 100 words and have to be trained to recognize each individual speaker. IBM has a prototype that recognizes thousands of words, but it has to be trained for each speaker and is too expensive for general use.

fully understand how features are stored in memory or how stored features are matched against features found by the eyes.

Feature extractors are good enough that vision systems can be used for certain kinds of quality inspection and measurement and can read letters written clearly in several different fonts. Computer vision is at a stage similar to robots: If it worked well in factories there would be an enormous market, but it does not.

Like robots, vision systems are difficult to use. Camera placement is critical, light levels have to be adjusted precisely, focus must be maintained, lenses must be kept clean, and many other finicky details must be attended to. When vision systems work, they work well, but keeping them working seems to be beyond the capabilities of most factory maintenance people.

Automatic Programming
Programming is the act of telling a computer how to do a task. Human programmers must first understand the task, then explain how to do it in a language the computer understands. Computers always do exactly what they are told. The difficulty is telling them exactly what we mean.

Computers are unbearably literal minded. When a dog is on the other side of a fence and I tell it, "Come here," the dog usually goes away and runs around the fence in order to carry out the command. If a dog were no more intelligent than a computer, it would run straight at me until it hit the fence, then keep pawing away trying to "Come here" until its legs wore off.

The computer obeys the letter of the command and either comes straight to me or busts a gut trying. The dog does not do *exactly* as it is told—it starts out by going away when told to come—but owners prefer that dogs obey the spirit of the command rather than the letter. Teaching children and subordinates to do what I mean rather than what I say is difficult and frustrating, so it should come as no surprise to learn that teaching computers to do what users mean instead of what they say is difficult and frustrating.

There are signs that computers will be able to generate certain kinds of programs automatically. Some mechanical design systems generate tapes to guide computer-controlled machines to cut out parts. Programs called "application generators" translate pseudo-English task descriptions into computer programs. Application generators do not quite go directly from a memo describing the task in English to a completed program but are moving in that direction.[1]

Technologies That Will Not Work Soon

There are some problems in imitating human capabilities that seem so difficult that nobody has any idea when they will be solved. That makes them worthwhile for research. There is almost no chance that a researcher in human cognition will have to worry about making a career change.

The difficulty with these areas is not lack of memory or computing capacity, but lack of insight. We need many major intellectual breakthroughs—no one knows how many—before we will know how to build intelligent computers. Breakthroughs are notoriously difficult to predict, so it is hard to say when computers will start to think.

Common Sense

Nobody can define common sense, but everybody knows immediately when someone else fails to exhibit it. Computers not only do not know when to come in out of the rain, they cannot even tell it is raining without instruments to measure moisture and programming to interpret the data.

Life is so complex that parents cannot give children exhaustive lists of what to do under every possible circumstance. Parents teach general principles—rules, if you will—and hope for the best. Expert systems are beginning to be able to operate from rules, but the rules have to be extremely detailed. Expert systems have a long way to go before exhibiting common sense.

Planning

People plan so often and so naturally that we seldom notice when we do it. Simply rising from a chair and leaving a room requires that many separate motions be carried out in order: leaning forward, raising the body, turning toward the door, walking to the door, turning the handle, swinging the door, walking through it, closing it, and so on. Independent of the fact that robots lack the mechanical dexterity to perform such

---

1 Applications generators are becoming common in electronic data processing. Most transaction processing applications are similar enough that the code to handle transactions can be generated once the user fills in a form telling the computer what to do. Referring to this as "automatic programming" is a bit of a misnomer because overall directions of what to do still come from a human who understands the task well enough to explain it to the computer.

stupendous feats, computers cannot figure out the steps to move from point A to point B.

Factory managers must plan how to move equipment and materials. Large items are rotated and occasionally moved backward in order to get to the proper place. People do such things easily, but computer programs for planning are still a major research area.

Learning from Experience
A few game-playing programs record victories and defeats and attempt to draw on the records for hints of how to play. Expert systems learn, but only by having humans fix bugs in rules or write new ones. No computers learn automatically, even from carefully chosen examples.

Humans are born knowing how to learn, and that seems to be enough to get started. Our learning is extremely flexible, but it is conditioned by what we must learn. People who grow to maturity in jungles where the horizon is not visible have difficulty seeing horizontal lines. Eskimos raised in the Arctic have difficulty seeing vertical lines. Adults find it hard to learn the sounds of a new language, but children find it easy.

Analogies
People understand analogies well—apt analogies are an effective way to explain unfamiliar concepts. Computers cannot generalize their abilities from one task to the next. Suppose that a robot is programmed to paint doors in an automobile factory. If the design changes, engineers would like to say, "Just like the one last week, except a little more paint along the bottom," but this does not work. Programming starts from scratch as if the robot had never seen a door before.[1]

Creativity
Human creativity seems to be based on unforeseen combinations of existing ideas. Henry Ford combined the idea of the automobile with assembly line techniques developed by Sears Roebuck, and the mass automobile industry emerged. Automobiles had existed for a long time and Sears had been

---

[1] Patrick Winston, director of the MIT AI Lab, has written a program that draws analogies between situations in different Shakespearean plays. This work is described in *Learning and Reasoning by Analogy* (AI Lab Memo 520, April 1979) and *Learning by Augmenting Rules and Accumulating Sensors* (AI Lab Memo 678, May 1982).

using assembly line methods to fill catalog orders for years, but no one had combined these ideas before Ford.

Thomas Edison developed the electric light bulb by running electricity through a carbon thread enclosed in a vacuum to keep it from burning up.   Carbon arc lights were well known but the electrodes burned too fast to be practical for homes.   Vacuums had been investigated for a hundred years before Edison, but he was the first to put the two together.

Computers with unlimited disk storage ought to be able to remember more knowledge than humans and therefore have more to draw on when making creative associations.   The difficulty is that the number of possible associations grows rapidly as the amount of knowledge increases.   It takes human insight to know which combinations to try.

Nobody knows how people limit the number of possibilities to a manageable number.   When researchers figure that out, it may be possible to generate creativity mechanically.   Until then, we have to make do with human creativity, erratic as it may be.[1]

The State of the Art

To speak of the "march of science" is to speak nonsense.   Science does not march; it crawls on its belly, tripping over every leaf and twig in its path.   AI researchers originally thought that they could knock off vision and speech recognition over a summer or two, then get on to the *real* problems.   It has not turned out that way; vision and speech recognition remain mysterious.   Human input/output devices are complex enough to baffle the most intense scrutiny, to say nothing of the CPU itself.

AI techniques and ideas work well enough for a number of commercial applications, however, and some of them are discussed in the next chapter.

---

[1]   Doug Lenat developed a program called "AM," which makes mathematical discoveries.   AM rediscovered many truths already known to human mathematicians but has not come up with anything people did not already know.   See *Knowledge-Based Systems in Artificial Intelligence,* by R. Davis and D. Lenat (New York: McGraw Hill, 1982).   Lenat also wrote a program called "Eurisko," which could learn to play certain games well enough to defeat human players.

4
Applications of Artificial Intelligence

The main question that fans of artificial intelligence must answer is, Who needs it? AI experts have trouble handling this question well. AI is such a fascinating subject that technical people study it for its own sake and forget that the people who supply the money want tangible results. In this chapter I describe several commercially successful uses of AI technology.

A major part of the problem of convincing skeptics that AI is useful is the unfortunate fact that the main thrust of AI research—the emulation of human intelligence—has yielded few if any results. Skeptics such as Hubert Dreyfus write books about the limitations and failures of AI research.[1] This sort of background noise makes it difficult to persuade anyone of the merits of AI.

Another difficulty is that most AI programs are written in Lisp. Although it is not necessary to use Lisp to take advantage of the lessons of AI research and users rarely care what language

---

[1] Hubert Dreyfus is a vociferous critic of the part of AI that deals with human emulation. His thesis is that computers can never become intelligent because they are made of transistors, whereas minds are made of neurons. This argument is bolstered by the fact that there are no computer programs that exhibit any intelligent behavior. On the other hand, when Lord Rutherford stated that no one would ever split the atom, he was wrong.

a program is written in so long as it works, most of the useful ideas from AI research are most easily expressed in Lisp.

Lisp is covered in detail in chapters 5 and 6. It is strikingly different from any of the programming languages people are accustomed to. Engineers forget how much it costs for a firm to adopt a new programming language. New compilers and other software tools have to be investigated, selected, and purchased. People must attend classes and usually have to abandon large parts of their prior experience. New and different equipment must be put in the capital budget, argued over, specified, purchased, then finally installed and maintained.

Switching from C or Fortran to Lisp is a much rougher transition than going from Fortran to C or vice versa. Management has had enough experience with unexpected costs during changes in technology to be skeptical of any claimed benefits.

Problems with Management

There are a number of problems associated with using AI that have nothing to do with technology. Cultural difficulties are often harder to deal with than technical problems. Technical problems do not fight back; cultural problems keep cropping up.

Short-Term Outlook

A major factor holding up adoption of AI ideas and techniques is that American management demands a quick payback from new technology. Depending on the current interest rates, a new paper mill or new automobile assembly plant with an eight-year payback period may be acceptable. New technology, on the other hand, seems to require an almost guaranteed instant payback for management to be interested.

Preoccupation with Perfection

AI projects that are allowed long development times tend to stay in a research environment forever. Developers are reluctant to let a system out the door. They always want to add "just one more rule."

Most large expert systems developed in the United States are concerned with medical domains.[1] Our society expects absolute

---

[1] People argue about how many "large" expert systems have been developed and then argue some more about whether or not these expert systems have paid back their development costs. DEC has an expert system called "XCON" that they claim is saving them $20 million per year. GE developed an expert system to help repair diesel locomotives, but because it runs on a PDP-11, it is probably not a "large" system. British Petroleum has an expert system called "GASOIL"

perfection from the medical system, and customers sue for vast sums when perfection is not forthcoming. No computer programmer wants to be hit with a medical malpractice lawsuit. Programmers would rather keep on tweaking than let their creations out the door to face the cold, cruel, litigious world.

It is natural for technical people to want to keep a project under wraps until it is perfect, but the search for perfection delays the payback. One of the more difficult management decisions is knowing when to say, "Shut up and ship it."

A Different Culture
The American preoccupation with short-term returns is not as strong in other countries. The Nanjing College of Traditional Chinese Medicine has been working on an expert system for traditional Chinese medicine since 1978. The project has incorporated about one-fifth of the knowledge of a group of senior physicians into a computer program.

Even though the system is only 20% complete, it has been field tested in ten Chinese provinces. In the first two years after the system was installed in Xinjiang province, over 800 patients were treated for liver disorders. The college has also developed software for using acupuncture for weight loss and has treated many outpatients there.

American management typically allows about six months for a prototype system to be developed, and then another six months for the system to achieve perfection. It is hard to imagine an American corporation allowing a group of doctors and programmers to spend eight years on 20% of a project.

Field tests of a partial system are also a departure from American practice. China has a more forgiving legal system than America. Giving patients access to a computer program only one-fifth as knowledgeable as a human expert is better than the level of medical care that would be available without the computer, so releasing the program benefits society as a whole.

It would be ironic indeed if the latest and greatest in software technology—AI and expert systems—are first used in low-tech areas of the world because of such cultural problems, but things could turn out that way.

---

that is reputed to have more than 8,000 rules. The IRS is working on an expert system to help decide whose tax returns to audit, but this system is not yet in use. Regardless of how "large" expert systems are defined, it is inarguable that the earliest large systems were developed for medical applications.

The Proof of the Pudding

The only way to prove to management that AI techniques are worth investigating is to point to the results of other AI projects. Although there have not been as many different kinds of expert systems developed as one might like, there are enough successful examples that it might be possible to induce management to take a flyer or two on new technology.

A study by Arthur D. Little Inc. showed that more than half of the increases in industrial productivity throughout history have been due to new technology. The only way for average consumption to increase is for productivity to increase—if the goods do not exist, it is hard to consume them, regardless of government policy. AI is a new technology. Like all new technologies, adopting it brings risks but also offers opportunities. The uses of AI described in this chapter may suggest ways in which AI can bring benefits to other firms.

Applications

AI ideas are not unique to AI professionals, and some of the applications in this chapter used AI ideas without knowing it. Many customers think that AI is strange, exotic, and hard to manage, so these companies vehemently deny that they have anything to do with AI. I categorize them as accidental AI.

Profit, of course, has no respect for technology. Customers do not care how a product works, so long as it works and keeps on working. Even a world-class ideologue like Chairman Dengof China was pragmatic enough to ask, "Who cares what color a cat is so long as it catches mice?" Accidental AI is as worthy of economic success as deliberate AI. Lucky is just as good as smart and often better.

I include some examples of conventional projects that use AI tools or Lisp machines to cut costs because extremely advanced software tools were an outgrowth of AI research. Better software tools reduce the cost of developing software. A large enough cost reduction can make the difference between a project being possible and being impossible.

These applications are deliberately difficult to categorize because I want to give an idea of the range of potential uses of AI. Applications are discussed in alphabetical order by the name of the firm that paid for the work.

Andover Controls: Building Energy Management

Andover Controls was founded during the energy crisis when it seemed that every American home would need a solar energy system to keep warm during the winter. Solar energy systems are considerably more complex than conventional oil burners and need much more elaborate controls.

An oil furnace has two thermostats, an oil burner, and a fan. The first thermostat tells the burner to turn on when the house is cold. When the furnace heats up, the second thermostat turns on the fan to blow hot air at the customer.

Solar systems are much more difficult to control. The solar collector makes heat only when the sun shines. The harder the sun shines, the more heat available but the less heat needed. Solar heat must be stored, usually in a tank of water or a pile of crushed stone.

The control system drains the water out of the solar collector at night so that it will not freeze and pumps hot water out of the tank to heat the house. When there is not enough heat in the tank, the controller runs the backup heater.

Andover needed a control system with enough computer capacity to handle the problem and that heating, ventilation, and air conditioning (HVAC) engineers could program without having to earn a degree is computer science. In the early days, nobody knew how to control solar systems. Engineers would install a collector and its associated pumps, valves, and plumbing on a house, then spend the next year or two tweaking the control system to make it work properly.

One of the most important attributes of the controller was that it had to be programmed in a language that could be taught to building engineers. Building engineers are smart enough to learn how to program computers, but they do not want to. If they liked computers, they would not be in the HVAC business.

Given the year of tweaking and tuning that went into a working solar system, Andover could not afford to keep sending programmers to the building site. It was imperative to develop a controller language that was simple enough to be taught in less than a week but powerful enough to express complicated pump and valve control algorithms.

Another problem was caused by staff turnover. A building project uses many HVAC engineers over time. When one leaves, a successor must step in without spending much time figuring out what the previous engineer was doing. Not only did the language have be understandable, it also had to prevent engineers from writing programs that were hard for others to understand.

After two or three weeks thrashing around with different ideas, my client and I had the idea of basing the programming language on the imagery of a sequence drum. A sequence drum is a rotating cylinder like a Swiss music box. Pins stick out of the drum and turn switches on and off as they rotate past. HVAC engineers have used drums for years to control external lights and change thermostat settings. Andover reasoned that engineers could understand a language based on drums.

Drum programs are divided into many drums, each with up to 100 lines. A drum line can turn switches on or off, then rotate to another line based on external conditions. The following two line program keeps a temperature between 55 and 65 degrees:

| Line 1 | OFF > FAN, HEATER | Exit to Line 2 If T1 < 56 |
| Line 2 | ON > FAN, HEATER | Exit to Line 1 If T1 > 64 |

Line 1 turns the fan and heater off. "Fan" and "heater" are user-assigned names for a motor that drives the fan and a valve that lets hot water flow into a radiator. "T1" is the name given to a sensor that measures the temperature in the room heated by the fan and heater.

If T1 says the room is too cold, the program exits to line 2, which turns the fan and heater on. The program stays on line 2 until T1 says the room is warm enough, then goes back to line 1. Giving names to switches, fans, and temperature sensors makes it easier to understand a program.

Completely by accident Andover used a logical structure for drum programs that is similar to rules in expert systems. As explained in chapter 10, expert systems use if/then logic. If some condition holds, then the program carries out an action.

Andover's logic could be described as then/if. When the program enters a line, it takes an action such as turning a fan on or off. The program stays on that line until some exit condition occurs; then it rotates to a different line and does something else.

An expert system acts as if all the rules are processed at the same time. Each rule is a separate "program," and all programs run at the same time. Andover gets the effect of simultaneous parallel processes by running many drums. Each drum runs its own program independently of all the others. The drum that controls the temperature in one room has nothing to do with the drum that controls temperature in another room. Andover re-invented the logical structure of expert systems and also discovered the feature of processing many rules at once.

So Andover Controls made a fortune in the solar energy business and everybody lived happily ever after. Well, not quite. The government decided to help the solar energy business by offering customers a tax credit. During the eighteen months between the time they started talking about the credit and the time it was finally voted, nobody bought any solar energy systems because they were waiting for the tax credit. Andover quit selling solar systems during this dead period and decided to sell controllers instead.

Andover controllers were ideal for environmental management in small commercial buildings. Nobody wanted solar collectors, but everybody wanted to put a computer in existing buildings to improve comfort and save money at the same time. There are millions of old buildings in the United States. Andover sold controllers for a lot of them and is now the third largest company in the building energy management business.

Beckman Instruments: Lab Management

Beckman Instruments makes ultracentrifuges—machines that go "whir" in the lab. Beckman centrifuges spin at up to 100,000 rpm and separate liquids and solids according to density by using centrifugal force to generate up to 600,000 times the force of gravity. Running samples through high-performance centrifuges is rather complicated. Operators must choose the sample spin time, the number of sample tubes to put in the rotor, the rotor shape and loading, sample tube material, gradient fluid in which to suspend the sample, best sample temperature, and proper sample placement in the fluid.

Using the optimum rotor instead of a merely adequate rotor can reduce spinning time by many hours, depending on sample composition and accuracy of the separation. Lab technicians and researchers have to know so much about so many different subjects that it is unreasonable to expect them to become centrifuge experts as well.

Beckman had a centrifuge expert who spent about a third of his time on the telephone to customers working out solutions to problems and the rest of his time on the road developing new techniques. In order to make his expertise more generally available, Beckman used Gold Hill Common Lisp to write a centrifuge expert system called "SpinPro."[1]

This was a complex project. The team spent about six staff years writing more than 25,000 different rules in order to arrive at a final working set of 800 rules. The problem domain seems to have been suited for expert systems technology even though the final rule set exceeded the initial estimates by a factor of 4.

---

[1] *An Expert System for Optimizing Ultracentrifuge Runs,* by Martz, Heffron, and Griffith, ACS Symposium Series 306 (Washington, D.C.: American Chemical Society, 1986).

The user interface took up about 50% of the code in SpinPro. SpinPro asks questions about the experiment and recommends the minimum time separation based on its table of centrifuge rotors that are available in the lab. SpinPro then computes the fastest spinning time given the best rotor available and compares it to the fastest time given the best rotor in the catalogue. If the best in the catalogue is enough faster than the best in the lab, the lab technician may call Beckman and order the better rotor.

Whether this purchase is cost-effective or not depends on how many samples the lab will run. If there are a lot of samples to be done, buying the more productive rotor is often a good idea. Making timely suggestions is like having a centrifuge expert permanently stationed at the customer site.

By helping lab technicians use Beckman's equipment more efficiently, SpinPro effectively makes it spin faster. The $2,600 selling price of the program does not return much money directly, but it increases centrifuge output just as if a newer, better centrifuge had been designed. Military folk call this effect a "force multiplier." Shells don't go "bang" any louder, they just go "bang" nearer the target.

Campbell's Soups: Sterilizer Expert
Every can of Campbell's Soup passes through a sterilizer after the can is sealed. Soup sterilizers are over 70 feet tall, process between 450 and 480 cans per minute, and hold 55,000 to 65,000 cans at a time.

An empty can comes out of the washer at about 250°F. The "filler" pours in the soup, the "closer" seals the can, and the can enters the sterilizer at about 190°. The sterilizer heats the soup to 250° for four minutes to kill harmful bacteria.

Sterilizers are full of belts, pulleys, and chains that move cans through the process. There are valves and heaters to maintain the proper temperature profile. The sterilizer is riddled with temperature and pressure sensors so that operators can figure out what is going on inside in order to control and diagnose it.

No one can see what is going on inside the sterilizer. If a chain breaks or an obscure belt sticks, it can take quite awhile to figure out what is wrong. The plant staff handles routine maintenance, but the tough problems get passed to Aldo Cimino, who has worked with sterilizers for fifteen years.

Aldo solves most problems by telephone but occasionally flies out to reason with a particularly recalcitrant sterilizer. Campbell's operates 130 sterilizers at 8 different sites in the United States and England, and losing production while the soup waits for Aldo costs money. As Aldo neared retirement, Campbell's decided to capture his knowledge in an expert system. Texas Instruments supplied a knowledge engineer who worked with Aldo for about 6 months, writing about 150 rules such as

if the symptom is temperature deviation
 and the problem temperature is T30 cooling spray
 and the input and output air signals for TCV-30 are correct
 and the valve on TCV-30 is not open
then TCV-30 is not working properly. Check the
 instrumentation and the air signal.

The sterilizer expert was developed using a product from Texas Instruments called "Personal Consultant," which runs on an IBM PC. The expert system does not know as much about sterilizers as Aldo does, but it handles about 95% of all maintenance problems with the cookers. This gives Aldo time to design new equipment before he retires. New equipment will invalidate all the rules, of course, but by then Campbell's can train a new expert.

This is an example of leveraging an expert. Aldo can handle sterilizer problems, but there is only one of him. Putting his knowledge in a computer makes it available to all the plants.

Corning Glass: Lehr Planner and Simulator

When liquid glass is cast in a mold, the molten glass solidifies so fast that thermal stress is induced, making the glass too fragile to be sold. Glassware is passed through a furnace called a "lehr" in order to relieve the stresses. A lehr is about 10 feet high and 180 feet long. The air at the front is heated, and there are vents along the sides that let hot air out or cool air in. The wider a vent is open, the cooler the lehr is beyond it.

Glassware passes through the lehr on a conveyer. The glass must get hot enough to reach its "annealing temperature," the temperature at which it is soft enough to relieve stress but not so soft as to flow and lose shape. The glass must stay hot long enough for all the stresses to work themselves out.

After annealing, glass is cooled slowly to avoid new stresses but not so slowly as to exceed an acceptable exit temperature at the end of the lehr. If the glass does not get hot enough or comes out too hot, it cracks. If the lehr gets too hot, the glass sags. Production people adjust the controls to send glass through as fast as possible without breaking or sagging.

Lehrs have so many interacting controls that few people understand them well enough to prepare for a new product. Lehr experts fly to the plant site to set up the lehr. They wait twelve hours for temperatures to stabilize, run some glass through, and see if it breaks, sags, or cracks. If it does, they tweak the lehr, wait twelve more hours, and try again. It usually takes three or four cycles and a lot of broken glass to get things right.

Corning tried to develop a thermodynamic model of the lehr to help figure out how to set the controls, but this turned out to be impossible. There were too many variables for an exact simulation. Texas Instruments developed a lehr management expert system that runs on a DEC VAX 11/780. The program met the original goal of helping operators reduce breakage, but minimizing breakage turned out to be less important than the rule-based planning system that was added later.

The expert system uses empirical rules to predict the curve of temperature versus position in the lehr and tells how adjusting the vents or conveyer speed affects the temperature curve. TI developed a planning expert system that vent settings for new products given the desired annealing temperature, maximum rate of cooling, and maximum exit temperature. The planner makes a guess, calls the simulator to determine the temperature curve, refines the guess, and tries again.

Corning was extremely surprised to find that the rule-based program could simulate lehr behavior because they had spent so much effort attempting to write an analytical model to simulate it. The empirical model based on rules of thumb gathered from lehr experts worked much better than the analytical model and cost far less to develop.

Software development began at the end of 1984 and was completed in January 1986. The program has been installed in Corning facilities. Lehr operators like it because when something goes wrong, they can fix it without expert assistance.

Eloquent Systems: Resort Marketing

Eloquent Systems was started by an entrepreneur who wanted to improve service in hotels and expensive restaurants through the use of AI. There is such a large market for hotel and restaurant skills that colleges offer degrees in hotel management and there is a salary premium paid to skilled food service managers.

The food service manager's skills have a strong effect on profitability. A hotel with a poorly managed dining facility does well to break even on food service. A hotel in the same chain with the same customer traffic can net as much as $200,000 on food service with adequate management and up to $400,000 with expert management.

Moving managers around while holding other factors constant has shown that the difference is indeed due to the manager's expertise. A good manager is worth between $200,000 and $400,000 per year more to a hotel than a mediocre manager. The theory was that hotels would pay for a computer that offered world class food management expertise.

The First Plan Eloquent's original idea was to develop a total food manager expert system. Fine dining restaurants with high prices and over $1 million in annual sales and hotel chains would surely buy expertise that maximized profits. A little back of the envelope work convinced everybody that developing a complete food expert would cost more than the investors were willing to spend and would require a computer too big for enough customers to afford.

Dropping back a bit, Eloquent found that there were many restaurant computer systems on the market. Potential customers said that their major problem was theft in the bar and that no existing computer system solved that problem. If Eloquent had a "really good" bar expert, they would buy it.

The "Bar Wars" project had surprising results. Restaurant and hotel managers flocked to ogle the fancy electronic bartender and shower the software team with compliments. *But nobody bought it.* Whenever the sales force asked for purchase orders, everybody grabbed their wallets and ran. This demonstrated yet again that just because customers express interest in a new marvel does not always mean that they will buy.

The Second Plan While trying to sell Bar Wars to a resort hotel, the chef told Eloquent that the system might be useful for reservations. Resorts have a problem because people do not have to go there. Giving guests a good enough time that at least 50% of them come back is what the resort business is all about.

Part of giving guests a good time is remembering them and treating them personally. "Well, last time you stayed in 243 overlooking the pool. Would you like a mountain view this time? Should we make your wife an appointment with the hairdresser? Will you want your usual tennis court?"

Customer friendliness requires prodigious memory, indefatigable tolerance for guests requests, and intimate knowledge of what the hotel facilities can accomplish under combat conditions. Resorts rely on people who have worked at the hotel for thirty years and know every guest by sight, but such people are dying out. How can hotels capture the necessary expertise despite staff turnover?

The answer, of course, is with an expert system. Eloquent installed a Lisp machine and appropriate software at The Balsams, a 232-room resort in Dixon's Notch, New Hampshire, and put it to work helping reservation clerks. Hotel management expected a lot from the computer.

• Even when the hotel was full, there were small gaps in room occupancy. Filling the hotel more efficiently would generate more revenue without adding much to costs.

• The system had to remember and respond to the personal preferences stored in 50,000 guest histories going back 16 years.

• Resorts have many seasonal policies on prices, deposits, changing rooms, and checkout times that are hard for the staff to apply consistently when the cashier's desk is busy. Harried staff sometimes give customers the benefit of the doubt, which costs money. The computer enforces all the rules consistently even when it is busy.

• The Lisp machine software allows hotel management to write their own rules. Management can make changes in the hotel operation, something they could not afford if they had to hire a programmer.

The computer fits more guests into the hotel than people do. During the peak season, "completely full" means that the reservations desk cannot rearrange room assignments to put any more people in, given commitments of certain rooms to favored guests, odd lengths of stay, and the fact that the staff is too busy to juggle the room chart again.

The computer reduces empty rooms by about 50% by making better room assignments. This yields six or seven more guest nights per day during the busy season when room rates are at their peak. The computer also suggests alternatives when callers cannot have exactly what they want because it is already booked. Searching the records manually to find another time when a caller could have a particular room and a favorite tennis court at the same time took so long that it was seldom done. The combination of tighter scheduling and suggesting alternatives increased daily guest count by 19.

The extra cost of a few more guests is nothing compared to the extra income, so the computer generates almost $2,800 per day in extra profit. It is as though someone gave the Balsams five or six new rooms at no cost *and filled them*. The Balsams expects to earn back the $100,000 cost of the system in less than a year.

Soft benefits are equally important. Training new reservations clerks to use the manual system took about a month. Since the computer was installed, training time has fallen to about a week and the reservations office is a much more relaxed place to work. The computer helps identify guests who might bring new group business and targets group members who might return as individuals. All of this enhances the Balsams' marketing efforts and makes the operation more profitable.

Future Plans The Balsams plans to use the new rule-writing capability to further enhance their marketing. They plan to keep closer track of the results of soliciting past guests and people who call in to make inquiries.

Better information pays off. Another resort found that 17% of the callers who asked for a reservation decided not to come when told the room rate. Cutting rates for everyone would have reduced profits, so the hotel developed a "phantom family plan." If the reservation was for a period when the hotel was not likely to be full, the clerk would say, "Wait! You might qualify for one of our discount plans!" and offer a 15% to 25% price cut. This ploy persuaded all but 2% of the callers to come, resulting in a great deal more profit.

Converting 15% more inquiries into customers generated a great deal of extra profit despite the discounts. As the resort business becomes more competitive, this sort of strategy becomes more important but is extremely difficult to implement without tight controls. The Eloquent system provides tight control while letting management change the strategy at any time.

Federal Bureau of Investigation: Bank Note Processing

The FBI crime lab is often asked to help solve bank robberies in which a substantial sum is taken or someone is killed. Many bank robbers walk up to a teller and pass them a note asking for money. If all goes according to plan, the robber grabs the swag and disappears, never to be seen again.

Although bank robbers try not to leave the note behind and often include instructions demanding that it be returned, notes are often left behind in the confusion. Detailed analyses of the handwriting, ink, paper, and phrasing provide information about the robber.

Finding similar notes from two different robberies lets the FBI suggest that police pool information about what may be the work of one felon. By collating information in this way, the FBI helps police build a picture of the robber and nail him.

The FBI maintains a file of thousands of such "bank notes." Whenever they receive a note from a law enforcement agency, an examiner pores through the file looking for similar notes. This became rather tedious, and examiners turned to computers.

Instead of using pattern recognition software, the FBI has humans identify important features of bank notes to develop a note index. The computer retrieves notes based on the index, and the examiner has fewer notes to search.

The domain expert for the project was Examiner Bedie Yates, who probably knows more about bank robbery notes than anyone else in the world. She identified twenty-nine attributes, such as use of banking terms, how the money to be handed over is described, whether the robber claims to be armed with a gun, explosives, acid, gas, a knife, or other weapon, whether the note refers to a "heist," a "holdup," a "stickup," or whatever. After the notes are indexed, they are photographed and stored on a laser disk.

I watched her process a new note. After she indexed it, the computer found about fifteen notes that might match it. The computer displayed them on a screen in order of diminishing similarity to the target note. Yates scanned candidate notes at about two per second and found an almost identical note in about five seconds.

This is *not* an example of the use of artificial intelligence; it is a clever use of computers to enhance genuine intelligence. Yates' vision system is a better pattern matcher than any computer, but she cannot retrieve thousands of notes as fast as the computer can. The computerized index reduces the number of notes Yates must search; her built-in pattern matcher finds the right note, and the noose tightens around another miscreant. In fiscal 1987 Yates examined 597 notes and got 174 hits.

Computerized indexing works so well with bank notes that the FBI is thinking of applying it to matching faces. Even when a victim gets a good look at a perpetrator, finding the right picture among thousands of mug shots is a daunting task. Faces change with the growth of facial hair and age over time.

There is a system of life-sized plastic templates of various eyes, noses, hair lines, chins, and so on called Identikit™.[1] The victim looks through the ears for a match, then finds the best chin, and so on. When the pieces are put together, the result is often a reasonable likeness.

The FBI is attempting to build on existing feature indexing systems to retrieve good matches from a photo file, but progress is slow. Human features do not have simple yes/no attributes as bank notes do. The FBI is working on an expert system to

---

[1] Identikit™ is a trademark of Smith & Wesson.

generate softer match criteria so as to include the perpetrator without overwhelming the victim with photos.

Ford Motor Company: Quality Monitoring
The Ford Taurus is selling well, and Ford management wants to keep sales at record levels. Automobile customers have become much more quality conscious than in the past, and Ford executives constantly scrutinize Taurus field repair records. The immediate goal is to cut warranty costs in half, and the only way to do this is to improve manufacturing quality.

Ensuring zero defects in installing side molding is difficult for all auto manufacturers. Side trim attachment must be firm enough to hold the trim in place for the life of the car, but too much pressure can bend the side panels. If the trim is not glued on properly, water seeps behind the trim strip and freezes, causing the trim to come off.

The Chicago Taurus factory decided to develop a quality monitoring system to make sure that trim moldings were applied properly. The total cost of the sensors, interface wiring, and computer hardware had to be kept below $20,000 in order for the project to be cost-effective. The system used an IBM PC/AT, which runs data collecting and monitoring software written in Gold Hill Common Lisp.

The computer is attached to twenty-seven different sensors that monitor every step in the process: A special paper towel soaked with an alcohol mixture is wiped along the length of the body where the trim is to adhere; heat lamps along the sides of the car warm the body to the required temperature; molding strips are heated to bring the glue to the right temperature; molding strips are placed on the car using special alignment fixtures; the car passes through rollers that press the moulding onto the sides of the car.

The computer drives a color monitor that shows an animation of the assembly line. Operators can see the position of each car and the value of each process variable. Normal green displays turn red when a variable is out of tolerance, and an alarm sounds. Data on 500 recent vehicles is stored on the disk. The system works so well that Ford has installed duplicate systems at the Atlanta Taurus and Ohio Thunderbird plants.

This application is not a direct use of AI because computerized process monitoring dates back almost twenty years. However, this system had to be installed in six weeks. It would not have been possible to develop the process monitoring software on such a tight schedule with conventional programming languages. The Lisp development tools described in chapter 6 effectively doubled programmer productivity during the project. This is an example of using the indirect results of AI research to increase productivity on a conventional project.

GigaMos Systems Inc.: Process Control

GigaMos Systems Inc. (GSI) designed a specialized expert system called Picon to monitor and control real-time processes. GSI labored to make Picon easy to use. Customers can develop the rules for their own applications within weeks of installing a Picon system.

Picon is one of the few commercial expert systems that was designed for real-time process control. Most expert systems are not fast enough to handle data that change as rapidly as process variables in a chemical plant.

A chemical plant has as many as 20,000 variables. Alarm monitors look at most variables and notify people if a variable moves out of a specified range. Operators must decide what to do about each alarm. They can ignore an alarm because they feel that the sensor has malfunctioned or because the process will settle down by itself, or they can decide to intervene.

Power plants and chemical refineries are collections of large subassemblies that interact in complicated ways. When something goes wrong in a subsection of the plant, its variables drift out of tolerance and alarms are signaled for those variables. Fixing the problem would be easy if the rest of the plant continued to work properly, but the problem usually spreads beyond its point of origin. It is quite common for the first alarm to come from a part of the plant that is actually OK but that has been disturbed by a problem somewhere else.

Alarm processing gets exciting—a nuclear power plant can generate as many as 800 alarms within 2 minutes of a major disturbance. The control panel has as many as 3,000 lights on it, and within 5 minutes, essentially all the lights turn red.

Without paying close attention to the exact sequence in which red lights come on, there is no way to figure out what caused the problem quickly enough to do anything about it. Picon remembers the order in which alarms occur and uses its process knowledge to advise the operator what to do.

Picon cannot scan 20,000 variables fast enough to analyze all the alarms, so it uses a process called "focusing" to decide which data to collect. Focusing rules look at a few variables that characterize major subsystems and ignore other variables. When the major variables indicate that a part of the plant is not behaving well, Picon reads the rest of the variables for that subsystem and uses more detailed rules to see whether there really is a problem.

Chemical plants use holding tanks to handle variations in reaction rates between successive steps in a process. A focusing rule to tell Picon to worry about fluid level in a tank might be:

if tank-level > 80%
   or tank-level > 60%
      and rate-of-increase > 10% per minute
then focus-on-tank-level-high

This rule tells Picon to worry about the tank level being too high if the tank is more than 80% full or if it is more than 60% full and increasing at more than 10% per minute. If the focusing rule does not fire, Picon ignores detailed rules that figure out why the tank is too full. When it needs to examine these rules, Picon obtains data about reaction rates before and after the tank to decide if the tank level is really a problem.

When Picon decides that there is a reason to intervene, it notifies the plant operator. Because it makes a detailed analysis of the reasons why variables are out of tolerance, Picon is able to reduce the number of alarms operators must handle. Without Picon, operators would have to respond to every variable that drifted out of tolerance and decide whether or not to do something about it. Picon helps separate transient alarms and failed sensors from real problems.

Focusing lets Picon concentrate on the data and rules that are relevant to a particular situation instead of collecting all the information and examining all the rules all the time. Focusing conserves data collection bandwidth and rule-processing capacity, making it possible for Picon to handle more complex processes than if it always looked at everything at once.

Badger Engineers Badger designs and installs process plants. Badger used Picon to simulate the operation of a proprietary process for making styrene. Simulating the process helped Badger to improve its productivity by about 6%, resulting in substantial savings. After a two-week training period, engineers at Badger were able to develop and maintain the simulation system with no further background in expert systems.

Oak Ridge National Laboratories Oak Ridge National Laboratories is developing an autonomous remote-controlled robot called "Hermes." Picon gives the robot the flexibility to plan exploration strategy and to work out detailed navigation tactics.

The robot sends information to Picon's data handling module. This module makes most of the tactical decisions, invoking rules only when strategic decisions are needed.

The robot uses sonar to scan for obstacles and to check its position against the navigation plan. If the robot finds an unexpected obstacle, it stops and waits for Picon to figure out what to do. Picon collects further information by asking for more sonar scans. Planning rules in Picon use this information to decide how to handle the obstacle. When Picon figures out what to do, it passes the information to the robot.

Oak Ridge anticipates that a robot navigation system that works in the field will require a large number of rules. Picon's ability to focus its attention on a small subset of its rules is absolutely essential. There are far too many rules for the computer to examine all of them all of the time.

Gould Programmable Controllers: Factory Automation

Until the early 1970s, machinery in automobile factories was controlled by large banks of relays. Relay panels got as large as 8 feet high by 20 feet wide because the large machines that make such complex parts as engine blocks require a lot of control.

The principle behind an engine block machine is simple. Machining operations such as drilling, tapping, and milling are done at machining stations bolted to the floor. Each station has a set of clamps and several slides that carry tools. While the clamps hold the casting still, the slides are driven forward to remove strategically selected bits of metal, then retract out of the way. The clamps release, and a transfer bar shoves the casting to the next station, as shown in figure 4.1.

A group of stations lined up so that many castings are moved at once by the same transfer bar is called a "transfer line." A casting starts at the first station at the bottom of figure 4.1 and is transferred from station to station until it emerges as a finished part at the top. Machining stations all work at the same time, so this is highly productive. Such machines make one engine block per minute so long as operators feed in castings and keep the tools sharp.

Transfer lines use many microswitches that tell the control system whether a clamp is open or closed, whether a part is present at a given station, whether a slide is fully retracted, and so on. A medium-sized control system reads up to 1,000 microswitches and uses about 200 outputs to drive motors or hydraulic cylinders to make the machine go.

Controlling a big machine gets complicated. It is not a good idea to send the slides forward until all the clamps are closed, because cutting into a casting that is not clamped may throw the casting across the factory. Cycling the transfer bar before the clamps open breaks things. There are many such interlock rules that must be followed so that a transfer line can make engine blocks without tearing itself to pieces. The control system must check all thousand microswitches before it turns on an output to move a clamp or slide.

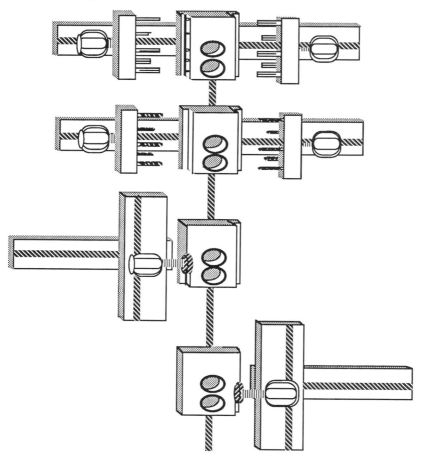

Figure 4.1
A transfer line for machining engine blocks.

Relay panels to control transfer machines were designed and documented using relay ladder diagrams. This notation was invented in the late 1880s and spread throughout the automobile industry. Although every plant electrician knows how to wire relays and relays are relatively cheap, relays are not ideal for control systems. It can take as long as six months to wire and debug a large relay panel. Even after a machine is working, a sticking relay can put it out of action.

In 1969 a startup company called Modicon introduced the programmable controller, a hardened computer programmed to imitate a bank of relays. Programmable controllers (PCs) were programmed in the same relay ladder notation that was used for wiring relay panels. Using familiar notation minimized user training. So many electricians know the relay ladder language that it is fair to call it a "natural language."

The major advantage of PCs over relays was not cost—early PCs cost several times as much as equivalent relays. Customers bought PCs to get machines working faster. It was much simpler to change the ladder program in the PC than to rewire relays. PCs reduced programming time from six months to six weeks. Starting to use a $50 million transfer machine five months sooner is worth the extra cost of the programmable controller.

The relay ladder language uses if/then notation just as expert systems do. Each line specifies the conditions under which an output is to be turned on. Horizontal and vertical lines in a ladder diagram represent wires that carry current when the switches associated with each line are in the conducting state. The relay ladder program

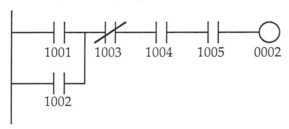

could be expressed as

if (switch 1 or switch 2) and not switch 3 and switch 4 and
    switch 5
then turn on output coil 2

If switch 1 is closed, it conducts electric power from the power rail at the extreme left to the switch to its right. The diagonal line at switch 3 means that power flows when switch 3 is open and not when it is closed.

Either switch 1 or switch 2 can get electricity to the input to switch 3. From there, electricity gets to the output coil only if switch 3 is open and switches 4 and 5 are closed. If all these conditions are met, the output coil is energized.

Programmable controllers are expert systems that run fast enough to operate machinery in factories. They are programmed in a language that many people know, so they have a natural language interface. PCs were thus one of the first real-time natural language expert systems on the market.

Modicon was so successful that it was bought by Gould Inc. in 1976, and sales rose to nearly $200 million per year. As other vendors entered the market, the PC became the foundation of a $500 million per year business in digital machine control.

The recent popularity of the IBM Personal Computer showed the folly of Gould's not registering the acronym "PC." Personal computers have become common in factories. Nobody knows if "PC" means personal computer or programmable controller. But humans get used to that sort of thing. After all, "AI" means "artificial insemination" to farmers.

ICAD Inc.: Intelligent CAD Systems

In chapter 2 I pointed out that computer-aided design systems do not design any more than word processors write. The computer draws and erases lines like a fancy pencil but does not design.

ICAD is a new concept in CAD systems. Instead of storing the arcs and lines for a specific design, ICAD stores the engineering rules for a whole class of *potential* designs. Users ask ICAD to generate specific designs by entering parameters, and ICAD generates performance data, part geometry for drawings, bills of materials, cost estimates, and manufacturing information.

ICAD's system acts as a front end for a conventional CAD system—it knows enough about parts, design rules, and manufacturing to verify the design and passes geometric information to the CAD system to generate the drawings. ICAD describes parts in terms of their features and relationships with other parts. Once all the parts in a subassembly are described, ICAD can generate drawings, cost estimates, and other manufacturing data.

One of the better results of designing in terms of relationships between parts is that designs can be parameterized. Changing the size of one part automatically resizes other parts, and an updated drawing comes out rapidly.

Semi-automatic design is important to Houston Engineering, a firm that sells large heat exchangers to the process industry. Engineers give design parameters to ICAD, and ICAD figures out part sizes and generates drawings and cost estimates.

Combustion Engineering installed five ICAD systems at their steam boiler division and saves thousands of staff hours per month. A large steam boiler is a rat's nest of welded pipe. Engineers used to sketch each piece of pipe and hand the stack of drawings to manufacturing. Manufacturing would claim that some bends were too sharp and that some of the welds were located where nobody could reach. Negotiating the trade-off between heat transfer efficiency and manufacturability consumed valuable time and delayed delivery.

The ICAD system knows the design and manufacturing rules for pipe assemblies and verifies designs before engineering gives them to manufacturing. ICAD generates control tapes for the pipe cutting and bending machines, bypassing the drawing stage.

TrueSports Automobile Racing: Data Display and Analysis
TrueSports designs, builds, and operates high-performance race cars. Professional auto racing is extremely competitive. All the top racing teams have access to unlimited funds, use essentially the same technology, and must conform to the same rules. Racing is mature enough that all the obvious ways to make cars go faster have been tried. There appear to be few breakthroughs left, and improvements come in small increments.

Race car design uses sophisticated analytical techniques such as wind tunnels and finite element analysis, but tuning the cars is not an exact science. Wringing the best performance out of a car is based on experience, intuition, and detailed knowledge of the driver, the track, and the engineering team.

Sophisticated teams use telemetry systems that send back reams of numbers representing performance factors such as gear speeds, engine rpm, ride height, wheel travel, and air pressure at various points on the skin. The problem is not collecting data, as existing telemetry systems grind out all the data anyone could want. The problem is turning data into information.

TrueSports wanted data displayed as a function of the position of the car on the race track rather than as a function of time, but this was difficult because the computer would need a map of each track. TrueSports bought a Symbolics system and hired a consultant to help with data reduction and display.

The consultant spent the remarkably short time of twenty-one days developing a software package that knew about track layouts and used the Symbolics window system to display the telemetry data in a much more informative way. This could not have been done without the graphics and windowing software that comes with the Symbolics computer.

Being able to understand the results of a test run quickly is immensely helpful because a team can make adjustments and try another test immediately. Being able to make more tests makes it more likely that the best adjustments for a particular racing situation can be found. This helps a car win.

While preparing for the Indianapolis 500, analysis of telemetry data suggested adjusting one of the car's front wings by eight tenths of a degree. This increased the lap speed from 205 mph to 210 mph. Two percent is not a huge increase, but in the competitive world of auto racing, any small advantage is significant. TrueSports won the Indianapolis 500.

US Coast Guard: AMVER

The US Coast Guard operates the Automatic Mutual Assistance Vessel Rescue System (AMVER), which keeps track of the positions of oceangoing vessels all over the world. About 32% of the world's merchant fleet participate voluntarily in AMVER by sending position reports to the Symbolics computer at Governor's Island in New York. Most ships cruise at 15 knots, or 18 mph, and report to AMVER about every 48 hours. The usual steaming distance for that period is 700 to 1,000 miles, so AMVER has a reasonable idea where the ships are located.

AMVER pays off when a ship disappears. The most recent position report gives a starting point for a search. AMVER is also useful for less spectacular incidents. If a crew member is hurt or falls ill, the captain calls AMVER. Depending on the location of the ship and traffic in the neighborhood, AMVER provides information so the Coast Guard and other rescue agencies can arrange evacuation by helicopter or rendezvous with another vessel to get the patient to a hospital more quickly.

About three years ago the International Maritime Organization developed a standard form for reporting a ship's position to AMVER. About 70% of the 2,200 daily messages follow the standard format, but the rest use what AMVER staff euphemistically refer to as the "old format," meaning no rules at all. A ship going from New York to Tokyo via the Panama Canal may send a message "New York to Tokyo via Panama" or "Tokyo from NY via canal" or "NY to Tok" depending on how the radio operator feels at the time.

The official language of AMVER messages is English, but more than 34,000 ships from 94 countries participate in the program. Many radio officers have only rudimentary acquaintance with English, and the best that can be said for old format messages is that they are "Englishlike."

There are more than fifty different ways of entering time: Greenwich or local with or without seconds, abbreviated month names, day/month/year, month/day/year, and so on. The same chaos holds for reporting latitude, longitude, and just about everything else about a ship's situation. Disentangling such messages requires knowledge of where the ship was, individual characteristics of radio operators, nautical terminology, standard routes between ports, and many other factors.

The Coast Guard tried to write a computer program to understand messages in Fortran but converted to Common Lisp. When the Lisp program showed signs of working, the Coast Guard spent three days converting it to Symbolics Common Lisp. They chose the Symbolics system because it was the only computer available that could handle the complex processing needed to understand a message every two minutes. The Symbolics computer decodes the messages and updates a database on another computer. This frees the staff members from the task of entering position information so that they can work on improving the system.

USDA: Cotton Management Expert System
The United States Department of Agriculture developed a cotton crop management system that maximizes cotton yields by computing the best schedule for irrigating, fertilizing, and harvesting. Putting too much water on the plants is costly and promotes rot. Giving too much fertilizer reduces yield because the plants do not grow properly. Harvesting early produces inferior cotton, and harvesting late increases the risk of rain, which damages the crop and makes harvesting more expensive by muddying the fields.

The cotton management expert, known as Comax,[1] is written in Gold Hill Common Lisp and runs on an IBM PC. Comax uses a plant simulator that was written over a period of twelve years. The simulator accepts information on soil and climate and predicts how a cotton plant will grow under those conditions.

Comax has about fifty rules that decide how to run the simulator. The first step is to assume dry weather and determine when the cotton plants will need water. This gives the earliest irrigation date. The program then runs the simulator assuming normal weather and finds the expected irrigation date, then assumes wet weather and simulates again to find the latest irrigation date. After the irrigation schedule is predicted, Comax

---

[1] Hal Lemmon, "Comax: An Expert System for Cotton Crop Management," *Science* (4 July 1986), 233:29-33.

runs the simulator assuming cold weather and minimum plant growth to determine minimum fertilizer requirements, then expected and maximum fertilizer needs.

Simulations are run everyday during the growing season. Comax asks the farmer to enter the weather each day and calculates new predictions. For example, on August 1 the program might say that irrigation will be needed on August 10 if the weather is hot and dry and on August 17 if it is normal. When the program is run on August 2, the hypothesized weather for August 1 is replaced with the actual weather. If August 1 was cold and wet, the August 2 simulation may say that irrigation is expected on August 12 if the weather is hot and dry or on August 19 if it is normal. Conversely, if August 1 is hot and dry, the hot and dry irrigation date is still August 10, but the normal weather irrigation date may move to August 15 instead of August 17.

When tested during the 1985 growing season, Comax suggested that the farmer apply 50 pounds of nitrogen per acre. The farmer had not planned to add any more nitrogen, but applied 20 pounds per acre, leaving a 6-acre plot for comparison purposes.

Comax predicted an increase in yield of 200 pounds per acre if 50 pounds of nitrogen were applied. Comparing the rest of the farm with the test plot showed an increase of 180 pounds per acre, valued at $71 per acre. Applying nitrogen cost $9 per acre, for a net gain of $62 per acre on a 6,000-acre farm.

Lessons to Be Learned

There are lessons to be learned from these applications:
• Getting a prototype running *quickly* is important. When Texas Instruments started working with Campbell's Soup, the sterilizer expert knew little about computers. Once the first few rules were working, he understood the project goals and could help more effectively. An ounce of illustration is worth a pound of explanation.
• Management faith and commitment is essential. Nobody at Campbell's could prove that an expert system could fix sterilizers—no computer had ever done that before. Management had to be willing to overlook initial problems and forge ahead.
• Listening to end users can change the product thrust completely. Eloquent's electronic bartender did not sell, but they found a market niche while trying to sell it—a customer told them what to do. Some people claimed that Eloquent wasted money developing the bar management software, but if they had not been trying to sell Bar Wars, they would not have discovered the market for improved reservations systems.

• Amazing things happen when end users get direct access to technology. Andover Controls and Eloquent Systems brought computers to heating engineers and to hotel reservations staff. These people understand their jobs much better than the programmers do. Giving them control of their tools made them much more effective in their jobs.

• An expert system project dies unless experts cooperate. There is no other source of expertise, and without knowledge the program will not work.

• Displaying information more clearly can be worth a great deal. TrueSports did not develop an expert system or obtain any new information; they developed software to display data they already had. Making data more accessible to engineers led to improvements in their operation.

• Expert systems can make conventional programs easier to use. The cotton simulator was an extremely accurate program but was difficult to use. The expert system helped farmers run the simulator, and that made the simulator more useful.

• The FBI bank note file works without AI . This is a reminder that an ounce of insight is worth a pound of technology.[1] The fact that the same technique does not work with mug shots is a reminder that standard technology has limits and that new technology is sometimes needed to do the job.

Applications of AI technology pop up in surprising places. Few people would expect to find a Lisp machine at the India-napolis 500. In the next few chapters, I go into the technology behind AI in more detail. This should help you recognize opportunities to use AI when you run across them.

---

[1] Engineers should need no reminder not to use flashy technology for its own sake. I was reminded of this by Eugene Charniac, of Brown University, when I was discussing an AI project with him. He said, "AI software costs a *lot* more than conventional software. You should never use AI unless there is no alternative." That was years ago and the cost of AI has dropped considerably, but his point stands.

"The reasonable man adapts himself to the world,
the unreasonable man adapts the world to him.
All progress depends on the unreasonable man."
— George Bernard Shaw

5
The Lisp Programming Language

Defining artificial intelligence as a programming style based on
data, rules, and goals may make intellectual sense but is not very
satisfying. People are accustomed to processing data with
computers but find it hard to grasp rules and goals. In this
chapter I explain rules, define symbolic programming, then
describe programming languages that process symbolic data.

I am not trying to teach you how to write Lisp programs.
There are many books available for that, and some of them are
listed in the bibliography of this book. My purpose in this
chapter is to convince you that data, rules, and goals make an
interesting programming style and to convey enough of a feeling
for symbolic programming that you can make an informed
decision whether or not to learn more.

Data, Rules, and Goals

A rule contains human knowledge such as "If a lamp does not
light, check to see if it is plugged in before replacing the bulb."
Data are facts: "It is dark in the room." "Most rooms have
lamps." "Lamps produce light." The goal is, "Let there be light!"

Humans know thousands of rules. It has been estimated that
a chess grandmaster uses more than 50,000 rules when playing

chess.[1] The more rules we know, the better we play the game of life. Learning the rules is called "growing up."

No one can prove that humans use explicit rules when thinking, but only AI researchers care whether people really think in rules or not. Writing programs in terms of rules can be an extremely cost-effective way to put computers to work, which is enough to interest engineers.

When people program computers, they must understand the task the computer is to do. After a human understands the task, the task must be expressed in a program the computer understands. The program specifies a list of steps needed to carry out the task. Once the computer knows how to do a job, people no longer have to do it, which is the point of writing the program.

The easier it is to explain a task to the computer, the less it costs to write a program. Rules are a good way to express certain kinds of information to computers. Writing rules, as opposed to some other kind of program, may or may not save money depending on the circumstances. The more ways an engineer knows to express knowledge to computers, the more tasks computers can be programmed to do and the easier life becomes.

Symbolic and Numeric Processing

Shortly after computers were invented, researchers realized that computers could process symbolic information as well as numbers. This was not a particularly profound insight. Arithmetic uses symbols to represent ideas, so symbol processing is involved even in arithmetic.

In arithmetic notation, the character "2" stands for the abstract idea of "twoness," the character "3" stands for "threeness," and so on. The earliest computers could not understand the symbols 0 through 9 and did arithmetic using the binary symbols 0 and 1 instead. Computers were soon modified to use human symbols to represent numbers because that was easier than persuading everybody to learn the computer's symbols. Given that numbers are represented by symbols, numeric processing is a subset of symbolic processing.

This was an early example of "user friendliness." Even computer experts found the symbols 0 and 1 to be intolerably inconvenient. They programmed computers to handle the rest of the numbers, then the alphabet.

The process of making computers easier to use has been going on for a long time. Each improvement in convenience increases

---

[1] Herbert Simon, *The Sciences of the Artificial* (Cambridge, Mass.: MIT Press, 1982), p. 106.

the market for computers. This makes computers available to more people, whose frustrations lead to further improvements, and so on. "Ease of use" is an implied goal of AI research. If computers were as intelligent as humans, we could just tell them what to do. In the process of trying to make computers more intelligent, researchers made them more useful.

Rules of Arithmetic

One of the problems with the "data, rules, and goals" definition of AI is that all programming involves rules and goals. The purpose of a payroll program is to compute paychecks according to the law of the land. There are even rules for arithmetic. For example, carry when the total in a column of addition is greater than 9; borrow when subtracting a big number from a small number, and so on. The rules of arithmetic are built into computers so that they can add, subtract, multiply, and divide.

The major advantage of arithmetic processing over symbolic processing is that only a dozen or so rules are needed for arithmetic. There are so few rules that vendors build them all into the computer's hardware, where they run fast. Computers do arithmetic rapidly because the rules are built in.

Computers such as the IBM 1620 or 1401 with memories smaller than 10,000 words could do cost-effective numerical tasks such as bookkeeping. Customers bought these computers in order to have such tasks done. IBM grew to be a huge firm by offering computers that performed simple arithmetic tasks, such as record keeping, which people are willing to pay for.

Commercial Success and Failure

Lisp was invented in the early 1960s; Fortran was developed a few years earlier in the late 1950s. Fortran was a commercial success because useful Fortran programs could run on the small computers that were all that could be manufactured given the state of the art of electronics at the time.

Tasks such as figuring out how to turn on a lamp require so many rules and so many facts that computers big enough for worthwhile reasoning were not available until the early 1980s. Throughout the 1970s it cost several million dollars to buy a computer big enough to run even the smallest AI programs, so few organizations had any interest in AI at all.

This is an example of the "so what" reaction that often hurts engineers' feelings when they bring a wonderful new technology to management. Lisp programs are *extremely* interesting. Writing Lisp programs for symbolic differentiation is much more fun than writing programs to compute payroll or keep accounts. The commercial world would pay for computers big enough to run accounting programs, but not for computers big enough to run Lisp. IBM prospered selling business machines while AI researchers starved.

In 1980 special-purpose AI computers called "Lisp machines" costing about $120,000 were put on the market. By 1987 small Lisp machines had dropped to $36,000, which is about the same as large engineering workstations. AI programs can also run on personal computers costing less than $10,000.

The recent interest in AI is not because AI has improved all of a sudden but rather because computers that can do AI are available for a reasonable price. This once again demonstrates that form follows finance.

Discussing programming languages without explaining computer technology is futile, so in the next few pages I provide a bit of background in general computer concepts.

Telling Computers What to Do

Telling computers what to do is the foundation of the computer industry. The easier it is to tell computers what to do, the more people can use computers and the more computers can be sold.

It was difficult and tedious to tell early computers what to do. They were programmable in that they could do different tasks, but tasks were described by strategically rearranging wires between parts of the computer.

These computers stored numbers in memory. Attaching wires directed the computer to add, subtract, accumulate totals, and do other operations to these numbers. Programmers told computers what to do by routing wires. This was quicker and easier than building a special machine for each task, but manipulating wires was boring and error prone. The "stored program computer" was a seminal advance. Instead of using memory only for data storage, the memory also stored instructions.

Computer memories can only store numbers, so both data and instructions are expressed as numbers. Computers not only read data from memory but also read instructions for processing the data. Programs are changed by changing numbers in memory. This was so much more convenient than moving wires that it became economical for computers to be given many more tasks.

Program Storage and Execution

Computer programs are lists of instructions stored in memory that the computer carries out one at a time. Computer memory is divided into "words." Each word has a number called its "address." Addresses are assigned starting with zero for the first word in memory, increasing by one for each successive word until the last word in memory.

Programs are stored in a simple way. Successive instructions are stored in successive words. The computer has special hardware called a "program counter" that remembers the address of the next instruction to be executed. The computer reads the word whose address is in the program counter, carries out the instruction, and increments the program counter to go to the next instruction. The cycle of fetching an instruction, executing it, and incrementing the program counter to go to the next instruction happens over and over until the computer is stopped.

The Software Development Process

Software development evolved a mystical choreography all its own. Computers were so expensive that they had to be kept running twenty-four hours a day. A programmer dashed up with a program punched as a series of numbers on a paper tape, read the numbers into successive words in memory, set the program counter to the beginning of the program, started the computer, and tested the program. Programmers used their precious access time to find as many errors as possible, then retired to fix the tape while others took their turns.

Tapes were punched by hand. Getting the right numbers punched was not easy. Humans have trouble remembering that 32 means add, or maybe it is 33.

The solution was to let the computer take care of such clerical details. Programs were written to change words representing instructions such as "add" to instructions like 33. In order to load word B into a register, add word C to it, and store the result in word A, a programmer wrote three instructions to the computer:

```
LOAD    B
ADD     C
STORE   A
```

Programs were becoming symbolic! Instead of using numbers to represent instructions and data, programmers used symbols like LOAD to represent instructions and variable names such as A, B, and C to represent data. The computer translated the symbols into the appropriate numbers to put in memory.

Programming Languages

Programmers quickly grew tired of writing so many instructions, and algebraic languages such as Fortran were developed. Computers now understood programs such as

A = B + C,

which the computer translated into instructions to load B into a register, add C to it, and store the result in A. Instead of writing three lines of instructions, the programmer wrote one. This improved productivity because programmers can write only a certain number of lines of code per day. The number of lines depends on the complexity of the task, but does not depend on the programming language. The more work a line of program does, the more a programmer can accomplish per day.

The only profitable uses for computers were based on arithmetic, so most of the effort of designing computer languages was directed toward numeric programming. Fortran, Pascal, Cobol, PL/1, Ada, and C are slightly different implementations of the same basic ideas.

With the exception of a few operations for manipulating character strings, these languages are designed to carry out arithmetic operations as fast as possible. Programmers combine simple arithmetic operations into more complex units called "modules" or "subroutines," but all that these languages do is turn the computer into a large adding machine.

Expressing Programs Symbolically

Conventional programming languages are symbolic. The sentence

A = sine(B) + sine(C)

is a symbolic representation of the sequence of arithmetic operations needed to compute the sine of B, the sine of C, add the results together, and store the sum in A. The computer cannot understand a symbolic instruction such as sine(B), so the symbols must be translated into the proper sequence of numbers that stand for the instructions to carry out the calculation. Programs that translate symbolic representations of calculations that people understand into numbers that computers understand are called "compilers."

Compiling is a symbolic process, in that symbols in the program are turned into numbers. About the time the first compiler was developed in the late 1950s, researchers realized that symbolic manipulations other than changing names of arithmetic operations into computer instructions might be interesting. In particular, people interested in how the human mind works needed a language that could manipulate symbolic information such as "Fred is the father of George," or "Cows are mammals," or "Roses are beautiful."

Such concepts can be manipulated by conventional programming languages. Programmers could assign one number to the symbol "Fred," another to the relationship "father of," and another to the symbol "George."

Unfortunately there are far more objects like "Fred" and relationships like "father of" in real life than instructions in a computer. Knowing how difficult it was to remember numbers representing computer instructions, researchers realized that it would be impossible to remember numbers representing more complex ideas. Before AI could get underway, researchers needed a programming language to manipulate symbols and the associations between them.

Why Lisp Was Invented

Lisp was invented to keep track of relationships between different kinds of information. Information is represented by symbols that stand for ideas, just as the symbol "gerbil" stands for the idea of a furry domestic animal. Programming in terms of relationships between symbols is called "symbolic programming." Writing bigger, better, and sometimes more intelligent symbolic programs has been the key to research efforts to understand human thought.

Lisp expresses information that is difficult to express in other languages. Purely by accident, Lisp turned out to be commercially useful as well as academically interesting.

That is the main reason engineers ought to know about Lisp. The more tricks in our bag of tools, the easier it is to perform stupendous feats. Ninety percent of engineering is knowing where the flat rocks are so that we can walk on water on command. Lisp is just another flat rock, albeit a nice, big, round one.

There are a number of other reasons to learn about Lisp:

• Lisp is the major programming language used in AI research. Hundreds of clever student-years have been invested in Lisp programs to try out theories of how the brain works. It is hard to understand these experiments without knowing Lisp.

• Lisp offers better software development tools than any other language. Software is becoming an important part of products such as microwave ovens, toasters, and automobiles. The ideas behind the Lisp software tools would reduce the cost of software developed in other languages.

• Lisp is extensible in that it was designed to grow as research took different directions. Extensibility has let Lisp adapt to new theories of how programs should be written without changing the language in any fundamental ways.

• Lisp is a superb tool for writing new programming languages. The programming language chosen for a project limits the way in which developers think about the problem. Many researchers invent new languages, implement them in Lisp, and write experimental programs in the new language.

• Common programming languages such as Ada, Cobol, Fortran, PL/1, and C are all based on Turing machine theory; Lisp is based on recursive function theory. Explaining these theories is beyond the scope of this book, but they are *very* different ways of looking at calculation. Some problems are much easier to solve in Lisp than in other languages.

Programming Language Theory
Programming languages are made of operators and data types. Data types are the kinds of information programs can manipulate—integers, real numbers, characters, symbols, rules, relationships, vectors, matrices, or whatever. Operators are what programs do to data—add them, subtract them, invert them, read and write them, and so on.

Fortran was the first widely successful programming language. Its data types are integers and real numbers. Integers are numbers without periods; real numbers have periods. Fortran programs can add, subtract, multiply, and divide numbers. Fortran makes a computer act like a large pocket calculator.[1]

Fortran programmers assign symbolic names to data and refer to them by name. The Fortran compiler decides where to locate data and instructions in memory so programmers do not need to worry about that. As computer memories became larger and as programs dealt with more variables, automatic memory assignment became more and more important. Symbolic references to operators and to data are included in all computer languages.

Program Control Structure
Computers would not be useful if they always started with the first instruction in a program and ran straight through to the

---

[1] Languages can also be described in terms of efficiency and expressiveness. Expressiveness determines how easy it is to describe a task using the language, efficiency determines how fast the computer can do the task once it has been described. Fortran expresses numerical calculations well, Cobol describes accounting transactions, and Lisp describes symbol manipulation.

end. Programs execute some instructions and not others based on the values of data. For example, social security payments depend on a person's age at retirement. The benefit program chooses different methods of computing benefits depending on the value of a variable that stores the person's age.

The control structure determines the order in which operators are executed in a program. Operators determine what happens to the data; the control structure determines when the operators are carried out. The classic way to express choices between two alternatives is the if/then/else statement.

Suppose that there are two ways to compute social security benefits, Formula1 and Formula2. A program to choose between these formulas might look like

```
if   AGE > 65
     then Formula1
     else Formula2
```

This social security if-statement tests to see if a condition is true. In this case, the condition is "AGE > 65," meaning that a person's age is greater than 65. If the test is true, it is said to succeed, and the instructions following the "then" are executed. If the condition is not true, the test fails and the instructions after the "else" are executed instead. This program fragment executes either Formula1 or Formula2 depending on the value of the variable AGE.

How If/Then/Else Works

Computers choose between alternatives by using instructions that change the program counter instead of doing arithmetic. The program counter holds the address of the next instruction to be executed. Most instructions simply increment the program counter to go to the next instruction. This forces the computer to execute instructions in the order in which they appear in memory. When a decision-making instruction modifies the program counter, however, this order is changed.

When the compiler finds an if-statement in a program, it first generates code to perform the test, then the instructions that follow the "then," finally the instructions that follow the "else." If the test succeeds, the program executes the code following the "then," which is the normal order of instruction execution. If the test fails, however, the program counter is modified to contain the address of the code following the "else."

The following table shows the memory addresses and the code that the compiler generates when it reads the social security if-statement:

Address	Contents
100	Code to compare AGE with 65
.	
.	
.	
108	Last part of the "if" test
109	Conditional jump to location 150
110	"then" clause (Code to compute Formula1)
.	
.	
.	
148	Last instruction in Formula1
149	Unconditional jump to location 160
150	"else" clause (Code to compute Formula2)
.	
.	
.	
159	Last instruction in Formula2
160	First instruction after the if-statement

The if-statement starts at location 100 in memory. The instructions to compare the value of the variable named AGE with 65 are stored in words 100 through 108. The then-clause runs from word 110 to 148, and the code after the "else" occupies words 150 through 159.

After comparing AGE with the number 65, the program decides whether to continue on to location 110 and execute the then-clause or jump to location 150 and execute the else-clause. The instruction that makes this choice is called a "conditional jump" because it may or may not modify the program counter depending on the result of the test. The conditional jump instruction goes in word 109, right after the code to compare AGE with 65.

Whenever the program executes the then-clause, it jumps over the else-clause. This requires an instruction to change the program counter to the address of the instruction after the else-clause. This instruction is called a "jump" because it always modifies the program counter. The jump is put in location 149, immediately after the code that follows the "then." It changes the program counter to 151, so that the rest of the program after the if-statement is executed.

Early compilers often generated incorrect code. Programmers had to know what the code should look like so that they could make sure the compiler had translated their intent properly.

Modern compilers are reliable and programmers rarely worry about where the compiler puts code in memory or what it looks like, but it is interesting to know what the compiler is doing.

If/then/else statements are all compiled in essentially the same way. The compiler generates code for the test, a conditional jump, code for the "then," an unconditional jump, then code for the "else." Modern compilers look for special cases such as an if-statement without an "else" so that they can omit the unconditional branch, but these are refinements. The basics are the same in all programming languages, including Lisp.

Other Control Statements

Modern control structure include something called "loop" or "while" or "repeat-until" or "do" that repeats a group of instructions until a condition is met. This is useful in computing averages. The program keeps adding until it sums all the data, then drops out of the addition loop and divides by the number of data to get the average. Languages such as Pascal and C include a "case" statement for choosing one alternative from among many alternatives.

Unfortunate Realities

Fortran is based on arithmetic concepts—addition, subtraction, multiplication, and division. As many engineers have learned to their sorrow, there is a world of difference between arithmetic on paper and arithmetic in a computer.

Numbers on paper can have as many digits as necessary, but numbers in a computer occupy part of a finite amount of memory space. If we compute 1/3 of a number and multiply the result by 3, we expect the original number back again. This does not always happen in computers. Dividing 1 by 3 gives 0.3333333 or perhaps 0.333333333 depending on how many digits are used to store each number. Multiplying by 3 gives 0.999999999, not 1.

Such differences may seem unimportant, but round-off errors have a nasty habit of accumulating during complex calculations. In extreme cases the result of a calculation depends more on the round-off error than on the input data and is essentially random. We can minimize round-off to whatever degree we wish by using more memory to store more digits for each number, but we cannot eliminate it entirely.

Any computer calculation is an approximation at best. The accuracy of the approximation depends on how the calculation is done. If multiplication is done before division in the example, the error goes away. Multiplying 1 by 3 gives 3, then dividing by 3 gives back exactly 1.

So multiplying before dividing solves the problem. Right? In this case, yes, but suppose that the original number is 30,000 instead of 1. Small 16-bit computers use so little memory for numbers that memory cannot hold numbers bigger than 32,767. Multiplying first should give 90,000, but 90,000 is too big for the memory location assigned to it. The result is an overflow error whose value depends on the design of the arithmetic circuits in the computer.

Overflow and round-off errors confound programmers.[1] The more memory the computer uses for each number, the fewer overflow and round-off problems there are, but the fewer numbers can fit into a given memory size. The less memory used for each number, the more numbers that can be stored in memory at once, but the more likely users are to get inaccurate results.

There are rules of thumb for how much memory is needed to store enough digits to get reasonable results. The numerical analysis needed to figure out whether a calculation involving a given program, set of data values, and memory size will generate accurate answers is a real pain. Most programmers ignore the problem and get away with it most of the time. From an engineering point of view, the only way to tell if the computer's numbers are accurate is to see if the bridge stays up.

Data Types in Lisp
For all that AI is regarded as a mysterious field, the Lisp language is simpler than Fortran. Fortran has three basic data types, whereas Lisp has only two: *Atoms* are character strings bounded by spaces. "Fred," "father-of," and "3.14159" are atoms. *Lists* contain atoms held together by parentheses. A is an atom, (A) is a list containing the atom A. The list (A B C D) has four elements—the atoms A, B, C, and D.

Atoms are similar to variables in other languages in that Lisp atoms may be assigned values. The value of the atom A might be set to 3, or the value of the atom AGE might be set to 65. The value of an atom can be a list—CITIES-TO-VISIT could have the

---

[1] A symbolic mathematics program called MACSYMA avoids problems with precision and round-off error by storing quotients as the ratio of two numbers. MACSYMA stores the fraction "1/3" as the number "1" divided by the number "3." If this fraction is later multiplied by "3", MACSYMA cancels the "3" in the denominator and returns the exact result "1." MACSYMA stores mathematical constants symbolically, remembering the symbol "PI" instead of the approximation 3.14159... MACSYMA knows rules for integration, differentiation, and simplification and saves a great deal of time in mathematical analysis.

value (Boston Chicago Detroit). This value is a list instead of a number or an atom because it is surrounded by parentheses.

Lisp programmers got tired of coping with inexact numbers, round-off errors, and overflow and developed facilities for handling large numbers called "bignums." When a Lisp number grows so that it has too many digits for the word in which it is stored, Lisp automatically allocates more memory to hold the number. If the number later becomes small enough to fit into a single word, Lisp recycles the extra word because it is no longer needed. Automatically adjusting the amount of memory allocated to different-sized numbers is extremely convenient.

Recursive Lists

Lists are recursive in that one list may be put inside another. The list ((A B) C) has two elements. The first element is the list (A B), and the second element is the atom C. "Recursion" describes processes that may be repeated indefinitely. Each step in a recursive process is based on the value of the previous step.

Complicated lists can be built using recursive processes. One recursive rule for making complex lists from a simple list is "Make a two-element list, where both the first and second elements are copies of the original list."

Applying this rule to (A B) produces the list ((A B) (A B)). This new list is a two-element list, and each element is a copy of (A B). Applying the rule again gives (((A B) (A B)) ((A B) (A B))), another two-element list. The next step gives ((((A B) (A B)) ((A B) (A B))) (((A B) (A B)) ((A B) (A B)))). Picking through such monstrosities to find where the parentheses balance is a task that only a computer can love.

List structure is useful for maintaining relationships between information. By convention the meaning of the list (Father-of Fred George) means "Fred is the father of George." (Bigger-than dog mouse), (Color-of elephant gray), and (Price-of books excessive) are similarly easy for people to interpret—each list represents a fact that means something to a human.

Meaning is assigned by the programmer, not the computer. (Father-of Fred George) might mean "George is the father of Fred" to another programmer. Meaning is in the programmer's mind, not inherent in the program.

Facts that are represented as lists can be collected into lists. For example, the value of the atom Author might be a list of information about me:

((height 6')
(hair-color brown)
(job AI-consultant) ...)

Each element of this list is itself a list containing a fact about Author—hair color, job, and so on.

Property Lists

Maintaining information about properties of atoms turned out to be such a useful procedure that special facilities were added to Lisp to make it easy to manipulate such lists. The "property list" maintains information about an atom. Each property has a name and a value. The name of the property is an atom, and the value of a property may be an atom or a list.

In describing this property list, we would say that the value of the height property of the atom Author is 6'. The value of the job property of the atom Author is "AI-consultant" and so on.

The same structure can also store Author's address. An address is a list containing a street address, a city, a state, and a zip code. Adding Author's address to the property list gives

((height 6')
(hair-color brown)
(job AI-consultant)
(address ((Pinnacle Hill Road)
          (New Hampton NH 03256))) ...)

The value of the address property of the atom Author is the two-element list ((Pinnacle Hill Road) (New Hampton NH 03256)).

Although computers have no trouble with nested lists, a nested list is hard for people to understand unless it is indented to display its structure. This is called "pretty printing" and was developed soon after Lisp was invented.

Lisp Operations

There are three basic operations that can be performed on lists:
• CAR returns the first element of a list.
• CDR returns all of a list except the first element.
• CONS takes two atoms or lists and combines them into a bigger list.

If Lisp is asked to compute the CAR of the list (A B C), it returns the atom A, which is the first element of the list. The CDR of (A B C) is the list (B C), which is the original list minus the first element. The CONS of the atom A and the list (B C) is the list (A B C).

CONS reverses the effects of CAR and CDR. Feeding the list (A B C) into CAR gives the atom A. Feeding the list (A B C) into CDR gives the list (B C). If these two results are given to CONS, it combines them into the list (A B C).

Atoms can be thought of as playing cards, and parentheses are like rubber bands holding cards together in decks. CAR pulls the first card off the top of the deck, CDR returns all of the deck except for the top card, and CONS stretches the rubber band and puts a new card on top of the deck.

What CONS does in this case is stretch the rubber band holding (B C) together and stick A inside it. More formally, CONS always produces a list. The first element of the new list is the first argument passed to the CONS function, and the rest of the new list is the second argument.

CONS collects small units of information into bigger units. Lisp programmers often say, "I'll CONS something up for you," when they are about to gather existing information or functions into something you have asked for.

The names "CAR" and "CDR" are a historical misfortune. The first Lisp was implemented as a set of subroutines that could be called by Fortran programs. It is amusing that Lisp was first written in Fortran because Fortran is not normally the language of choice for writing new languages.

The second Lisp system was written for an IBM 709 computer at MIT. CAR and CDR were names of two particularly important 709 instructions—"contents of the address register" and "contents of the decrement register."

Those two names became part of the Lisp language, and we are stuck with them. The Common Lisp standard defines an operation called "First," which is the same as CAR, and another called "Rest," which is the same as CDR. Programmers are being urged to use First and Rest instead of CAR and CDR, but this is regarded as an affectation by traditionally minded programmers who like their Lisp raw.

Recursive Lists and Organization Charts

To repeat a little, Lisp lists are recursive in that one list can be put inside of another. If we have a deck of cards rubber banded together, we can stretch the band and stick another deck anywhere inside. This can be illustrated by an organization chart, which is a common recursive data structure in real life.

Organization charts are recursive because a box representing an organization can be replaced by the chart for that organization. We can put one chart inside another and nest them as deeply as we like. Consider a simple organization in which engineering, marketing, and manufacturing all report to the president:

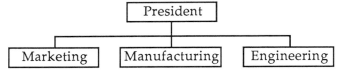

"President" is the title of an individual, so the chart cannot go any higher than that box. "Marketing" is the name of an organization with its own chart:

These two charts can be combined by replacing the Marketing box with the marketing chart, which produces a new chart:

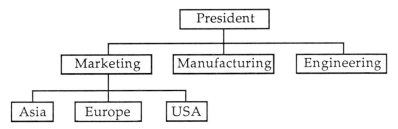

Representing Organization Charts in Lisp

Users can store this information in a Lisp data structure by defining the "over" and "under" properties that contain lists of parts of the organization that are over or under a given position on the chart. The value of the "over" property of the atom President is NIL, or nothing, because there is nothing over the president. The value of the "under" property of the atom President is the list (Marketing Manufacturing Engineering), because they all report to the president. The chart is stored as values of the "over" and "under" properties of all of the atoms in the organization as shown in the following chart:

Atom	Properties	
	Over	Under
President		(Marketing Manufacturing Engineering)
Marketing	(President)	(Asia Europe USA)

This pattern can be continued as deep as necessary. Values can be specified for the "under" properties of Asia, Europe, and so on until the very bottom of the pile.

The structure can also handle matrix organizations in which an individual may report to more than one boss. The value of the "over" property can store a list of all parts of the organization to which each person reports.

Recursive Functions and Counting Atoms

Just as Lisp data are recursive, Lisp functions are also recursive, in that a function can call itself. A recursive function needs a self-reference and an exit. The exit is needed because if a function goes on calling itself forever, the computer eventually runs out of memory and stops. The exit gives a way to escape from the function.

One simple task is to count the atoms in a list. All that Lisp offers for pulling lists apart is CAR and CDR. Suppose it becomes necessary to count the atoms in the list constructed by using the recursive procedure ((((A B) (A B)) ((A B) (A B))) (((A B) (A B)) ((A B) (A B)))). Taking the CAR of this list gives (((A B) (A B)) ((A B) (A B))), which is simpler, but not much. Since a program has no idea how complicated a list it will be given, it cannot rely on doing any fixed number of CARs and CDRs to isolate the atoms so that they can be counted.

Let's start writing the Count-the-atoms-in function even though it is not yet clear exactly how it will work. Remember, the function isn't done until the parentheses balance.

(DEFUN Count-the-atoms-in (A)

"DEFUN" tells Lisp that a new function is being defined. The new function is called "Count-the-atoms-in," and it expects the function that calls it to pass it one parameter called "A." If A is an atom instead of a list, the answer is 1. If we solve the simple part of the problem first, the function becomes:

(DEFUN Count-the-atoms-in (A)
        (COND ((ATOM A) 1)

COND stands for "conditional," which is the Lisp word for "if." ATOM is true if A is an atom. If ATOM is true, the value of the COND statement is 1, Count-the-atoms-in returns 1, and the problem is solved. Suppose that A is not an atom. Then what?

Suppose that there were a function to compute the number of atoms in the CAR of a list or in the CDR of a list. Call this function "Future-function," because it will be defined later. The

number of atoms in a list is the sum of the atoms in its CAR and
the atoms in its CDR. If Future-function were available, Count-
the-atoms-in would look like

```
(DEFUN  Count-the-atoms-in (A)
        (COND   ((ATOM A) 1)
                (ELSE (Add-the-results-of
                      (Future-function (CAR A))
                      (Future-function (CDR A)))))))
```

Count-the-atoms-in first tests to see if A is an atom. If A is an
atom, the answer is 1. If A is not an atom, A must be a list. The
"else" part of the COND computes Future-function of the CAR of
A, computes Future-function of the CDR of A, and adds the two
results. Because Future-function can count atoms in the CAR or
CDR of a list, Count-the-atoms-in is now complete.

The solution is nigh. The only task left is the mysterious
Future-function. What does it do? It counts the atoms in the
CAR or CDR of a list. But the CAR of a list is either a simpler list
or an atom, and so is the CDR. Future-function's job is to count
atoms in a list, which is exactly what Count-the-atoms-in does.
Future-function is already available—it is the same as Count-
the-atoms-in! The final program is

```
(DEFUN  Count-the-atoms-in (A)
        (COND   ((ATOM A) 1)
                (ELSE (Add-the-results-of
                      (Count-the-atoms-in (CAR A))
                      (Count-the-atoms-in (CDR A)))))))
```

Figure 5.1 shows what happens when Lisp tries to Count-the-
atoms-in the list (A B C). The Count-the-atoms-in at the top of
the diagram first checks to see if it has been given an atom
instead of a list. (A B C) is not an atom, so the COND asks Add-
the-results-of to sum the result of Count-the-atoms-in the CAR of
(A B C) and Count-the-atoms-in the CDR.

The second Count-the-atoms-in is passed A, which is the CAR
of the original list (A B C), and the third Count-the-atoms-in is
passed the CDR of (A B C), which is the smaller list (B C).

The second Count-the-atoms-in finds that A is an atom and
returns 1. The third Count-the-atoms-in notices that (B C) is not
an atom and calls Count-the-atoms-in twice more, once for B
and once for C. Each of these calls to Count-the-atoms-in finds
an atom and returns 1. These 1's are summed to get the number
of atoms in (B C), which is 2. This 2 is summed with the
number of atoms in A, which gives the final answer of 3.

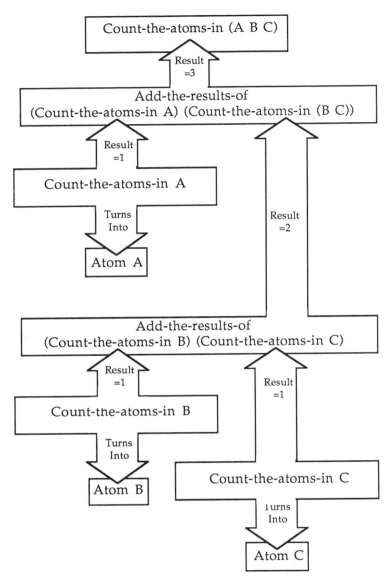

Figure 5.1
A diagram of how Lisp can Count-the-atoms-in the list (A B C)

Lisp keeps track of all the calls to Count-the-atoms-in, passing the correct lists to each one and returning the values from each call. Managing many calls to a function is easy for computers.

Recursion is a simple idea—all it means is that programs can call themselves—but the details are messy. It is seldom worth the trouble to figure out what goes on during recursion.

The important point is that programs can be used before they are complete. Count-the-atoms-in calls Count-the-atoms-in to do a part of its job. When writing Count-the-atoms-in, we *assumed that it already worked.*

Lessons from Recursion

Assuming that programs work before they are complete bothers many programmers, but it is central to the AI programming style. The major lessons from this example are:

• Start programming before the task is fully understood.
• Handle simple cases first (divide and conquer).
• When a problem is not simple, simplify it and pass it on.

This is how people solve problems. We usually start work on the part of the problem that we understand. If we cannot solve a problem immediately, we break it down into simpler problems and solve each part.

This is a recursive process. When we break down a problem, each part becomes a separate problem to be further broken down and simplified. Provided that we keep track of all of the pieces, solving the individual parts solves the overall problem.

Count-the-atoms-in delegates simplified lists to itself instead of to another function, but the principle is the same. The Lisp system worries about the bookkeeping and programmers write functions that call themselves with gay abandon.

Other Data Structures

Although atoms and lists were the only data types in early Lisp systems, language developers soon offered other ways to organize data. Mature Lisp systems offer all the data structures offered by conventional programming and some that are not.

The data type most peculiar to Lisp is called a "structure." A structure is an object that contains smaller objects. For example,

```
(DEFSTRUCT ship
        (speed :initial 0)
        (cargo-capacity :initial 0)
        (passenger :initial 0))
```

defines the structure of a new class of objects called "ship." Each ship has three attributes—speed, cargo-capacity, and passenger—in which programs record information about each ship.

Once the structure is defined, Lisp knows how to allocate memory when a program creates a ship instance. When a program asks for a new ship, Lisp allocates memory, giving the new ship space to store the values of its speed, capacity, and passenger attributes.

Attributes could be stored in lists, of course. Suppose that data about ships were in a list (speed cargo-capacity passenger). A programmer would have to remember that speed was in the CAR of the list, cargo capacity in the CAR of the CDR, and passenger in the CAR of the CDR of the CDR. Finding elements in long lists by using CARs and CDRs is error prone.

The major advantage of using structures instead of lists is that programs can manipulate attributes by name. Defining a structure not only tells Lisp how to make a new ship, it also defines functions that extract attributes from it. The function (get-speed a-ship) finds the speed attribute, (get-cargo-capacity a-ship) extracts the cargo capacity attribute, and so on. Details of how data structures are implemented are hidden and the programmer does not have to worry about how they work.[1] If someone discovers a better way to record and retrieve attributes, Lisp can change the way in which ships are implemented without affecting ship users.

Review of Lisp

Atoms and lists are the two basic Lisp data types, although many others have been added. Atoms are character strings bounded by spaces, and lists are atoms grouped by parentheses. An atom may have a value and any number of named properties. The value of an atom or property may be an atom or a list.

Lists can be put inside other lists. The CAR and CDR functions pull lists apart to get at the atoms inside; CONS puts lists together.

Lisp offers conditional statements that let programs decide which instructions to execute based on values or properties of data. Lisp is a recursive language because lists can be put inside

---

[1] Hiding implementation details is a powerful idea. Lisp keeps track of recursive function calls and allocates memory to store numbers as they grow bigger. The more details that are handled automatically, the more a programmer can concentrate on the task instead of worrying about the program. The real advantage of Lisp over other languages is that the Lisp environment handles far more details than other programming environments.

other lists and because functions can call themselves. One difficulty programmers have when adapting to Lisp is learning to assume that programs work before they are complete.

The preferred Lisp programming strategy is to handle simple cases immediately. Difficult problems are simplified and delegated. Problem simplification and delegation is a recursive process, so the Lisp programming style mimics the recursive steps by which engineers decompose problems.

Property lists record information about variables and can also record relationships between facts. Property lists are one of Lisp's most important features. In the next chapter I tell more about property lists, then explain how Lisp is used.

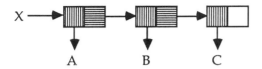

6
Using Lisp

Using Properties: "Is" and "Has"

Properties are useful for storing information about atoms and for keeping track of relationships between them. In the organization chart in chapter 5, the "over" and "under" properties recorded rank relationships between atoms. The next example introduces the "is" and "has" properties, which deal with more complex knowledge.

Knowledge processing can be illustrated by defining a simple database about circus-elephant, elephant, performer, and other objects. This illustration of the use of property lists is based on an exercise from an introductory Lisp course at Brown University. Humans know that "circus elephant" refers to a single object. Lisp defines an atom as a string of characters bounded by spaces, so Lisp thinks that "circus elephant" is two atoms. Linking the words with a hyphen and referring to "circus-elephant" instead of "circus elephant" tells Lisp that it is dealing with one atom instead of two. Let's start with the facts:

is   Circus-elephant   Performer
is   Circus-elephant   Elephant
is   Elephant   Animal
has   Elephant   Head
has   Elephant   Trunk
has   Head   Mouth
has   Animal   Heart
has   Performer   Costume
is   Costume   Clothes

This small database says that a circus-elephant is a performer and also an elephant. An elephant is an animal and has a head and trunk. A head has a mouth and so on. These facts can be recorded using "is" and "has" properties of atoms such as circus-elephant and elephant as shown in the following table:

Atom	Properties	
	Is	Has
Circus-elephant	(Elephant Performer)	
Elephant	(Animal)	(Head Trunk)
Head		(Mouth)
Animal		(Heart)
Performer	(Costume)	
Costume	(Clothes)	

The value of the "is" property of the atom Circus-elephant is the list (Elephant Performer) and so on.

Inferring New Facts from Old Facts

Once the computer has recorded these facts, it can infer more facts. A circus-elephant is a performer because "performer" is a member of the list that is the value of the "is" property of circus-elephant. A circus-elephant is an animal because a circus-elephant is an elephant and an elephant is an animal. The database does not record the fact that a circus-elephant is an animal, but that fact can be inferred from the facts that are in the database. Inferring new facts from old ones is one of the key ideas behind expert systems, as explained in chapters 8 and 9.

If a user asked whether a circus-elephant is a clown, the program says no because "clown" is not a member of the "is" property list of anything in the database. This is an illustration of the closed-world assumption—anything the computer does not know to be true is regarded as false. Programs do not know the limits of their knowledge. To an AI program, "No" and "I don't know" are the same.

A person usually knows that they have no information about clowns. Getting AI and database programs to realize when they are approaching the limits of their knowledge is an open research topic.

Complex Inference
It is interesting to follow the process by which the program deduces that a circus-elephant has clothes. The "has" property list of circus-elephant is empty, but a circus-elephant is an elephant. An elephant is an animal that has a heart but no clothes. An elephant has a head and a trunk and a head has a mouth but still no clothes. However, a circus-elephant also is a performer, which has a costume, which is clothes.

Whenever the search does not find what it is looking for, it calls itself to repeat the search on some member of the "is" or "has" list where it just failed. When the search fails to find clothes on circus-elephant, it looks for clothes on elephant and on performer. Failing to find clothes on elephant, it looks for clothes on animal because an elephant is an animal and on head and trunk because an elephant has a head and a trunk. The program calls itself until it either finds what it wants and succeeds or gets to a point where it can go no further and fails.

An Unexpected Bug
Now that the program works, suppose that an entry clerk adds the new fact

is   Clothes   Circus-elephant

The database now looks like this:

| Atom | Properties | |
	Is	Has
Circus-elephant	(Elephant Performer)	
Elephant	(Animal)	(Head Trunk)
Head		(Mouth)
Animal		(Heart)
Performer	(Costume)	
Costume	(Clothes)	
Clothes	(Circus-elephant)	

There is a loop in the data—when looking at circus-elephant, the program examines performer, which leads to costume, which leads to clothes, which leads back to circus-elephant. When a request refers to any item in the loop, the program runs forever. The code has not changed; the error is caused by new data. Data are often harder to debug than programs. AI researchers spend a lot of time debugging data in addition to debugging programs.

What This Example Means
"Is" and "has" properties are the core of an inventory control program. A computer is a product; a computer has a power supply; a power supply has a circuit board and components and so on. This program can answer questions such as "Does a model B use a #14 power supply?" Finding out what goes into what is called "parts explosion." It is often used in factories to figure out how many parts to buy to fill an order.

The program to construct the database and answer questions about it takes about a page of Lisp. This is the first problem in many beginning Lisp courses. When people learn Fortran, one of the first assignments is to write a program to compute the area of a triangle given the lengths of the three sides. Solving triangles takes about a page of Fortran, whereas solving the is-has problem would take many pages of Fortran.

This is not to say that relationships are inherently more important than triangles. The point is that solving some problems in Fortran may take longer than solving them in Lisp. That is why Lisp belongs in an engineer's tool kit—it makes some problems easier to solve. If we have a problem for which Lisp is appropriate and we use Lisp and competitors do not, we gain a competitive advantage.[1]

Reduced programming cost is really the only reason to adopt a new programming language anyway. Buying a new language, installing and maintaining the compiler, and learning to use the language are time consuming and expensive. A new language has to repay this cost through reduced programming cost if the exercise is to be worthwhile.

---

[1] It is hard to overemphasize the point that different programming languages are merely tools designed for different uses. Arguing that Lisp is better than Fortran is like arguing that a Phillips screwdriver is better than a standard screwdriver. There is no general answer to such questions. It depends on the problem.

Semantic Nets

Property lists were put in the Lisp language in order to record attributes of objects. The is-has example shows how property lists can record relationships between objects and facilitate deductions about objects.

The usefulness of the "is" and "has" properties led to the idea of using semantic nets to store knowledge. Humans use knowledge about general object categories to make deductions about specific objects. German shepherds are a breed of dog, and are usually black and gray. If someone mentions a specific German shepherd such as Rin Tin Tin, people know that he is a dog and assume that he is probably black and gray without being told. Making assumptions on the basis of general categories leads to an occasional mistake, of course, but seems to be the basis of many human thought processes.

A Subtle Problem

The simple logic rules used in the is-has example—the assumption that A is B and B is C imply that A is C—leads to errors when dealing with larger collections of facts. People would say that an elephant is gray and that gray is a color, but when these facts are added to the database, the program infers that elephant is color.[1]

People would say that an elephant has color, but this sort of distinction is difficult to incorporate into our simple database and inference mechanism. Investigators learned that the rules humans use when categorizing objects are complex and that getting a computer to do it the way humans would is difficult.

Object Types and Subtypes

In order to simulate this process in a computer, investigators developed the ideas of object type, subtype, and instance. An object type contains information that is true of some general class of object. As shown in figure 6.1, "dog" is a-kind-of object type. The object type dog records facts that are true of all dogs— that they are mammals, that they have puppies, that they have hair, and so on.

A subtype is a category of object that shares attributes with another type but may differ in detail. "German shepherd" is a-kind-of dog. Knowing that a dog is a German shepherd provides

---

[1] This is really a bug in the English language. Saying that an elephant is gray is syntactic shorthand. It is more precise to say that an elephant has gray as the value of its color property. Semantic nets often use "has-color" instead.

additional information. It would not be useful to specify a color attribute in the definition of "dog" because dogs vary in color. The definition of German shepherd can record a default hair color because most shepherds are the same color.

An "instance" is an object that is a member of some class. Rin Tin Tin is a German shepherd, so he is an instance of the German shepherd subtype of the more general object type dog.

Relationships between types, subtypes, and instances are often recorded in a data structure called a "semantic net." A sample semantic net is given in figure 6.1

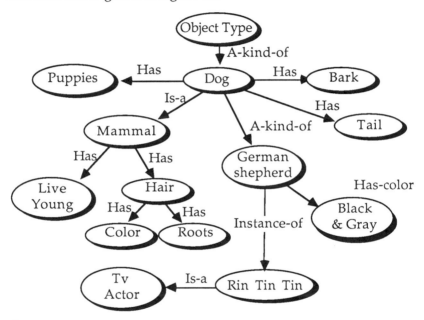

Figure 6.1
Relationships between object types, subtypes, and instances in a semantic net.

German shepherd could be defined as a separate object type rather than as a-kind-of dog, but the network would have to repeat all of the properties of German shepherds that are also true of dogs. Whenever a new attribute was added to dog, it would have to be added to German shepherd as well. It is much simpler to define German shepherd as a-kind-of dog than to repeat so much information.

Attribute Inheritance
German shepherd "inherits" properties from dog because a German shepherd is a-kind-of dog. A dog is-a mammal, which has live young. A program can deduce that a German shepherd

has live young even though that fact is not recorded in the German shepherd object type. Making such deductions is a little more complex than deducing that a circus-elephant has clothes because the program has to deal with a-kind-of in addition to "is" and "has" relationships, but the overall process is similar.

Whenever a program needs information about an attribute of an object, it first looks in the object to see if the information is found there. If not, it looks for the information in the type definition for the instance. If the attribute is found, it stops. If not, the program looks in the next type up and keeps going until it either finds the attribute or reaches the most general type definition and fails.

Instances and Object Classes
An instance of an object type is a specific example of that type of object. "Rin Tin Tin" is an instance-of the object type German shepherd, which is a-kind-of dog.

Instances of the same object type are referred to as members of the class of objects defined by that object type. Rin Tin Tin is a member of the German shepherd class. Lassie is a member of the collie class. Both Lassie and Rin Tin Tin are members of the dog class. Although they both have individual characteristics, they inherit many attributes from their class definition.

Exceptions to properties of object types are recorded as properties of specific instances. If Rin Tin Tin is a hairless German shepherd or if his color is other than black and gray, this is recorded as a property of Rin Tin Tin because it is not true of all German shepherds. Although chihuahuas are a-kind-of dog, hairlessness is an attribute of the chihuahua subtype, because it is true of most chihuahuas. If a member of the chihuahua object class has hair, that exception to the general properties of the class is recorded as a property of the individual object.

Multiple Inheritance
Rin Tin Tin is an unusual German shepherd in that he also is-a TV actor. In addition to inheriting properties from German shepherd, Rin Tin Tin inherits attributes from the TV actor object class. Most real objects fall into many categories. When a person is thought of as an engineer, their professional attributes and skills come to mind. When thought of as an employee, topics such as salary and responsibilities are important. The ability to treat an object as a member of many different classes is extremely helpful in making useful deductions about it.

Limitations of Semantic Networks

One major problem with semantic nets is that most properties are not recorded with the objects. Rin Tin Tin has bark, but this fact is not found in the Rin Tin Tin instance. In order to learn about "bark," the program searches through the definition of German shepherd and then through the definition of dog. This can take quite a long time in a complicated semantic net. If the program searched TV actor first instead of German shepherd, finding "bark" would take even longer.

The most general properties are needed most often. Because the most general properties are stored in the highest-level definitions, the properties that are needed the most often take the longest to find.

Copying properties into the object definitions reduces search time. The main reason not to specify common properties in objects is that it becomes difficult to maintain the network because it is hard to ensure that all object definitions are updated correctly. It is easy, however, to write a program to wander through the network and copy attributes from each type into all of its subtypes and from subtypes into objects. Humans can divide data into types and subtypes that are easily maintained and have object attributes updated automatically.

Copying information into objects makes properties easy to find but takes a great deal more computer memory. The trade-off between search time and storage space has not yet been solved in a satisfactory way. The human brain searches object definitions quickly so this is known to be possible, but no one knows how it is done.

Misinterpreting Semantic Networks

There is another, more subtle difficulty: Semantic networks are easy for programs to misinterpret. Programs do not really understand the information in semantic networks and can make ridiculous deductions.

Suppose that it becomes necessary to add chimpanzees to the network and to record the fact that they have arms and legs. Mammals have legs, so it seems reasonable to make legs a property of mammals, but chimpanzees also have arms and mammals in general do not. Being lazy, the programmers record that mammals have limbs instead of legs, because limb covers both arm and leg.

There is a problem. Figure 6.1 shows that Rin Tin Tin has bark, he has roots, and now he has limbs. It is easy for a program to confuse Rin Tin Tin with a tree! Humans would not make that error because we know so much more about trees and dogs, but the computer knows only what we tell it. On the basis of what the computer has been told, trees and dogs seem similar.

This specific error is too simple to happen in a real network, but such errors crop up all the time as networks grow and get more sophisticated. Semantic networks are a useful programming technique and can record a great deal of information. However, semantic networks are no longer used very much in AI research because they fall apart long before storing enough information to duplicate human knowledge.

Object-Oriented Programming

Semantic networks make mistakes because words do not always mean the same thing. "Bark" has different meanings when discussing dogs and when discussing trees. "Is" has different meanings in the facts "Elephant is gray" and "Gray is color." Processing the information in semantic networks properly requires that attributes be treated differently depending on the type of object. Attributes require different processing because they have different meanings depending on the context in which they are used.

Processing attributes according to object type leads to a new definition of object. An object is a list of properties *and code to manipulate them.* It is not enough to say that dogs have limbs— the object also needs a program to manipulate the attribute. The code to manipulate the limb property of objects of class dog is different from the code to manipulate the limb property of objects of class tree even though the properties have the same name.

Semantic networks define properties of object classes but cannot easily associate instructions with attributes of classes. Linking data and the code to process the data to form an object class is called "object-oriented programming."

Object-oriented programs are organized into objects that combine both data and code. Objects have attributes that are referred to as "variables" and programs called "methods," which are applied to the attributes.

Processing happens when a "message" is sent to an object. The message tells the object which method to perform and supplies any parameters the method requires. The method accepts the parameters, changes object variables as needed, and returns a value.[1]

An object's attributes can be manipulated only by its methods, and messages are the only way to invoke an object's methods. This forces programs that manipulate objects to stick to standard methods. Forcing programmers to use approved interfaces makes programs easier to maintain.

Incremental Programming

Objects act very much like subtypes. When a new object class is defined, variables and methods from other object types may be included in the definition of the new object. This makes it easy to define objects that are similar to existing objects because the new object inherits variables *and methods* from any object types included in its definition.

The programmer defining a new type of object does not need to rewrite methods that can be used with the new object. Only methods that differ from previous methods need to be written; all others can be used without change. This is a form of "programming by exception."

Suppose that a computer application defines "cargo-ship" objects. Objects of class cargo-ship have a "population" method that tells how many people are on board. When a "passenger-ship" class is defined, the programmer includes all the variables and methods for cargo-ship, then adds new variables to record the number of passengers, number of cabins, and other information needed for passenger ships.

Passenger-ship requires a new "population" method that returns the sum of the number of passengers and crew instead of just the crew. Methods for navigation, fuel capacity, and any other calculations that are the same for both kinds of ship need not be written for passenger-ship because they are inherited from cargo-ship.

This is the major difference between object-oriented programming and semantic networks: Objects define both attributes and code, which are inherited; semantic networks define only attributes. Attribute inheritance saves having to reenter attri-

---

[1] There is nothing magical about the term "method." A method is simply a software function that can be applied only to certain types of object. If a programmer writes a method to deal with automobiles, the object-oriented programming system keeps the code from being used to process airplanes by mistake. The software management system that is inherent in the idea of objects and methods reduces the cost of developing and maintaining software.

butes when a new object is created; code inheritance saves having to write new code.

Code inheritance permits incremental programming. When new objects are added, existing methods can be used to begin with and new methods added over time.

Uses of Object-Oriented Programming

One of the best uses of object-oriented programming is in developing graphics systems. Windows, lines, displays, and text strings are defined as objects that respond to messages such as "move," "erase," and "redraw." So long as any new class of objects responds to these messages, little code is needed to add new capability to the display system.

Object-oriented programming could also be useful for computerized manufacturing. Engineers could define objects such as machines and operations such as drilling and send messages such as "Make a hole."

If a transportation management system is defined in terms of objects, adding new kinds of vehicles is easy. The code to select an appropriate transportation mode needs to examine cost per ton per mile, ability to reach both the origin and destination, speed, time until pickup is possible, time until delivery, and other attributes of each potential mode of transportation.

Once the master scheduling program is able to deal with objects of type truck and railroad, it can handle aircraft and even space shuttle objects without changing the master program. So long as any new object classes respond to the same methods, the scheduling program need not even know that a new class of object has been added to the system.

Memory Management in Lisp

Property lists are one of the two major facilities that distinguish Lisp from other programming languages. Lisp has one other major distinguishing characteristic—automatic memory management. Letting programs call themselves is not unique, as recursion is offered in C, PL/1, Pascal, and Ada.

Automatic memory management is a spectacularly useful feature. No computer ever has enough memory—programmers are always running out, no matter how much memory management buys. In order to make up for limited memory, programs must recycle memory. The same memory words are used to hold different programs or data at different times.

Many languages permit manual memory management. Programs ask for more memory when they need it and return it when they are finished with it. Memory is allocated from a stock of available memory and goes back to the free memory inventory when the program returns it.

Forcing users to write programs that manage memory causes a great many mistakes. If a program returns some memory that it is not really finished using, this memory will sooner or later be given to another program for its use. Now, two different programs try to store information in the same memory words. The resulting chaos is similar to crossed telephone wires.

Lisp assumes the burden of memory management. Whenever a program needs memory, it is allocated automatically without the program having to ask. When a program stops using part of memory, the unused memory is reclaimed automatically. In this section I explain memory management to show how useful automatic memory management really is.

Function Call and Return

The memory management facility keeps track of how functions should return to the programs that called them and manages the memory used for data storage.

Tracking function calls is illustrated by the example in figure 6.2. Suppose that I write a program to compute the sine of variable X. The code looks like

A = sine(X)

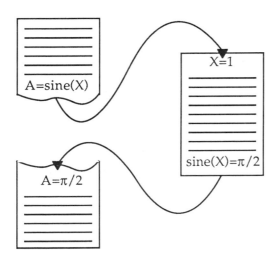

Figure 6.2
Function call and return.

The compiler translates this code into a call to the sine function. The instructions in the sine function take X as an input parameter and compute its sine. The result is the output from the sine function. When a function is called, the address of the instruction following the call is passed to it. When the function finishes, it uses this return address to jump back to the proper place in the program that called it:

At the same time, another program computes the sine of Y:

B = sine(Y)

Both programs use the same sine function. The function gets its input from two different variables: X in the first case and Y in the second. Because the same sine routine is called by many different programs, there can be many different return addresses floating around at the same time.

Memory Stacks
Managing return addresses and parameters is complicated because functions call each other. When the sine function calls the square root function, the computer must keep track of separate return addresses and parameters for the call to sine and for the call to square root. When recursive functions call themselves, the computer must distinguish the different sets of return pointers and parameters.

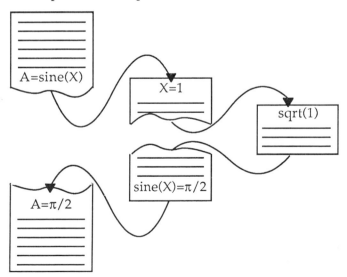

After trying many ways of passing return pointers and parameters, computer designers settled on memory stacks. A stack is a memory area that grows and shrinks like a pile of papers on a desk. Information is put on top of the stack or taken off the top. Putting data on the top of the stack is called "pushing" and taking data off the top is called "popping" as illustrated in figure 6.3

When a function calls another function, the return address is pushed on the stack followed by the parameters as shown in the diagram on the next page. The function gets its parameters by popping them off the top of the stack. When the answer is ready, the function pops the return address off the stack, pushes the result onto the stack, and returns.

When my program computes the sine of A, it pushes a return pointer on the stack followed by A and calls the sine function. The sine function pushes a return pointer and A onto the stack and calls the square root function, and so on. From the point of view of the calling program, parameters on top of the stack are magically turned into results on top of the stack.

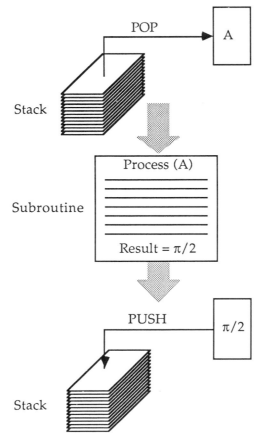

Figure 6.3
Pushing and popping data in a memory stack.

Stack Frames
The part of the stack where the parameters and return address for a function are stored is called its "stack frame." Functions also store temporary variables in the stack, so that they do not have to allocate any fixed storage in memory.

Storing variables in the stack means that functions can be used by different calling programs at the same time. When my program asks for the sine of X and your program asks for the sine of Y, we use the same sine function but different memory stacks. My program puts my return address and X in my stack and calls the sine function; your program puts your return address and Y in your stack and calls the same function. As long as the function uses my stack while computing the sine of X and uses your stack while computing the sine of Y, there is no difficulty in using the same code for different purposes.

Many computers have a special register called a "stack pointer" in addition to the program counter. The stack pointer stores the address of the memory word at the top of the stack. The computer has special instructions that push data onto the stack and pop it off. When the computer is running my program, it sets the stack pointer to point to my stack area, and sets the stack pointer to point to your stack when running yours.

When my program has run long enough that it is time to give yours a turn, the computer saves my stack pointer and program counter in memory somewhere and puts yours back the way they were when your program's last turn ended. Having a computer run many different programs by giving each of them turns in succession is called "multiprogramming."

Functions Calling Each Other
Functions often call each other. The function that computes sines needs square roots, so the sine function calls the square root function. This does not cause any problems. The return address and arguments to the square root function are pushed onto the top of the stack above the information pushed for the call to the sine function.

As long as the stack does not get too big for memory and each function always takes exactly as much information off of the stack as is put on for it, functions can call each other to any degree. Having one function call another is called "nesting."

This saves memory space and programming time. Once someone writes the square root function, any other function that needs square roots can use it. No matter how many functions call the square root function, only one copy of the function need be in memory, and all callers use the same copy.

The program that calls the sine function does not know that the sine function calls the square root function. If the sine function is changed to compute sines in another way and no longer needs square roots, calling programs do not care so long as the new version gives correct answers.

Managing Variable Values in Memory

Variables in conventional programming languages are assigned fixed memory addresses by the compiler or assembler. When our program refers to sine(X), the compiler looks up X in a table to find the memory address where X is stored. The compiler then generates code, which uses that address to retrieve X and push it on the top of the stack to pass X to the sine function.

Lisp data cannot be stored in fixed memory locations because the memory used to store a value changes frequently. As numbers get too big for one word, they are given another. Lists need more memory as elements are added and they need less as elements are deleted. Because there is no way to know in advance how much memory will be needed for a list, the memory allocated to lists must be changed as the program runs.

Automatic memory management grew out of the need for Lisp variable values to occupy different amounts of memory at different times. It is hard enough to write programs to compute correct values. It would be much more difficult to write programs that not only compute correct values but also allocate memory to store the new values.

Having Lisp assume the burden of making sure that values have enough memory to store whatever a program computes made it easier to write large Lisp programs. If programmers had to worry about memory allocation in addition to computing correct values, writing large programs would be too expensive and take too long.

List Structure

The classic way to store a Lisp list in memory is to link elements together using memory blocks called conses. Each cons holds for two pointers—one pointer gives the memory address of the word containing the car of the list, and the other pointer gives the address of the cdr.

Lisp experts use the word "cons" to refer both to the cons function and to a block of memory containing car and cdr pointers. I use CONS to refer to the function and cons to talk about memory blocks, and similar notation for car and cdr.

Figure 6.4 shows how the list (A B C) is stored in memory. Each rectangle represents a cons. The arrows coming out of each half of the rectangle show where the pointer in that word of the cons points.

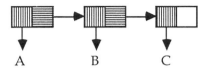

Figure 6.4
Storing the list (A B C) in memory.

The first pointer in the first cons in the list points to A, so A is the car of the list. The second pointer in the first cons points to another cons, which is the first cons in the sublist (B C), so (B C) is the cdr of the list (A B C).

The cdr pointer of the rightmost cons does not point to anything because there are no more conses in the list. A pointer to nothing is called a "NIL pointer," or "NIL." A list ends with a cons that has a "NIL cdr."

Finding Elements in Lists
Knowing the memory address of the first cons in a list is all that is needed to find any element—computing enough CARs and CDRs eventually locates any element in the list. For example, the cdr pointer of the list above points to the list (B C). The car pointer of that list points to B. Computing first the CDR and then the CAR of the list finds B. Finding C is similar, except that it requires one more CDR before taking the CAR. The first CDR returns the list (B C), the second CDR returns the single element list (C), and the final CAR returns the atom C.

Processing information in Lisp usually requires long sequences of calls to CAR and CDR to find the right data. The fundamental Lisp operations manipulate pointers instead of doing arithmetic. If a Lisp system is running on a computer where pointer processing is slow, Lisp runs slowly.

Constructing New Lists
When the CONS function is passed a list and an element to add to the list, it allocates a new cons in memory to hold pointers to the car and cdr of the new list. Suppose that CONS is given the list (B C) and the atom A:

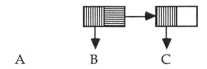

A   B   C

CONS constructs a new list by allocating a new cons from the free memory list and storing pointers to the car and cdr of the new list in it:

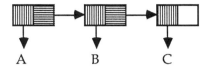

A   B   C

The CONS function not only manipulates pointers, but also allocates a new area of memory. Memory allocation is relatively rare in conventional languages, and memory is allocated and reclaimed in large blocks of as many as 4,096 words each. Lisp allocates memory whenever any program calls CONS, and memory is allocated and reclaimed in terms of blocks of two words.

It takes more processing power to keep track of memory in two-word increments than in 4,096 word blocks. Lisp uses more computer capacity for memory management than other languages do. This is not unreasonable, as large corporations spend as much time filing and managing information as they spend collecting it in the first place. Libraries spend as much money putting cards in the card catalogue, sticking a label on the back of each book, and putting books on the right shelves as they spend buying books.

Setting and Changing Symbol Values
Suppose that the symbol X has the value (A B C). X is represented in memory as an entry in a table listing all symbols that have been defined by a Lisp program. Each symbol table entry stores the name of the symbol and a pointer to its value:

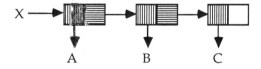

X   A   B   C

When Lisp computes the CAR of X, it first looks up X in the symbol table to find where the value of X is stored in memory. Lisp then follows this pointer to find the first cons in the list (A B C). CAR returns the first pointer in the cons, which points to A, the first element in the list.

Lisp proceeds in exactly the same way when computing the CDR, except that it returns the second pointer in the cons instead of the first. Instead of pointing to a symbol, this points to another cons because the cdr of X is the list (B C).

When a program changes the value of the symbol X to the list (D E F), Lisp automatically allocates three conses to store the structure information and memory to store the elements D, E, and F. After X is changed, memory looks like

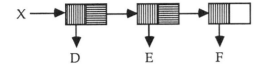

The value pointer for X now points to the list (D E F) instead of the list (A B C). The memory that stores (A B C) is no longer in use because it is no longer pointed to by the value pointer for X. Changing the value of a variable allocates new conses and results in the original conses not being pointed to. Conses that are no longer pointed to can be recycled.

Garbage Collection

Recycling conses that are no longer pointed to is called "garbage collection" and is a necessary evil in a Lisp system. Garbage collection is simple in principle: The garbage collector scans memory for conses that are not pointed to by any other cons or symbol value pointer.

Simple garbage collectors use the "mark and sweep" method. The garbage collector first marks all conses as "not pointed to." It then follows all pointers in the values of all symbols, flagging all conses it encounters as "pointed to." After scanning all the symbols, the garbage collector makes a final pass through memory, recycling all conses that are still flagged as "not pointed to."

One difficulty with mark and sweep is that the Lisp program stops while the garbage collector monopolizes memory. This is tolerable in a research environment because no one minds if an experimental program pauses every so often. It is not acceptable in a factory environment. If a program controlling a machine tool pauses to get its act together, disaster results.

There is another garbage collection technique called "reference count." Whenever a pointer is set to point to a cons, a counter telling how many pointers point to that cons is increased by one. Whenever a pointer is changed so that it does not point to a cons anymore, the count for that cons is decreased by one. If the cons's reference count is reduced to zero, there are no more pointers to that cons, and it is recycled immediately.[1]

Tag Bits

When a program follows pointers to the bitter end and finally finds data, it needs to know what to do with it. Knowing what to do with data is easy in conventional languages—the value of a variable always occupies the same memory location and does not change to a different kind of data while the program is running. The compiler knows what kind of information is stored in each variable and generates the right instructions to manipulate that type of data.

Lisp variable values need more memory during execution as lists grow or numbers get bigger. When Lisp changes the amount of memory used to store a value, it must leave some sort of record behind so that it can figure out how to deal with the value the next time it is needed.

Lisp uses "tag bits" to record what kind of information a pointer points to. When X was assigned the value (A B C) in the example, X's value pointer gave the address where the list started and also included tag bits that indicated that the value of X was a list. If the program later sets X to 2, the value pointer is changed to point to 2 and the tag bits are changed to indicate that the value is a single-word integer. If later calculations increase the value of X so that it no longer fits in one word, an extra word is allocated, and the tag bits are changed to indicate that X is a number that occupies more than one word.

Special-purpose Lisp computers often incorporate extra bits in each word to hold tag information. Lisp systems on conventional computers store data type information in other ways. As long as Lisp programs run fast enough that speed is not a problem for the application, it does not matter how Lisp stores data type information.

Summary of Lisp

Lisp has property lists for recording information about symbols and relationships among them. It also incorporates automatic

---

[1] Garbage collection imposes such a heavy burden on the computer hardware that it is worth some effort to avoid it. It is possible to write Lisp programs in such a way that they do not generate surplus conses. This programming style is called "garbageless Lisp" and makes it possible to run Lisp programs on conventional computers without paying a heavy performance penalty for garbage collection overhead. It is much more trouble to write garbage-free Lisp, however, which negates some of the advantages of using Lisp.

memory management that lets variable values change in size and eliminates many programming errors. These are the two major features that distinguish Lisp from other programming languages. Lisp also includes the standard control structure mechanisms developed for conventional languages.

Other Languages for AI

Lisp is not the only language in which AI programs can be written, but it is by far the most convenient most of the time. Chapter 13 describes Prolog. Heroic programmers have implemented expert systems and natural language parsing systems in C, Basic, Forth, and even Cobol. AI is a set of programming methods and philosophies; it is not tied to a specific language.

In the next several chapters I discuss Lisp's programming tools and then describe natural language and expert systems in some detail. Knowing how expert systems work is helpful in understanding Prolog, which is becoming popular for AI work.

Diagnosis:
Try Stress
Control. ..
... .

7
Software Tools for AI

Artificial intelligence problems are so difficult that researchers cannot afford to waste time wrestling with recalcitrant computers or software development tools. For the past fifteen years, researchers at MIT, Stanford University, Carnegie Mellon, Yale, Xerox Palo Alto Research Center, and other AI labs expended vast energy and cleverness on methods and tools to make it easier to write software. Until many of the staff left to form a company to sell computers designed specifically to run Lisp, an entire floor of the MIT AI Lab in Cambridge, Massachusetts, was devoted to software tool development.[1] The result was the most productive software development environment in the world.

Commercial products are becoming dependent on software. There are seven microprocessors in a recent model of a well-

---

[1] This company was Symbolics, which quickly became one of the leading vendors of Lisp machines, which are computers specially designed to run Lisp well. Most Lisp machine development was done at MIT with funding from the Defense Advanced Research Projects Agency (DARPA) with the explicit intent of spinning the results of the research out into a commercial company. DARPA has been funding AI research for twenty years. Finding a way to make Lisp machines available for only $100,000 or so would make other research projects a lot cheaper. Helping to found Symbolics saved DARPA a great deal of money by reducing the cost of AI research, but opened DARPA to the charge of unfairly subsidizing a commercial firm.

known luxury automobile, and two or three in self-focusing 35 mm cameras. Software bugs can keep the engine from starting, make the car handle poorly, or ruin irreplaceable wedding photographs. Office copiers and microwave ovens all have microprocessors. Washing machines, refrigerators, and other kitchen appliances are beginning to use microprocessors. These products depend on software for correct operation. This software must be developed in a timely manner at reasonable cost.

In this chapter I briefly introduce engineering design tools and software development procedures and describe conventional software tools. After that, I describe software development tools and methods which were derived from AI research.

Conventional Engineering Tools

Engineering tools have many tasks. They are used for prediction, performance evaluation, project tracking, design description, and problem analysis. Some tools predict how a design will work. Predictive tools include finite element analysis, simulation, modeling, and imagination. These methods help find design errors before the prototype is built. Errors caught at this stage cost less than at later stages.

Other tools show the engineer how a device is performing. Such tools include strain gauges, wind tunnels, test tracks, oscilloscopes, frequency meters, vibration probes, and thermo-couples. Knowing what a prototype is doing helps an engineer compare its performance with the design goals, which is the first step in refining the design.

Clerical tools keep track of changes. Design changes are sent to the factory, to field engineers, and to customers. Making sure that current information reaches everyone who needs to know is a daunting task.

Documentation tools help engineers describe designs so that others can manufacture or maintain the device. Documentation tools include cameras, drafting boards, word processors, CAD systems, electronic mail, and document tracking systems.

An oscilloscope graphs voltage versus time on a TV screen. Engineers attach a probe to a circuit, and the oscilloscope displays the instantaneous voltage at that point. This tells the engineers what the circuit is doing. By comparing what the circuit does with what it ought to be doing, the designers figure out how to refine the circuit until it works properly. When engineers adjust circuit parameters, new results appear on the oscilloscope screen at once. Cameras record displays for later use.

An oscilloscope contains ten or twelve circuit boards. Each board is about as complicated as a typical circuit an engineer designs using an oscilloscope. An oscilloscope is about ten times as complex as most circuits with which it is used. Electrical engineers use tools that are about ten times more powerful than the circuits they design.

Most software tools are much simpler than the programs being developed. When programmers want better tools, they usually write their own or do without. Inadequate software tools hold down productivity.

Although computers run relatively rapidly, software tools provide information slowly. Programmers usually find out what programs are doing by looking at the values of variables. When debugging a program that computes square roots, the developer needs to examine the input value and the result in order to check the answers. Many variables are written out in the course of normal program operation, but if a programmer needs to know the value of a variable that is not being written, it is necessary to insert a special WRITE command in the program, and then rerun the program in order to find out the value of the variable. How fast would circuit design go if engineers had to wait half an hour or so after moving oscilloscope probes before new data appeared?

The Software Development Process

Software development is pretty much the same, regardless of the kind of computer being programmed. I want to skip software design and concentrate on program debugging. Programming starts with "source code." Source code is a collection of symbolic program statements such as A = sine(X) that the compiler turns into numbers representing instructions.

Most computer programs are too big to be written by one person in a reasonable amount of time, so they are broken down into separate modules. Each module is assigned to a different programmer and contains source code for several different functions. Each module has a "source file," which stores the source code for the module.

Source modules are compiled into "object modules." Object modules store the instructions to perform operations described in source modules. Object modules must be combined so that the program can be run in the computer. A program called a "linker" reads object modules and produces a single "load module," which can be read into memory and run. Reading a load module into memory before running it is called "loading."

Fixing Program Errors

After the programmer figures out which source code in a test program need to be changed, fixing an error in a conventional software development environment involves many steps.

1.   Tell the computer to stop running the test program and start the program editor.   Most program editors operate like word processors and display parts of the program on a terminal screen so that programmers can enter changes from the keyboard.
2.   Tell the editor to start work on the source file containing the error.
3.   Find the instruction that has to be changed.   This may take a while if the file is large.   One reason to break a large program down into small modules is to minimize editing time.
4.   Make the changes.   This is often the fastest step, particularly if the repair needs only a simple fix such as changing a call to the sine function to a call to the cosine function.
5.   Tell the editor to write an updated copy of the source file.
6.   Leave the editor.
7.   Tell the compiler to read the updated source file and make a new object module.   Editing may introduce errors that the compiler finds.   If the compiler complains about the module, it is edited again.
8.   When the compiler accepts the module, it generates an object file.   This new object file is linked with all the other object files in the program to produce a new load module.
9.   Load the new module into memory.
10. Start the test all over again from the beginning.

Most computers can run the compiler and linker automatically after the source file has been edited, but it is easy to make mistakes.   Programmers often edit the wrong file or link in the wrong object modules, particularly when many people are working on the same project.

The worst aspect of this process is the time it wastes.   Finding the right file, making the change, compiling, linking, and getting ready to test again can take half an hour or more when the application program is large.   Short programs can be compiled and linked in under a minute, but few programs that small are found in commercial practice.

Multiperson Programming Projects

When a project is divided among many people, each person is responsible for writing and testing several different modules.

Keeping track of which source file corresponds to which object file is tedious, time consuming, and fraught with error in a multiperson project.

Modules written by someone else are usually needed before any programmer can test any module. Nothing works when the project starts, so no one can test anything until someone gets a few modules staggering well enough to test other programs. Once a few modules are working fairly well, the people who are responsible for them make copies for other people to use.

Suppose, for example, that I am writing a sine function, and you are writing the function which computes square roots. I store the code for sine in the same module with cosine, tangent, and other similar functions. You put SQRT in the same module with EXP that computes exponents, ABS for absolute values, and so on. My sine function needs to compute square roots, so I cannot test it until you get SQRT working.

You write a quick version of SQRT that works some of the time so that I can test SINE while you finish SQRT and work on EXP. I do not want you to give me a new version of SQRT very often because I am fixing bugs in SINE. If I got a new SQRT every day, it would be hard to tell if my program acted differently because of a change I made to SINE or a change you made to SQRT.

I need my own copy of SQRT that stays the same while you change yours. Every so often you come to a reasonable stopping point and give me a new version of SQRT that works better than the previous one. Being the suspicious type, I am not convinced that your new SQRT solves more problems than it causes, so I keep my old copy around until I use the new one enough to have faith in it. Only then do I discard the old version.

There are at least three copies of SQRT floating around: the version you are working on, the version you just gave me, and the older version I kept just in case. Multiply this by several hundred modules in a project and ten or twenty people working together, add staff attrition and turnover over a period of years, and you have the ingredients for utter chaos.

Source Code Control

How do we cope with multiple versions of the "same" program? They cannot all be named SQRT because computers have a nasty habit of demanding unique file names. Not only that, there are other functions in the file that contains SQRT—it also stores EXP, ABS, and many others.

We not only have to give the file a name that more or less describes all the modules in it but also give it enough different names for all the different versions. After we give each version a different name, how do we tell the linker which file to use when making a load module?

Hardware engineers have a simpler existence. No matter how often they change a circuit by adding new wires or removing old ones, the underlying printed circuit board remains the same. Making a new board is so much work that there are seldom many versions of a circuit lying around.

Computers can copy files quickly and easily, so source and object modules multiply like rabbits. It is as if each time a hardware engineer changed a circuit in the slightest, the board magically copied itself. The lab would be hip deep in *almost* identical circuit boards, and chaos would reign.[1]

Keeping track of which source file to use to compile each object module and which versions of each object module to link together is called source code control (SCC). There are many different SCC techniques, but the SCC systems developed for AI research are among the best available and are still being worked on. AI researchers must cope with the world's largest programs, and graduate students have high staff turnover. AI research is the worst-case software management problem.

Software Development Tools

Software engineers make relatively little use of analytical tools to predict how software designs will work. Software designers use statistical modeling techniques to analyze performance of transaction processing systems, such as airline reservations and order entry, but there are few tools available for determining whether software will work before it is built. Programmers write programs without doing much design validation, then tweak them to make them work as the customer wants.

AI researchers could not predict how programs to emulate human thought would perform because the purpose of writing the program was to determine if it would work at all, never mind how well. AI developers concentrated on tools to help write code quickly. If software can be implemented with little more effort than required to simulate it, a researcher might as

---

[1] Custom integrated circuits are changing this. New software tools let hardware designers churn out new chips so fast that hardware versions multiply almost as fast as software versions. One might hope that hardware engineers will keep better track of what they are doing than software people have in the past, but experience suggests that they will have to get burned a time or two before they learn to be careful.

well write the program instead of simulating and get accurate results instead of approximations.

Writing Programs Rapidly

Software development and maintenance are extremely labor-intensive operations. The laborers are expensive, hard to find, and even harder to retain and manage. There is a tremendous premium on the ability to write programs rapidly in order to save labor. In order to be able to write programs quickly, programmers need tools to:
- Find out if functions are computing correct results.
- Make sure functions are being called at the right time.
- Find the right place in the source code to change.
- Make changes quickly.
- Retest rapidly.
- Communicate with colleagues about problems and solutions.
- Keep track of different versions of source and object modules.
- Interact with the computer in a natural language.
- Find relevant system documentation quickly.

Each of these problems has been attacked with separate facilities in the Lisp software environment. The different kinds of software tools are described in what follows.

Finding Out If Functions Work Properly

In order to verify that functions are behaving properly, programmers must be able to find out symbol values and be notified when functions are called. Learning symbol values is easy in Lisp. Lisp environments are structured around a program called a "Lisp listener" which waits for the user to type something. Whenever a user types anything, the listener reads it, computes its value, and prints the result.

Typing the name of a symbol makes Lisp follow the symbol's value pointer to find the value in memory and print it. This helps programmers find out what a program did because it is easy to learn what values were computed for any symbol.

Typing an expression such as (CAR '(A B C)) makes the listener compute the CAR of the list (A B C) and return the symbol A. Functions can be tested by typing their names and arguments into the listener. The listener calls the function and prints the result.

If a programmer suspects that a function is not working right, one way to check is to find out what data are being passed to it and what values it returns. The Lisp "program trace" generates a message whenever a function is called. The trace lists the values being passed to the function, runs the function, and then prints the value that was returned. By comparing what the function did with what it should have done, developers can find whether the function works or not.[1]

Trace also gives clues about control structure errors. If the trace message does not appear, the function is not being called and the error is in the calling program instead.

Finding Control Structure Errors

Tracing functions is useful for finding whether functions compute correct answers but is not very helpful finding errors in control structure. When my SINE program calls the exponent function by mistake instead of the square root program, tracing SQRT does not find the problem. I need to know where SINE wandered off to and how it got there so I can fix the error.

Whenever a function calls another, Lisp builds a stack frame to hold the arguments to the function and the return pointer. The function also uses part of the stack frame to hold temporary variables needed for its work. When SINE calls SQRT, a stack frame for SQRT is built on top of SINE's stack frame. When SQRT calls ABS, a stack frame for ABS is built on top of SQRT's.

Suppose that SINE goes into an infinite loop. I eventually get tired of waiting for SINE to return and hit the BREAK key.[2] BREAK tells the Lisp listener to interrupt whatever function is running and enter a debugger.

The debugger displays the stack for examination and modification. I can examine the current stack frame, the one before it, and the one before that, all the way back to the initial function call. Each frame has a return pointer, an argument list, and the temporary variables for each function. The stack defines the state of my program at the time of the BREAK.

---

[1] In general, any function can be encapsulated with code that is run whenever the function is called and whenever it is returned. The tracer is a specific encapsulation that prints the argument list when a function is called and prints the result when it returns.

Programmers can write custom encapsulations to do things such as writing debugging information to a disk file instead of to the screen. The ability to run code whenever a function is called without changing the function is a very powerful technique. You can change what a function does without getting inside it by encapsulating it with code that implements the changes.

[2] The actual keys that cause a BREAK vary from Lisp vendor to Lisp vendor. On a Symbolics Lisp machine, the key combination for BREAK is called c-m-Suspend. To enter it, you hold the "control" and "meta" keys down while pressing "Suspend." Other environments use different keys. One of the difficulties with Lisp is that nobody has standardized the keyboard layout.

The top frame on the stack is a call to ABS. I know that the loop is in the ABS function and examine its arguments. ABS was passed the list (A B C) instead of a number. Why passing ABS a list instead of a number should make it loop I do not know, but is clearly an abuse of the function. Looking at the prior stack frame, I find that SQRT called ABS and passed it the offending datum. Aha! It's probably your problem, not mine, since you wrote SQRT. I scan the next few stack frames. SQRT was passed the argument (A B C) by my SINE routine, and SINE was passed a reasonable value.

Sigh. The bug is in my sine routine, not your SQRT or ABS. I mentally discard the scathing memo I was about to write and examine SINE's temporary variables to find out what SINE thought it was doing when it passed a list instead of a number.

Locating Current Source Code

There are two possibilities when figuring out where to change a program: Developers either know which source file has to be changed or have to guess. Because most bugs are found by whomever wrote the function, the name of the source file is usually known, but when someone encounters a problem in someone else's code, they often haven't a clue where the source code is stored.

Lisp programmers do not have to remember the names of source code files. The Lisp editor remembers the source file for every function that has been loaded into the Lisp system and retrieves the current version of the file containing the code for SINE when anyone asks for SINE. The editor reads the source file and displays SINE on the screen.

Suppose that you are on vacation, and I encounter a bug in SQRT that I must fix before I can proceed. I do not know the names of the functions that SQRT calls, but the editor helps me find out. The editor can search through the list of functions for names that match any character string I type.

I suspect that SQRT calls a function to compute an absolute value. Asking the editor to display the names of all functions that contain the text strings "absolute" or "value" generates a list of such functions. Tracing these functions shows me which one is called when the error occurs. I find that SQRT calls a function named "temporary-absolute-value" instead of "absolute-value" and look there.

If project members give functions long descriptive names, this process usually finds the right function rather quickly. It is as if an oscilloscope could read a schematic and trace a circuit—engineers could say, "Find all circuits affecting this signal."

The editor also knows which source file corresponds to the version of the function that is being run at the time and warns me if there is a more recent version available. This keeps me from wasting time finding bugs in an obsolete version of SQRT, and helps me find the current version.

Making Changes Quickly

Once a function is displayed on the screen, the editor helps make the changes. The Lisp editor is aware of Lisp language syntax: It knows where lists start and end, how parentheses should be balanced, and so on. The editor automatically indents source code in order to clarify the structure. Automatic balancing of parentheses and automatic indenting prevent many syntax errors and reduce conceptual errors in programs.

More exotic editors can execute functions, list required and optional arguments for functions, and expand macros. The function results or the macro expansion are displayed in a part of the screen that temporarily writes over the text being edited. When the user finishes with the temporary display, the original text is restored.

Recompiling Quickly

When I fix SINE to keep it from passing lists instead of numbers to SQRT, I do not have to recompile the entire source file—I can ask the editor to compile SINE alone. Compiling one function at a time instead of compiling all the functions in a file is called "incremental compilation."

After the editor compiles the function, it automatically replaces the old object code. Linking is never needed and all of the other object code stays in place. This fast edit-compile-test cycle makes it possible to change programs and start testing again in a few seconds.

Retesting Programs

After a change is made, the new program must be tested to see if the change fixed the problem. In a conventional system this requires loading the program into memory again and running the test from the beginning.

Lisp preserves the function call and return stack when an error or BREAK occurs. The stack records all of the function calls that were made up to the time of the error. After fixing the bug, I can test again without starting over.

In order to find the bug, I worked back in the control stack to the stack frame where SINE was called. After recompiling SINE, I can ask Lisp to restart the test from the stack frame created by the function call that produced the error. This throws away the calls to SQRT and ABS which were passed bad parameters.

Lisp passes the original argument to the new version of SINE. If my change fixed the bug, SINE runs correctly and the program proceeds as if the error never happened. If the error happens again, I can try another fix.

Data Inspector and Window Debugger
Debugger commands are complicated enough that most programmers prefer to use the window debugger. This program displays the top few stack frames on the screen and lists the names and values of the variables being processed by the function at the top of the stack. As programmers wander up and down the stack, the debugger generates new variable displays.

The inspector is useful in examining data structures because it is easy to see relationships between different data. Users can edit data on the screen before restarting programs. The ability to see all variables that are related to a function at once saves a lot of time. Programmers do not have to ask for variables one at a time; they can check them all at a glance.

Communicating with Colleagues
Interaction between programmers is very important. Staff members must be kept informed of design changes, test programs, module status, management desires, and other matters. I point out gently that your program ought not to loop when it gets bad data. You riposte that testing for bad data makes your program run slowly and that my program should be more careful. Conventional projects spend a lot of time in meetings.

Meetings are not possible in most AI projects. AI research teams are small and usually scattered all across the country. AI centers at MIT, Stanford, Carnegie Mellon, and other universities must cooperate on research. University budgets seldom permit enough travel to keep people informed.

Fortunately the Defense Advanced Research Projects Agency (DARPA; funded an experimental data communications network connecting computers at many academic computing centers. This network is known as the ARPANET. It was one of the earliest large-scale computer networks ever created.

The original goal was to share computing load between universities. If the computer at MIT was busy, the network would automatically transmit the problem to Stanford, run it on an idle computer there, and transmit the results back to MIT.

Automatic load sharing never worked well, but the network let professors and students dial into computers at distant universities. Supplying projects with terminals instead of computers saved DARPA a lot of money, and the ARPANET was ideal for implementing an electronic mail system to help coordinate research projects.

Electronic Mail Researchers wrote rather fancy electronic mail software. The E-mail system lets users compose messages at terminals and send them to individuals or to mailing lists. The mail software worries about selecting the right telephone lines to send mail to each person and storing the messages until the recipient is ready to read them.

The volume of electronic mail quickly grew to the point that nobody could read it.[1] Programmers wrote filtering routines to examine their mail queues to identify important messages. It is not unusual for programmers at AI centers to spend 30% of their time reading and answering electronic mail. Experience shows that up to 50% of project design discussions are carried out by means of E-mail in organizations with well-developed systems. Only an accountant would care whether this constitutes design or mail processing.[2]

Bug Reports Once the electronic mail system was working, programmers specialized it to send software bug reports. When I find a problem in your square root program that I cannot fix, I can send you a bug report. The mail system automatically formats the function call stack so that you will know which versions of all functions were called and which parameters were passed. I can add comments to the message, such as a passionate plea for you to fix the bug quickly. The mail system stores the message until you return from vacation.

---

[1] There are people who get more than 200 electronic mail messages per day, and 100 to 150 is not uncommon. Useful as it is, E-mail requires discipline to keep from degenerating into an electronic backyard fence or gossip network.

[2] Publishing firms are beginning to use commercial electronic mail systems. *PC Magazine* in New York City communicates with its authors via E-mail, and authors submit articles the same way. Text is corrected on display screens by editors and typeset by computer. Articles seldom see paper until the magazine is printed and distributed. *PC Magazine* is developing software to let subscribers dial its computer and look for articles that interest them. Maybe paperless media are coming after all.

Some programmers send bug reports to themselves, particularly when they do not have time to fix a bug right away. Sending the message preserves all of the information that will be needed later to fix the bug.

Bug reports are a special message category that most programmers examine as soon as possible. You read my message, note that I asked an obsolete version of SQRT for the square root of minus one, and send a reply to the effect that the bug would go away if I would switch to the latest version of SQRT instead of insisting on using my old one.[1]

Keeping Track of Software Versions
As software projects grind on, it becomes more and more difficult to remember which file has the current version of which function. Lisp installations offer a "system definition file" that lists all of the files in a particular software application, tells the order in which they must be compiled, and lists the object files.

When a programmer loads a program into memory, the "make system" command reads the system definition file and loads the proper object modules into memory for execution.[2]

If a source file has been modified since it was compiled last, make system automatically recompiles it to bring the object module up to date. Making the computer handle these clerical tasks turned out to be worthwhile.

Patch Files After a software system has been distributed, customers find bugs and developers offer new features. It can be acutely painful to find that a customer suffered a costly problem because they did not receive the correct version of all the functions. Chasing bugs that have already been found and fixed is rather discouraging.

The conventional practice is to send out a complete set of new software and to expect that a knowledgeable person at each site will make sure everyone gets a copy. This is acceptable in data processing, because large computer centers employ systems programmers to keep software up to date.

---

[1] Automobile companies use electronic mail to send engineering changes, schedule changes, and purchase orders to vendors in order to adjust production schedules more easily.

[2] The problem of maintaining software systems is not unique to AI. The UNIX operating system has a "make" command that has no background in AI research. The need was more acute in AI labs than elsewhere, so the AI-derived version control facilities are more powerful than most.

AI labs cannot afford special people to maintain software obtained from elsewhere because they are too busy fixing their own programs. AI people took advantage of the incremental compilation facility to distribute program patches to help maintain distributed software.

The patch facility requires cooperation among the editor, compiler, and system definition system. The editor notices which functions are changed during an edit session and copies them into a special patch file. This file is then compiled, generating a patch module containing object code for functions that have changed. Patch files are sent to all customers.

When the patch file is copied into the customer's file system, the system definition is modified to include the new patch. When the next user issues a "make system" command, the patch is loaded into memory after the original program is loaded. Functions in the patch file replace earlier versions, and the entire system is brought up to date.

Interactive Documentation
The ability to find functions and learn their calling sequence by entering their approximate name is helpful but not adequate for programmers who have no knowledge of a project. Staff recruits start by reading documentation until they learn enough about the project to know what questions to ask.

Computer systems are notorious for generating a tremendous volume of paper.[1] Keeping documentation up to date is a monumental task and can consume more resources than keeping software current. Symbolics and Texas Instruments, two Lisp machine vendors, offer software for maintaining, searching, and displaying documentation in electronic form.

Interactive documentation systems store documents on disks instead of on paper. The computer establishes electronic cross-references between documents so that users can find related material across many separate documents. Whenever a reader scans a paragraph, key words representing links to other infor-

---

[1] When IBM's operating system for the 360 mainframe computer was introduced in 1964, a complete set of system manuals was "only" about six feet thick and I was able to read most of it. The documentation has grown faster than the software ever since. When I met one of IBM's documentation honchos at a seminar in 1983, he had no idea how thick the manuals were, but said it was probably at least 100 feet. He pointed out that IBM was second to the US government in annual publishing volume. I asked how he measured volume— titles, pages, words, or what? He said, "Forget all that. We measure in tons!"

mation are highlighted so that the user not only knows that there is related information available but also how to find it.[1]

The computer finds relevant material on the disk faster than most people can flip through books. Storing text on disk takes less space than on paper, and information is kept current by sending out document updates to go with software updates.

Experience is suggesting that electronic documents with automatic cross-references are qualitatively different from printed documents because they can be searched far more easily. If human editors and computers establish linkages between documents in a systematic way, readers can chart their own paths through the documentation forest and learn the minimum amount of information needed to do the task at hand.

Instant access to information helps make computers easier to use. It does not matter if a person forgets how to use a computer if the computer can retrain the user rapidly enough.

Natural Language Interfaces
The more useful a computer program becomes, the harder it becomes to use: The more useful a program is, the more tasks it can do; the more tasks the program can do, the more commands there are; the more commands there are, the longer it takes to learn to use the program.[2]

If research into natural language processing had produced computers that understood English, the user interface problem would go away because users could simply tell computers what to do. Unfortunately existing natural language programs are limited in scope as explained in chapter 3.

The most frustrating problem confounding users who are unfamiliar with a specific natural language system is knowing which words the computer understands. A friend of mine once spent an hour or two thinking up synonyms for "manager" to try to get information out of an employee database that had a natural language interface.

He asked about "boss," "manager," "leader," "group leader," and many others before giving up in disgust. The next day he

---

[1] Although documentation is developed on computer screens, most editors and authors prefer to scrutinize a printed copy for the final editing pass before publication. I have been using word processors for ten years, but I had to print this book for my last scan before publication. It is possible that a computer screen the size of a book page would eliminate the need for the final look at a printed page, but it might not.
[2] The Lisp machine software environment is perhaps the ultimate example of a powerful program with a great many commands.

found out that the database did not have information about hierarchical relationships. It told which employees worked on each project, but not who supervised whom.

Texas Instruments' Natural Language Menu (NLM; system is a form of "near natural language." Queries resemble English sentences, such as "Find parts whose weight is greater than 12 and whose supplier city is London," but instead of typing any old sentence from the keyboard, users build sentences out of phrases selected from menus.

Each menu lists phrases that can be used under certain circumstances. The comparison menu lists the phrases "between," "greater than," "less than," and "equal to"; the modifier menu has sentence fragments such as "whose part city is," "whose part color is," and "whose part weight is." Users can enter only those phrases that are listed in a menu.

The constraints imposed by the menus mean that users cannot enter sentences that the system does not understand. Because the entire vocabulary is displayed in the menus, there is never any doubt about which words the system can understand. My friend would have quickly noticed that there were no menu entries for "supervisor" or anything similar and concluded that the program did not know about employment hierarchies.

The major advantage of constrained natural language is that it offers nearly as much ease of use as full natural language at a small fraction of the cost. Application program developers specify which menu categories are allowed at various points in a sentence and tell which functions to call when a user chooses a particular phrase. The NLM system handles the user dialog and calls the appropriate functions when the user completes a sentence. The programmer does not have to develop the user interface because that is handled by the NLM package.

Was It Worth the Cost?

From an engineering point of view the software tools provided with Lisp machines are absolutely marvelous. I have worked in many programming environments, starting with typing programs onto IBM cards and working with just about every programming device that came down the road over the last twenty-five years. Productivity in a good Lisp environment is a factor of

10 better than in any other environment[1]—I get 10 times more work done per unit of effort than using any other set of tools.

This is a clearly worthwhile result. AI researchers may or may not have developed any intelligent programs, but they have produced some extremely good software development tools.

The Cost of High Productivity

Increased productivity does not come free, of course. Running Lisp makes *severe* demands on computer hardware. Remembering function call stacks and recording source files for each function take a great deal of memory and compute power.

IBM PC programmers can write useful programs in Basic, Pascal, or C for the IBM PC that run perfectly well in as little as 128,000 bytes of memory or even 64,000 or even 32,000. My first 10-page Lisp program[2] kept running out of memory on a 512,000-byte PC, and I needed 4 or 5 million bytes of memory to develop realistically large programs.

Storing many versions of program source files takes a lot of disk space, and interactive documentation requires yet more. Examining source code, input data, output data, and the debug stack all at the same time requires a big display screen. Lisp programmers' appetites are infinite in all directions.

An insatiable hardware appetite is acceptable because hardware is getting cheaper all the time. Using Lisp environments effectively also makes severe demands on human memory, and that is not as acceptable. Examining the debug stack requires special debug commands. Editing programs demands editing commands. Building new software versions requires version building commands. Even though the commands are structured into patterns to help make them easy to remember, users need either exceptionally good memories or constant practice to keep the commands straight.

The Space Cadet Keyboard

Lisp programmers are no more interested in expending extra effort than any other engineers, and they do not like to type command names. Lisp systems are set up to execute most commands by typing *one character*. On a Lisp keyboard the standard alphabetic shift turns lowercase letters into uppercase letters and the control key turns characters into commands.

---

1 There are many buggy, incomplete Lisp systems floating around. Developing a full Lisp environment is a monumental software task, so there are still relatively few Lisp environments that are reliable, powerful, and complete.
2 I implemented the rule-based query system of chapter 10.

Holding the "control" key while typing "a," for example, tells the editor to move to the beginning of a line of text. Holding both the control and shift keys while typing "a" tells the editor to recompile. A combination of keys that activates a function in this way is called a "function key." Because the control key changes the way in which other keys behave, it is called a "modifier key."

One modifier key allows at least thirty-six different functions—one for each alphabet and number key, and even more if punctuation is included. This number is doubled if the shift key is included. One modifier is enough for most uses, and a key labeled "control" has been standard on computer terminals since teletypes were invented.

A mere thirty-six or even seventy-two function keys is *far* too few for serious Lisp programmers. The MIT AI Lab designed a keyboard with modifiers labeled "control," "meta," "super," "hyper," "hand-up," "hand-down," "hand-left," "hand-right," and many more in order to relieve the function key shortage. The resulting keyboard layout was so formidable that it was named the "space cadet keyboard" by outsiders who did not appreciate function keys.

That many function keys turned out to be too many for even Lisp experts to remember, and the keyboard was simplified for production use. Modern Lisp systems scrape by with only four modifiers—super, hyper, control, and meta. There are 15 ways in which these 4 modifier keys can be combined to change the behavior of any other key. Including the standard alphabetic shift gives 31 ways to modify each key, giving a grand total of 1,116 possible functions without using punctuation. This seems to be adequate.

The Power and Glory of Function Keys
The Lisp editor has more than two hundred commands that can be carried out with one keystroke. I recompile with one key, restart the program with another, and break into the running program with a third. Hitting just three keys carries me through the compile-test part of the edit-compile-test cycle, but I had better hit the *right* three keys. If I make a mistake, some unintended but powerful command is likely to blow my program away.

The Lisp environment is extraordinarily powerful, but there is a down side to any powerful tool—I better use it right or it slices my fingers off.[1] The Lisp environment has the longest, steepest learning curve in the world, but the view from the top is absolutely stupendous. The climb is worth the effort.

What Next?

It is difficult to explain rules without contrasting them with other major approaches to software organization. In the next chapter I discuss rules, object-oriented programming, and function-driven programming.

If you are the kind of engineer who likes to know how things work, proceed. If you do not feel the need to know how expert systems work in detail, skip the next chapter and go directly to expert systems. You can always come back later.

---

[1] This problem is not unique to software. Consider the chainsaw, the AK-47, the nail gun, and other high-performance tools.

Style is the dress of thoughts.
— Lord Chesterfield

8
Programming Styles

Many different programming styles have been promoted in
recent years, but there are only three significantly different ways
of arranging computer programs: function-based programming,
object-oriented programming, and rule-based programming,
which is sometimes called "logic programming."

Many computer professionals feel that whichever programming style *they* favor is the only one worth considering. Rule-
based programmers feel that rules cover all needs and that no
other form of programming is worth the paper to write about it.
Object-oriented programmers feel that they and they alone
possess the Holy Grail of software and that all other metho-
dologies are doomed to the dustbin of history

I have been in engineering long enough to know that no
single tool, no matter how wonderful, can perform *all* jobs well.
I am happy to adopt ideas from logic programming or object-
oriented programming or function-based programming, but
experience makes me reluctant to abandon tools that have
served me well.[1] New technologies are seldom as good as their

---

1 Technological conservatism is not new. Alexander Pope said, "Be not the
first by whom the new is tried, nor yet the last to cast the old aside." Another
way to put it is "An ounce of imitation is worth a pound of invention." The
cutting edge of technology is where people and organizations bleed. Most of the

proponents claim, at least not until after years of pounding and refinement in the marketplace. AI ideas are yet young.

Function-Based Programming

Most computer programs are based on functions.[1] Depending on the language, a function is sometimes called a "subroutine," a "module," or an "entry point," but all these terms mean essentially the same thing.

A function receives control of the computer when it is called. Data called "arguments" are passed to the function and it computes a result that is returned to the calling function. If the programming language permits side effects, a function may change other variables in addition to returning a value.[2]

Large functions are built up by calling smaller functions that are constructed out of fundamental language operators just as my sine function called your square root function in the previous chapter. Fortran functions are built from plus, minus, times, and divide, Lisp functions from CAR, CDR, and CONS. Constructing large functions by calling smaller ones is the fundamental concept of most programming languages.

---

drag, or cost, of an airplane wing happens at the leading edge. The lift, or profit, comes a foot or two back from the edge. Panasonic's motto, "Just *slightly* ahead of our time" is good advice for innovators.

[1] A purist might say "procedural programming" instead of "function-based programming," but I use "function" instead of "procedure."

[2] The term "functional programming" describes a programming style in which functions may not have side effects. All that a function can do is return a value; it may not change any variables. Graphics functions that draw lines on the screen violate this rule. In addition to returning values, they have the side effect of drawing something the user can see.

Functional programming is wonderful in theory because lack of side effects makes software easier to debug. The Apple Macintosh programming environment is a good illustration of the evils of side effects. There are over 400 functions that programs call to create and manipulate windows, and most of them have poorly documented side effects. Writing Macintosh application programs is difficult because side effects interact in unexpected ways. On the other hand, writing functional programs that do anything significant is a monumental pain because side effects are so useful. As far as Apple's violation of programming theory is concerned, they only sell $0.5 billion worth of Macintosh products yearly. I wish I could write such lousy software! The counter argument, of course, is that if they had done the software *right*, they would sell $1 billion per year.

Functions are active; data are passive.[1] Functions run when called by another function, and they manipulate data. Most Lisp programs are collections of functions that call one another.

Object-Oriented Programming

Object-oriented programming was introduced in chapter 3. Briefly, data and functions to manipulate the data are associated in an object. An object definition lists all the variables that define the object's state. For a ship object variables might include its latitude, longitude, crew size, and speed. After the variables are defined, functions that operate on the object's variables are defined.

The object definition describes attributes of a class of object. When a new object of a given class is created, it is said to be instantiated. When a new object is instantiated, memory is allocated to contain the values of the new object's variables, and it inherits specified properties from its class. Objects contain both variables that define their state and a list of functions that manipulate the variables.

Variables and functions from other objects may be included when a new object is defined. It is easy to define objects that are similar to existing objects: New objects "inherit" variables and functions from prior object definitions. This makes object-oriented programming ideal for programs that manipulate large collections of similar entities.[2]

The first commercial object-oriented programming system was called Smalltalk, which was running reasonably well by

---

[1] Like most generalizations about Lisp, this is not completely true. Lisp functions can be treated as data, in that the value of a variable can be a function. This function can be passed around just like any other value, and it can also be executed. This Lisp function returns a new function when it is called:

```
(DEFUN MAKE-NEW-FUNCTION (X)
     (LAMBDA (Y) (+ X Y)))
```

The value returned by Make-new-function is a function; "lambda" is a magic word which tells Lisp that the following code defines a function. This function can be assigned as the value of a variable:

```
(SETQ A (MAKE-NEW-FUNCTION 3))
```

creates a new function and stores it as the value of variable A. A full discussion of functions as variable values is beyond the scope of this book.

[2] The term "closure" is another way to describe the idea of tying programs and data together. The major difference between closures and objects is that closures do not inherit variables or methods from a class. You have to define each closure individually, so they are not as convenient.

1972. Smalltalk was developed by the Xerox Palo Alto Research Center, and the ideas behind Smalltalk were the basis for the user interface to the Apple Macintosh.[1]

The best-known object-oriented programming system is called "Flavors." It was embedded in the MacLisp system developed at MIT. Flavors became the basis for object-oriented programming systems offered by Symbolics and Texas Instruments. Xerox offers an object-oriented programming system called "Loops." Loops is unique in that it offers data-driven programming and rules in addition to objects and function calls.

Rule-Based Programming

Rules are the key idea behind expert systems. Experimenters found that rules are an effective way to write programs that exhibit human expertise. Rules are interesting because they can encode certain types of human knowledge that are hard to express in other languages.

The theory behind rules comes from mathematical logic, although the ways in which rules are used in expert systems differ from what mathematicians had in mind. Mathematical rules infer new facts, expert system rules carry out actions as well as inferring new facts.

Rules define condition-action pairs. Actions are carried out when the associated condition occurs. Rules have the same role as functions in that they operate on data, except that rules are triggered when patterns appear in memory instead of being called by another function.

A Touch of Theory
A rule takes the general form "if A then B." The conditions on the "if" side of the rule are called the "antecedents," and the actions on the "then" side are called "consequents."

The rule means that if the expert system knows that fact A is true, then it may conclude that fact B is also true. This is called "forward reasoning" or "forward chaining"—working from

---

[1] Untangling the history of an idea as powerful as object-oriented programming is difficult. People at MIT wrote a language called Simula before Smalltalk was developed. Carl Hewitt at MIT developed an early object-oriented programming system called Plasma, and Guy Steele's studies of Plasma were the foundation for the closures in the Scheme dialect of Lisp. Scheme is now available from Texas Instruments as a low-cost AI programming environment. Most engineers care little about who influenced whom. I concentrate on what is available, not where it came from.

known facts to facts that are not known but can be inferred from known facts.

The rule can also be used in reverse because there is no fixed direction in the statement "if A then B." Suppose that the expert system needs to know whether B is true. The rule says that it may conclude fact B if it can first prove fact A.

The system postpones the search for B and looks for A instead. If it finds A, the search for B succeeds. This is called "backward reasoning." Instead of looking directly for the facts it needs, the system looks for facts that would let it infer them.

Rules let computer programs infer facts that are not in the database from facts it knows. That is why the rule-processing part of an expert system is sometimes called the "inference engine." Some people talk about "deriving facts" instead of "inferring," but a rule by any name infers the same.

Rule interpreters get facts in about the same way people do. If I need to know something, I first try to remember it, then try to figure it out. If I cannot do either, I ask someone or go without the fact. Rule interpreters look for facts in the database, then look for rules that would let them infer the facts, and only then ask users for additional information.

One difference between mathematical logic and rules is what happens when a rule makes an inference. In logic, rules generate new facts. In expert systems, figuring out facts is not enough. The program must take action based on facts it infers. The consequents on the "then" side of expert system rules may include actions to be taken as well as new facts to be concluded.

Chaining between Rules

When a backward-chaining program finds the rule "if A then B" while looking for fact B, it temporarily suspends the search for B and starts looking for A. When it finds a rule "if C then A," it postpones the search for A and looks for C. This is called "backward chaining"—the program's interest in A is aroused because it was first interested in B, and interest in A leads to interest in C. Chaining continues until the program either finds a fact it needs or runs out of rules.

Rule interpreters also use forward chaining. If fact C appears, the rule "if C then A" lets the program conclude A, and the rule "if A then B" chains forward to conclude B.

Forward and backward chaining are used to control the interaction between a user and an expert system. Mathematical logic assumes that all known facts are available to rules. In most real consultations between expert systems and humans, facts are not available unless they are entered by the human. People resent answering questions that turn out to be irrelevant. The expert system not only has to figure out the answer, it must get the answer without asking for more facts than it needs.

Most experts ask a standard list of questions at the beginning of every consultation. A doctor collects low-cost facts such as weight, age, height, blood pressure, and gender from every patient, chains forward from these facts, and guesses the disease.

Suppose that the forward-chaining step infers the fact "patient has smallpox." Now the doctor collects more data by performing medical tests in order to prove or disprove the hypothesis. If the tests show that the patient has smallpox, the guess is verified and the doctor knows what to do. If the tests show that the patient does not have smallpox, the doctor uses the results of the tests and the original facts and forward chains to a new guess.

The forward-chaining step is important in minimizing the cost of diagnosis. It would be prohibitively expensive to perform all possible medical tests whenever anyone visited a doctor's office. Chaining focuses the doctor's attention on the most likely disease so that the answer can be found at minimum cost. When the doctor says, "We need a few more tests," you know that a hypothesis failed and that a new guess has been made.

Engineers forward chain from requirements to a design, then verify the design using tests suggested by backward reasoning. If the design fails, it is time to forward chain to a new design, knowing the reason why the first design failed, test the new design, and iterate until the bridge stays up. The ability to switch between forward and backward chaining is important in medical reasoning, engineering, and management.[1]

Triggers and Actions

Rules can also be described in terms of "trigger" and "action." The trigger arouses the rule interpreter's interest in a rule, and the action is what the interpreter does when the conditions in the rule are met.

In a forward rule the trigger is the "if" side. The interpreter does the actions listed in the "then" side when trigger conditions

---

[1] Knowing when to switch from forward chaining to backward chaining and vice versa is often tricky. Expert systems examine forward rules one at a time. As each rule fires, a new fact is inferred, which may make more rules fire, and so on. Most expert systems keep forward chaining until no new facts can be inferred; then they look at the rules that are *almost* ready to fire and see if there are backward rules which could infer facts to make these rules fire, and so on. The difficulties in controlling this process are discussed in chapter 12.

on the "if" side are met. In a backward rule, the "then" side is the trigger. The interpreter gets interested in a rule when its "then" side says that the rule might infer a fact that the rule interpreter needs. The actions taken by a backward rule are listed in the "if" side. When the interpreter decides that it wants the rule to conclude something, it examines the clauses in the "if" side to try to make the "then" side come true.

Using Rules

Rule notation is convenient for specifying responses to conditions outside the computer that are reflected in fact patterns in computer memory. Rule-based programs require data patterns in memory that reflect facts about the outside world and rules that carry out appropriate actions based on these data.

In order to be useful, of course, an expert system must include some means of getting facts about the outside world into computer memory and some way for the computer's recommendations to be carried out. The most common way for expert systems to communicate is to ask people for facts and then make recommendations for people to carry out, although diagnostic expert systems often try to get data directly from the equipment being repaired.

Rules for Equipment Troubleshooting

Many electronic devices have AC lights that are on when AC power is available and DC lights that are on when the power supply is converting the AC into DC power which the electronics can use. Diagnostic technicians know to check the AC wiring or circuit breakers on any unit whose AC and DC lights are both off. If only the AC light is off, the light is probably burned out, because it is rare for DC power to be available if there is no AC. Expert systems do not know these procedures unless rules are written to supply the knowledge.

The rule "Check AC power if the AC and DC light are both off" is triggered when "AC light off" and "DC light off" are both true. This combination of facts satisfies the conditions in the antecedent of the rule. In programming terms, fact patterns in the database match the "trigger pattern" of the rule, and it fires, issuing the recommendation "Check AC power." Having faith in the expert system, the user checks and tells the computer that the wiring is OK but the lights are still out.

In order to keep the system from making the same recommendation again, the trigger pattern needs the clause, "the AC wiring has not been checked," and the action clause must tell the database, "AC wiring is known to be good." The complete rule is, "Check AC power if the AC and DC light are both off and AC power has not been checked. After checking the power, remember that AC was checked and do not do it again."

People remember not to repeat actions so naturally that technicians seldom repeat the same test, but computers are not that reasonable. They have to be carefully programmed not to get themselves wrapped around the axle. Developing a large and consistent set of rules for a complicated domain is both expensive and time consuming.

Recycling Facts

The same facts can trigger many different rules. A fact helps trigger many rules if it matches part of their trigger patterns. For example, if the AC light is off but the DC light is on, the technician should replace the AC light instead of worrying about the wiring. This rule uses the same facts about the AC and DC lights but in different ways.

The fact about the AC light is not related to the fact about the DC light. Facts are independent pieces of information. Rules specify *combinations* of facts from which conclusions are inferred. Once there is a mechanism by which an expert system can get facts into its database, developers can add as many rules that use these facts as necessary.

Summing up Rule-Based Programming

Rules fire when facts that match their trigger patterns are available. Rule-based adaptive programs are relatively easy to write, and engineers can add new rules to provide new knowledge without affecting old rules.

New rules trigger when the right combination of facts appears without disturbing existing rules. Instead of having to write separate functions to handle every conceivable combination of circumstances, programmers provide general guidelines in the form of rules, and let the computer figure out the details of how to adapt to a given situation.

Summary of Programming Styles

These ways of organizing computer programs fall into two classes: demand pull and availability push. Procedural languages calculate values and store them in memory, so data are pushed into memory when they are available. Object-oriented programming also uses availability push in that functions compute and store values of instance variables, and storage occurs as soon as data are available. Forward-chaining rule programming is also based on availability push. Computation happens because a rule trigger pattern is satisfied. Actions specified by rules are carried out when the facts to fill in the trigger pattern become available. The appearance of the data in memory causes the action.

Backward chaining is demand pull, because the rule interpreter looks for facts when it is interested in a conclusion. Data can sit forever in memory and are not examined until the rule interpreter needs a fact in order to conclude some other fact.

Function programming has explicit control structure in that functions do not run until another function calls them. Rule programming has implicit control structure. Actions in forward-chaining rules are carried out when data patterns appear; backward-chaining rules are examined when interest is expressed in their conclusions. Both function-based programming and object-oriented programming require specific events, such as a request for an operation on an object or a function call, to start an action.

Object-oriented programming keeps variables and the code that manipulates them together because both are associated with an object class. This provides "implementation independence" for programs that use the objects because programs using the object do not care how it is implemented.

Conventional Device Independence

Programs writing data to disk files are not concerned with how data are transferred to a particular type of disk drive. Modern operating systems conceal any differences between line printers, magnetic tapes, and storage disks. If programs issue the correct operating system data transfer requests, data can be sent to different classes of devices without the program being aware of any difference. The destination where data are to be routed is chosen after the program is written, and the operating system assumes the burden of ensuring that data get to the right place.

This is extremely helpful when writing programs. A programmer knows that any differences between disks on the computer where the software is being tested and disks on the customer's computer will be masked by the operating system. It is not necessary for an application programmer to test the program with all possible disk drives. The interface standard that provides device independence in the operating system ensures that, once the program can write files at all, it can write to any device in the same way.

Devices As Objects

Data files are objects defined by the operating system. File objects have functions for opening, closing, writing, rewinding, and other I/O operations. If a new kind of device supports these functions, programs that wrote files on older devices can use the new device without change.

This is the major benefit of interfacing standards: Devices and programs can be plugged in, and they play together. Programs neither know nor care how files are written. So long as operating system services to perform standard I/O functions are provided, programs can use any new device. "Plug and play" is *extremely* valuable because I/O devices using new technology can be introduced without having to change existing software.

Object-oriented programming carries implementation independence beyond device independence. As long as all functions associated with an object manipulate object variables consistently and return the right answers, functions that are outside the object's definition do not care how it is done. Calling programs are independent not only of I/O devices but also of the details of other software as well. Object variables, functions, and even the object structure can be changed or moved to another computer without affecting programs that use the objects.

The Bottom Line on Programming

Unfortunately for passionate fans who argue that their favorite programming style is the latest and greatest, all known ways of organizing programs are mathematically equivalent. Mathematicians can prove that any computation that can be expressed as function calls can also be expressed as an object-oriented program or as a series of rules. Any computation that cannot be expressed as a series of function calls cannot be expressed as an object-oriented program or as a series of rules. All ways of programming can get the same answer, or the answer cannot be computed at all.

There is no reason to use one method over another except for convenience. The computer is a tool that must be told how to solve problems. The solutions to some problems turn out to be easier to express as a series of function calls, other solutions are easier to express as a series of rules, others as a collection of objects, and so on.[1]

---

[1] Differences in convenience can have great economic importance. A big enough change in ease of implementation may make the difference between a project that fits the budget and a project that is too expensive to even contemplate.

Pragmatic engineers should care about Lisp because of its potential to help get jobs done. There are two major reasons why Lisp is an efficient way to do many different jobs. Sometimes Lisp's built-in ability to store relationships between data makes it good for the task at hand. On other occasions the Lisp language itself is not uniquely helpful, but the Lisp development tools make it the language of choice.

Goal-Oriented Factory Automation Software

Programs designed around explicit function calls tend to be inflexible—everything the computer does is programmed in advance in complete detail. Rule-based programming may help simplify the software in future manufacturing systems. Rule-based techniques let programmers describe components such as machining slides, servomotors, and hydraulic valves, then assign the computer the goal, "Drill a hole here."

Once the computer is told what kind of machinery to use, it can make holes based on rules about machining practice and about how machines work. This is what human machine operators do—they know how machines work and twist the knobs to make parts.

Once computers know about standard machine components and how to make holes, it takes little more effort to assign a new class of goal, such as "Tap a hole there." Teaching the principles of machine operation to computers is similar to past efforts to teach computers how to read and write disk files.

Once a program can write data in a disk file, it can write data on magnetic tapes or on line printers without change. When factory computers achieve the same degree of "machinery independence" as commercial computers have "device independence," a program that knows which holes to drill in order to make a part will be able to use pretty much any machine to make the part. Differences between individual machines will be hidden by the "operating system."

Programming in terms of equipment and goals instead of coding limit switch closures and servomotor drive pulses is like programming in Fortran instead of assembly language. Higher-level languages improved computer software development productivity by an order of magnitude or more. Changing from low-level software written in terms of contact closures to goal-oriented software that describes holes will simplify factory software just as Fortran simplified mathematical software.

Goal-oriented knowledge-based programming is new, and researchers are just learning how to encode human knowledge of means and goals. The best-known way to describe goals and knowledge of how to reach them is in the form of rules, but it is not yet clear that this approach will win in the end. It is clear that knowledge-based programs that deal directly with machinery to achieve goals can be written much more quickly than programs that worry about such minutiae as contact closures, but other ways to represent knowledge might be even better.

This is what I mean when describing AI as programming with data, rules, and goals. Data are material properties and machining tables. Rules are machining methods, safety procedures, quality standards, and the like. The goal is to make parts.

Now What?

Having introduced three programming styles and emphasized rule-based programming, we are ready to tackle expert systems. In chapter 9 I explain what expert systems are for and discuss several examples without saying much about how they work. Chapter 10 covers the theoretical foundations of rule-based programming in detail.

Logic programming grew out of mathematical logic just as Fortran and other languages grew out of arithmetic. Most technical folk know arithmetic but are not familiar with mathematical logic. That is why logic comes before Prolog.

An expert is anyone from over 500 miles away.

9
Expert Systems

Whenever reporters discuss artificial intelligence, they pay the most attention to expert systems. This is partly because expert systems and logic programming seem to be the next technology that will emerge from the academic world of AI research into the crass, commercial world of engineering and partly because expert systems lend themselves to extremely impressive demonstrations under controlled conditions.

Expert systems are collected rules of thumb—human experience in a computer. This is close to cloning because once we capture an expert's knowledge in a computer program, we can make as many copies as we like. This is cheaper than hiring another human.

One reason writers get so interested is that the earliest expert systems tried to emulate medical reasoning. There is something intriguing about the idea of electronic doctors, particularly in this era of high medical costs.

Researchers also claimed that expert systems are somehow based on "knowledge," as if all prior programming was based on ignorance. All computer programs embody human knowledge of how to solve a problem or do a job. No computer can do anything unless someone tells it how. Expert systems are based on the idea that rules are an effective way to tell computers how to do certain kinds of things that people do.

Reasons for Developing Expert Systems

Expert systems capture human expertise that is scarce or expensive or both. Many firms have employees who have acquired valuable knowledge. As these people retire or move on, their expertise is lost unless it can be captured somehow. If the knowledge is captured in a computer program, fewer people will have to learn to solve that kind of problem in the future.[1]

The big reason for expert systems, of course, is to save money.[2] Even though many expert systems are too large to fit into today's computers, computers will continue to get bigger and cheaper. The trend of people getting more costly and computers becoming cheaper will result in many opportunities for expert systems.

The difficulty is knowing when to start applying AI technology. A firm that starts too early struggles with tools that have not been developed enough to handle worthwhile problems. Start too late and competitors gain an advantage.

Rules in Expert Systems

It is difficult to define rules accurately without introducing logic. Some of the ideas behind rules were introduced in chapter 8, and there is more detail in chapter 10. A rule specifies an action to be taken whenever a specific data pattern appears. A rule to remind a user to verify that a lamp is plugged in might be:

if   Lamp switch is on &
        Lamp is not lit
then   Check to see if the lamp is plugged in.

A real rule includes bookkeeping actions to prevent the rule from firing again:

---

[1] However much work they save, expert systems do not maintain themselves. Expert systems may reduce direct labor costs but require higher-priced systems analysts, knowledge engineers, and software maintenance staff. As always, technology creates more jobs than it destroys but *not for the same people*. Figuring out whether expert systems are cost-effective can be complicated.

[2] Some expert systems are intended to make money. Prospector is an expert system designed to locate mineral and oil deposits. Its owners do not say much about how well it works, but they smile a lot.

```
if     Lamp switch is on &
       Lamp is not lit &
       Cord has not yet been checked
then   Check to see if it is plugged in &
       Remember not to check it again.[1]
```

Human experts know a lot, so it takes hundreds of such rules to make an expert system that approximates human performance. It is not always necessary to make a computer as smart as the best expert. Most practitioners are not that good, so a program about 80% as good as the best human is often useful.

This leads to a management challenge. Technical people love to add to their creations—one more rule will make it wonderful! Managers may find that the hardest part of developing an expert system is getting the engineers to shut up and ship it.

Kinds of Expert Systems

There are three fundamentally different kinds of expert system: rule based, model based, and knowledge based.

Rule-Based Expert Systems

Rule-based expert systems are purely empirical in that the expert system knows nothing of any underlying causality. Rules encode experiential observations, such as "This disease is associated with fever," "That disease is accompanied by certain chemicals in the urine," or "Watch hydraulic pressure for a few hours after the pump is adjusted," without including any information about why these rules work. Such systems are called "shallow systems" and are said to use "shallow reasoning." Rule-based expert systems are common in medicine because doctors are not taught much about disease mechanisms.[2]

---

[1] It makes a huge difference in expert system development and maintenance costs whether such bookkeeping details are put in manually by a programmer or automatically by the expert system development tools.

[2] There is so much purely diagnostic information taught in medical school that there is little time to explain the underlying mechanisms of disease. Doctors seem not to need to know much about the causes of disease to make successful diagnoses; tracking down causes is left for epidemiologists. Medical school has been described as a place where students learn correlations and ignore causation. A student may be taught to treat gall bladder cancer with a certain drug. They are not taught that the drug is a metabolic poison that damages rapidly growing cancer cells more than it harms normal cells. This explains side effects such as hair loss because hair cells grow rapidly, but there are so many rules to learn that there is no time for such deeper details. Medical training is based on memorization of shallow rules.

Model-Based Expert Systems
Model-based expert systems supplement empirical rules with knowledge about the real world. Many electronic trouble-shooting expert systems are model-based. Having guessed a fault from the initial symptoms, the expert system simulates the fault in the circuit in order to discover more symptoms to prove or disprove the guess.

In theory, generalized troubleshooting rules should be enough for such an expert system—good technicians can fix unfamiliar equipment with nothing more than test equipment, circuit diagrams, and general knowledge of troubleshooting. In practice, general rules suggest too many potential faults, and such programs run too slowly to be useful. Practical programs need some specific rules about the particular circuit in order to fix it promptly. To be fair, humans are also more effective if they know something about the equipment they are trying to fix.

Knowledge-Based Expert Systems
Knowledge-based expert systems are the most active research area. One of the major difficulties in operating expert systems efficiently is choosing the next rule to examine. Knowledge-based systems have rules that tell which rules to look at next. This is a form of "knowledge about knowledge," which is sometimes called "metaknowledge," and such systems are sometimes called "meta reasoning systems." An investment adviser might incorporate metarules such as "If the client is older than 65, disregard rules about long-term investments." Model-based and knowledge-based expert systems are sometimes called "deep reasoning systems" in contrast to shallow rule-based systems.

Choosing Problems for Expert Systems

Expert systems are new enough that it is hard to predict whether the technology is applicable to a given problem domain. The situation is as it was when computer-aided design systems were first introduced—vendors said that CAD systems were good for anything, users were skeptical, and the whole truth has not yet emerged even after a lot of scurrying around.

Problem Size and Complexity
The size and complexity of typical problems are important considerations when designing expert systems. Expert system designers look for problems on which an expert spends a few minutes to a few hours. If problems are solved any more

quickly, the domain is probably too simple to justify the cost of an expert system. If problems take any longer, the knowledge required is probably too complex for current techniques.

Designing helicopters is too complicated; an expert system to design hydraulic systems for helicopters is possible. Designing hospitals or hotels is too complicated; suggesting locations for elevators and service cores is a problem domain that expert systems can handle.

Domain complexity determines the number of rules needed to solve problems. The more rules in an expert system, the more it knows and the more useful it is, but big systems cost more to write, run slowly, and suffer from unexpected rule interactions. The fewer rules in an expert system, the less it knows and the less useful it is but the faster it runs.

The trick is to pick a domain that is simple enough to write enough rules to at least suggest usefulness quickly.[1] Management gets impatient with new technology extremely quickly. Unless results come soon, the project may be shut down for lack of progress.

There is no good way to predict in advance how many rules will be needed to solve problems in a new domain. An area of expertise that takes humans six to nine months to learn is near the outer edge of what can be handled given the limits of today's expert systems.

Medical students spend a few months learning to identify and treat bacterial infections, but it takes years to learn to diagnose arbitrary diseases. An expert system for generalized medical diagnosis called "Caduceus" is still being worked on at Carnegie Mellon University after many years; an expert system called "Mycin" to treat bacterial infections works quite well. Domain simplicity made it possible to develop the bacterial infection expert system, whereas the complexity of general medical diagnosis made developing Caduceus difficult. It is usually best to attack a simple problem as an initial exercise.

The German experience in World War II demonstrated the folly of fighting two-front wars. Expert system technology is still rather new, and it can be difficult to figure out how to use it. It is

---

[1] There are three major attributes to any project: how much it costs, how long it takes, and how much it does. Fixing any two determines the third. Reminding management that the schedule does not constrain the problem and that, if there is any conflict between the schedule and the problem, the problem will win is not tactful. Predicting what an expert system can do or how much it will cost is hard. It is prudent to show results as fast as possible. The more momentum the project acquires, the harder it becomes to cancel it.

unwise to attack an unfamiliar set of powerful programming methods *and* a difficult, complicated problem at the same time. I chose a simple problem for my first expert system because I wanted to swing the hammer of AI around my head a few times and pound it on the floor before trying to drive real nails.

Jargon

An expert system project becomes much easier if the experts use specialized terms.[1] Computers have trouble understanding normal human speech because conversations are full of ambiguities. Expert terminology tends to be precise. A legal term such as "inter alia" or a medical term such as "gram stain" is easy for a computer to understand. The harder it is for humans to understand experts, the easier for computers.

Jargon also tends to constrain the domain. If the expert uses a well-defined vocabulary, the domain also tends to be well defined. One of the easiest ways to fail is to let the project domain grow. Leave related domains until later. Better a series of small independent successes than a large integrated failure.

Lack of Creativity

Computers are completely noncreative, so lack of creativity in solving problems is essential. Expert systems have no ability to develop new solutions to problems. What they do is match situations to conditions coded into rules and suggest a canned solution that matches the situation. In effect, expert systems act as automated reference manuals, and any problem that cannot be solved "by the book" is out of bounds.

Lack of creativity is such an important requirement that it can be asserted that expert systems do not exhibit intelligence at all. This opinion is based on the view that reasoning is only the mechanical application of rules of logic to facts. Marvin Minsky of MIT said, "Expert systems have nothing to do with AI because experts are not intelligent. They don't think—they *know*."

---

[1] Some scholars assert that there are no generalized skills and that all learning is domain specific. They point out that it is difficult to understand written material without knowing the subject matter. This argues that reading is specific not only with respect to alphabet, vocabulary, and grammar but also to subject matter. Learning to read is not just a matter of learning phonics and raw vocabulary; it requires knowledge of all the background ideas that the writer thought too basic to need explanation. See "Expert and Novice Performance in Solving Problems in Physics," by J. Larkin, J. McDermott, D. P. Simon, and H. A. Simon (*Science*, 1980, 208:1335-1342).

The most difficult form of creativity is common sense. The more obvious things are to people, the harder it seems to be to explain them to computers.

Problems with Many Possibilities

The more possibilities an expert has to consider, the better candidate a domain is for expert systems. Computers are better than people at searching through every fact and making sure that no possibility is overlooked. Programming the computer to make a systematic search through all the likely solutions, asking questions in the right order to minimize the cost of finding answers, often reduces the costs of solving problems, provided that the number of possibilities does not get too large.

Nontechnical Considerations

Cultural problems often affect expert system projects more than technical factors. Technical problems never fight back, but the Iranian revolution demonstrates that cultures may resist the introduction of new technology. It is difficult to do anything about corporate politics and management, but innovators should have enough knowledge of such factors not to take it personally when their projects are canceled.[1]

Risking Careers

Expert system projects tend to suffer from political fallout. If the people working on the project get fired after the company spends all that money, what has been gained?

Payback

Management demands some sort of return on any investment in expert systems. Bosses never seem to understand that exploring new technology is worthwhile for its own sake and keep wanting to make a buck from what engineers do. Financial types worry about how much money the project team will spend, and they even want to know how soon they will get it back. Management seldom reacts favorably to the engineer's budget: "Just put money in my hand until I say 'when.'"

---

[1] My first project was an expert system to find faults in an industrial computer called the Gould 584. We named the project DC-3 after the airplane to remind everybody that we wanted something simple, cheap, and reliable that would run for a long time. See "DC-3: An Industrial Expert System" (*Control Engineering*, August 1985, pp. 85-87). When the project was about 80% done, the division president quit. The new president was told to repair the division finances. DC-3 was canceled, and I was invited to leave a few months later.

Because there is no good way to estimate how difficult an expert system project will be before doing it, just pick one that would make a lot of money if it should happen to work. There are many opportunities for improving corporate operations if anyone looks.

Imperial Chemical Industries Ltd. (ICI) in England sells pesticides to farmers. Most pesticides have a short season during which they are worth applying. ICI wrote a small expert system to suggest when to apply chemicals to various crops. The system asks the farmer a few questions about crop, soil, and weather conditions, then calculates how much additional profit the farmer would realize by applying the recommended pesticides.

The program knows rules about crop prices, the efficacy of various chemicals, the cost of applying them, and so on. The payoff for ICI was not that people who knew about pesticides were particularly expensive but that there were too few of them. The season during which this expertise is useful is so short that people forgot the skills. It is not economical to train enough staff to serve all the farmers during the short spraying season. By smoothing the load on the expert and making more expertise available during the critical time, this expert system increased ICI's sales.

Payback considerations argue against applying expert systems to problems for which there are known formulas. If a formula has been developed to solve the problem, writing a conventional computer program is almost always cheaper than writing an expert system.

Inventory control used to be an art. Inventory managers knew how to keep enough stock on hand to be sure that the factory did not run out of parts. Now factories use "reorder points" and "economic order quantities" programmed into computers. This took enough skill from inventory control that an "inventory expert" would probably not be cost effective.

There are cases in which applying expert systems to formula problems is worth a great deal. Airlines sell more reservations than seats because some people fail to claim their reservations. Underbooking leads to empty seats, which is a calamity. Overbooking leads to annoyed customers, which is mildly distasteful, and to paying "bumping fees," which is anticommercial.

Airlines use formulas to calculate the right overbooking level on most flights. There are a few experts who study seasonal variations, traffic trends, and demographics and estimate *slightly* more accurate overbooking factors than the formulas. Airline tickets are so expensive that any improvement in sales is worth a lot to the airlines.

There are only enough experts to handle the most important flights. Adding just *one* more passenger on the other flights would be worth millions to an airline over the course of a year. Airlines are trying to clone this expertise so that they can balance empty seats against the cost of stranded passengers for all flights.[1]

Market Size

The size of the potential market is part of the payback calculation. Suppose that someone developed an expert system to design hydraulic systems for helicopters. The market is limited to a few helicopter makers. That is why there does not seem to be much of a market for most expert systems: Their domains are too narrow for broad market appeal.

Narrow expert systems appeal to firms that use them to further their business. ICI's pesticide expert helped sell pesticides; farmers could use the expert system for free, so it had no direct payback at all. Delloite Haskins Sells developed an expert system to help junior staff carry out client interviews to help make their product more uniform.

Involving Users Early

Many expert systems with excellent rules have failed because potential users refused to touch them. If users are involved from the beginning, they are less likely to reject the system.

Another reason to involve users is that introducing an expert system requires a change in traditional ways of doing things. Staff are apprehensive that the computer will eliminate their jobs. Unless they are convinced that they will benefit in some way from the expert system, users tend to make life difficult for system designers and implementers.

Availability of Domain Expertise

Getting information on which to base rules is partly a technical problem and partly a cultural matter. Expert systems mimic human reasoning, so it is not possible to write an expert system unless a human expert knows how to solve the problem. Or-

---

[1] According to *PC Expert Systems in Manufacturing* (Amherst, N.H.: Graeme Publishing, 1987), Sperry and Intellicorp developed a booking adviser called SEATS for Northwest Airlines. The prototype was demonstrated just as Northwest merged with Continental. This changed the route structure and invalidated the rules. To be fair, human experts also need time to adapt to such radically changed conditions—airline mergers often confuse employees.

ganizations have pressed ahead with expert systems even when no one could do the job. Success in such projects is unlikely.

Having a cooperative expert who knows the problem domain thoroughly and is also willing to talk to the "computer nuts" is essential. If the expert is not enthusiastic, the project will probably fail. Although few experts can resist the implied compliment of management finding their expertise worth copying into a computer, some feel that expert systems threaten their job. It helps if experts train apprentices because teaching ignorant humans makes them more tolerant of ignorant computers.

Because the program will probably never become as skillful as the designated expert, the project needs the best expert available. Management is seldom eager to take the best practitioner away from useful work for up to a year to talk to computer nuts, no matter how enthusiastic the expert.

Patient Money
Patience is *essential* if an organization's first expert system project is to succeed. After an organization absorbs expert system technology, it does not take long to crank out "just one more" for a reasonably simple domain.

Mars Confectionery (Mars Candy to colonials inhabiting the New World) has a group of programmers who develop expert systems to monitor and repair production processes. Mars has been developing manufacturing expert systems for several years and can grind out simple ones in a matter of weeks.

Getting the first factory expert system working was different, however. It took more than a year to train the right people, find appropriate software tools, learn how to use the tools, figure out how to get expertise from a domain expert, get the first system working, and gain enough user confidence that this new and untried technology could be accepted in the factory.

No matter how quickly an expert system is developed, management never concedes success until it has seen enough combat use that benefits can be compared to costs. Getting a system accepted often takes longer than developing it. Unless management is willing to wait at least two years for gratification, it would be risky to start an expert system project.

Delayed payback means that management must permit "failure" in the sense of false starts. When Digital Equipment Corporation was developing R1, an expert system that now saves DEC $20 million per year, there were periods when the amount of knowledge in the program *shrank*. Developers had to throw away rules when they realized that they were attacking the problem in the wrong way.

Temporary reversals are common when developing expert systems, especially when exploring new domains. It is not particularly stylish to use the term "floundering" to describe the brave forward march of technology, but all technical folk flounder a bit every now and then.

Operation of Expert Systems

The operating cycle of an expert system is straightforward: Get the facts, see if any rules fire, take the action implied by whichever rule fires, acquire more facts, repeat until done. There are five major parts of an expert system: (1) the user interface, which obtains information; (2) the database, which stores information about a specific problem; (3) the rule control structure, which decides which rule to use next; (4) the rule system, which checks to see if a rule can fire; and (5) the rules, which contain general knowledge about the domain.

The User Interface

The user interface is a set of programs that asks questions and accepts replies. A few diagnostic and process control expert systems obtain information directly from equipment. Equipment incorporating computer compatible sensors is rare, so most expert systems get facts by asking questions of human users.

Users *must* be considered when deciding how the expert system gets information from which to reason. If the questions are ambiguous or difficult to answer, users make mistakes and the expert system gets wrong data. If the questions seem poorly focused, users get frustrated and lie. The most wonderful rules in the world cannot give correct answers when reasoning from false data. Once users lose confidence in an expert system, getting them to use it again requires more tact than most engineers keep in stock. When it comes to user interfaces, form seems to be as important as function, if not more so.

An extremely good user interface backed by a few rules may intrigue users enough that they will use it even if it does not cover all the cases they want it to, whereas a poor interface may inhibit the use of some excellent rules.[1] It is not uncommon for

---

[1] Oncocin is a cancer treatment expert system developed at Stanford University Medical Center. The story goes that Oncocin was developed to the point that it could make correct recommendations rather quickly but that medical staff refused to use it. The computer wizards developed a series of

an expert system project to invest more effort in the user interface than in the rules.

The Database
After information is obtained from the user interface, facts are stored in some sort of database. A fact is a list of terms that are related in some way. The list (light-status ac-light on) means that the AC light is on. The fact (job Fred Secretary) means that Fred holds the job of secretary. Most systems put names of facts such as job and light-status at the front, and this is referred to as "prefix notation."

Humans prefer sentences such as "Fred's job is secretary" to gibberish like (job Fred secretary), so most expert systems translate between whatever notation is used internally and pseudo-English, which is displayed to users. Regardless of how information is obtained, it is converted to a fact in some internal format that can be stored and retrieved.

Essentially any method of storing facts is acceptable in an expert system. Relational databases work well, as does a simple list of facts. The main problem is that expert systems make many references to the database during consultations. If retrieving data is slow, the expert system runs slowly.

The Rule Control Structure
The rule control structure determines which rule is examined next or which question is asked to get more facts. It determines the strategy by which the expert system carries out its task.

Planning expert systems must decide which goal to pursue, whereas diagnostic expert systems work backward from the goal of fixing the equipment. Given that a piece of equipment is broken, a diagnostic expert system starts examining rules whose conclusions indicate the cause of the problem and see what conditions must be met for those conclusions to be true. This is backward chaining—the system works from a known goal to the steps needed to attain the goal. When a maintenance engineer decides that the CPU is broken, there are standard tests to confirm or refute the guess.

When the goal is not known, expert systems use forward chaining. Forward chaining works from available facts and tests the rules to see if their conditions are met. When an engineer

---

screen displays that mimic the appearance of the paper forms the medical folk were accustomed to using. Once given the new interface, users became much more willing to work with the program.

arrives at the site of a broken computer, there is a standard set of information collected. The engineer forward chains from these facts to a guess as to what the problem might be, and then works backward to test the hypothesis.

The control structure determines the order in which rules are examined and the order in which questions are asked in order to obtain facts. Backward-chaining systems tend to produce well-focused dialogues with users because all the questions about facts needed to satisfy a rule are asked at the same time. Forward-chaining systems seem to jump around, because the system has not yet settled on a direction.

The Rule Interpreter

The rule interpreter is sometimes called the "inference engine" because it infers new facts. It tests rule conditions against facts in the database to see if the conditions are satisfied. When all of the conditions are met, a new fact is inferred. Rules are examined when the control structure becomes interested in the rule.

Rules are expressed as "if A then B." Fact A is the condition of the rule, and B is the result. Rules can be used for either forward chaining or backward chaining. If a backward-chaining expert system needs to conclude B, it tries to find out fact A because A allows it to conclude B. If a forward-chaining system learns fact A, it immediately concludes B, because A implies B.

Rules are processed by the rule system when the control structure decides that a fact would be of interest to the consultation. Rules are written and debugged by the expert system developer. The other parts of the system—the rule system, the control structure, the database, and the information interface—are usually purchased as parts of an expert system tool kit called an "expert system shell."

Knowledge Engineering and Writing Rules

Knowledge engineering is the process of converting human knowledge into expert system rules. AI practitioners act as though there were something magical about knowledge engineering, but whenever computers are applied to a new kind of problem, there is always an acute shortage of people who understand both the problem and the software techniques to solve it.

In the early days of computerized accounting systems, there were few people who understood both computers and accounting. They were called "systems analysts" and were hard to recruit and keep. Now that computers are an accepted part of the accounting culture, such people are paid less.

The inverse of the lordly attitude of AI professionals is managers who think that the technicians "just have to throw some AI in and everything will be fine." It is not clear which viewpoint leads to the biggest disasters.[1]

Debugging rules is more like debugging ordinary software than AI people prefer to admit. Each rule has to be understood, coded, entered into the computer, compiled, tested, debugged, documented, and subjected to version control. The difference is that rules operate differently from functions. Instead of being examined when control is passed by a calling function, rules "operate" when information becomes available.

The interaction between rules is deliberately less explicit than interaction between functions. Debugging unexpected inter-actions is more common in writing expert systems than in conventional software.

Mycin: A Medical Expert System

Mycin is one of the best-known expert systems because it is one of the oldest and many papers were written about it. Mycin diagnoses bacterial infections and prescribes antibiotics. Mycin has about 450 rules, which look something like

if   the gram stain of the ORGANISM is negative &
       the aerobicity of the ORGANISM is anaerobic &
       the morphology of the ORGANISM is rod
then   there is suggestive evidence that the organism is
       BACTERIODES

The rule gives a number of conditions that help to identify the infectious organism. Mycin processes rules by matching clauses on the "if" side of rules with facts in the database or with the "then" sides of other rules. If all of the conditions in a rule are true, Mycin adds a new fact to the database. When a conclusive rule becomes true, it stops.

Mycin is a backward-chaining system, so it starts with the "then" sides of rules such as the rule in the example which would identify the organism if the conditions on the "if" sides were satisfied. If there are enough facts in the database for a conclusive rule to be true, Mycin can stop. If not, Mycin looks for other rules whose "then" sides match with a clause on the "if" side of the rule it is examining.

When examining the rule in the example, Mycin needs facts about the aerobicity of the organism. If there are no such facts

---

[1] "And they fled before the men of AI" Joshua 7:4, King James Version.

available, Mycin looks for a rule whose "then" side talks about aerobicity. If it finds such a rule, Mycin suspends work on the original rule and examines the conditions in the new rule in order to reach a conclusion about aerobicity.

If the aerobicity rule succeeds, Mycin goes on to the next clause and starts looking for facts or rules about morphology. If the rule fails, there is no information available about aerobicity. Mycin cannot make the bacteriodes rule succeed, so it shrugs its shoulders and tries another rule.

Asking Questions

Mycin asks questions when there is no rule whose conditions are true. The purpose of asking questions is to obtain new facts to make rules true. A dialogue with Mycin might look like:

Is the disease hospital acquired?
Why? [i.e., why does Mycin want to know?]
This will help identify the organism. It is known that:
  The morphology of the ORGANISM is rod &
  The gram-stain of the ORGANISM is negative &
  The aerobicity of the ORGANISM is aerobic
therefore
if The organism is hospital acquired
then There is evidence that the organism is pseudomonas
Is the disease hospital acquired?

Mycin displays known facts that satisfy clauses in the rule it is working on and turns the clauses for which there are no facts into questions. Mycin then repeats the question and hopes the user will get on with the job instead of harassing it for details.

If users get tired of answering questions about hospital-acquired diseases, developers can write a rule to infer whether the organism is hospital acquired or not. Mycin then uses the new rule instead of asking the user.

This is almost slick enough to slide uphill. The more rules Mycin knows, the fewer questions it asks. If rules are taken out, Mycin keeps working; it just asks more questions and handles fewer cases. Expert systems "work" as soon as they know *any* rules but answer "Don't know" when cases fall outside their meager knowledge. When it comes to evaluating demonstrations of an expert system project, an ounce of skepticism is worth a pound of regret.

Expert systems are never complete. The work of writing the rules helps people learn, so the expert always knows more. Developers should add rules until the expert system gets reasonable answers often enough, then stop. Programmers never want to stop, and expert system projects seem to run either forever or until the funding dries up, whichever comes first. That is called "management by resources."

Backward Chaining

Mycin chains backward because the doctor has done the difficult part and decided that the patient has a bacterial infection. Backward chaining minimizes the number of questions. Mycin asks only for facts that are needed to satisfy clauses in rules it is working on. If all facts were available from the beginning, Mycin could use forward chaining, but it is unreasonable to insist that all facts be supplied in advance.

Mycin's control structure decides the order in which rules are examined. This determines when questions are asked, which controls the order in which information is made available to rules. Experienced doctors often know which fact will determine the result of the consultation, but they cannot enter it until Mycin asks for it. It is frustrating to be forced to enter irrelevant facts while waiting for Mycin to ask the right question.

It would have been more convenient for users if they could interrupt Mycin and supply facts whenever they wanted to, but that would have made the control structure more complicated.

Explaining the Reasoning

Mycin explains its reasoning by playing back the rules or questions that led to the current question. This helps users gain confidence in Mycin and helps developers learn where Mycin went wrong. Instead of asking why Mycin wants to know a given fact, users can ask how Mycin arrived at the current question. For example:

Is the disease hospital acquired?
How? [i.e., how did Mycin get to this point?]
This will help satisfy Rule 123. I know that:
> The morphology of the ORGANISM is rod (Rule 117) &
> The gram stain of the ORGANISM is negative &
> The aerobicity of the ORGANISM is aerobic (Rule 42)
Is the disease hospital acquired?

Mycin explains that it is working on rule 123. The morphology fact was inferred by rule 117; the information about gram stain did not come from a rule and must have been the answer to a question, and aerobicity was inferred by rule 42.

Instead of answering the question, the user may reply

How 117 [i.e., how did Mycin satisfy Rule 117]

and Mycin prints the clauses and facts that satisfied rule 117.

Tracing the reasoning behind a decision is helpful to developers because they can find what went wrong when Mycin makes an incorrect diagnosis. One of the better techniques for debugging expert systems is to throw as many cases at them as possible. When the expert disagrees with the expert system, the knowledge engineer can walk the expert through the reasoning rule by rule to determine where the reasoning went awry and correct the errant rule.

Explanations can be informative to knowledgeable users, but most people accept the computer's word as gospel. Most users do not care how the computer gets the answer so long as it is right, much as most drivers don't care what makes a car go so long as it goes.

What Is in Mycin

Mycin consists of about a dozen different classes of object, such as organisms, gram stains, morphologies, and so on. There are about 200 attributes, such as gram stain, negative, and anaerobic, associated with objects. Most attributes are yes or no—a disease is either hospital acquired or it is not. Attributes such as blood pressure have numerical values.

In addition to the 450 rules, Mycin has between 500 and 1,000 other facts that are represented in coded functions instead of rules because rules are not always the best way to represent knowledge. It is important that expert system development tools permit programmers to write functions instead of rules when functions are more convenient than rules.

Identifying the objects is one of the first steps in developing an expert system. It is difficult to write questions and rules without having decided on the objects that questions ask about and rules reason about. Objects are patterned after things experts worry about, such as power supplies, diseases, stocks, and tax laws.

Growth and Development

Mycin grows when developers add new rules because there is no automatic mechanism for adding rules. Unlike humans, expert systems do not learn by themselves when they produce wrong answers. New knowledge must be put in by humans.

Writing rules is expensive, but once Mycin works on one computer, it is easy to transfer the knowledge to another computer by copying a disk.[1] Humans learn somewhat more

---

[1] Computers are like flatworms. If you grind up one computer and feed it to another, the recipient inherits some of the ground-up computer's memory. See

automatically than computers, but each one must be taught individually.

Symbolic Chaining between Rules

Mycin finds out which rules to examine by matching condition patterns in if-clauses with conclusion patterns in then-clauses. When examining the (hospital-acquired organism) condition clause in the "if" side of a rule, Mycin looks for a hospital-acquired conclusion in the "then" side of another rule. This process is difficult to understand when rules are expressed in English. It is easier when rules are written as Lisp lists:

```
if    (and  (gram-stain ORGANISM gram-negative)
            (morphology ORGANISM rod)
            (aerobicity ORGANISM anaerobic))
then  (evidence organism BACTERIODES)
```

When trying to match a clause about aerobicity, Mycin looks for another rule whose then-clause looks like (aerobicity ...). When working on the morphology clause, Mycin looks for a rule whose then-clause looks like (morphology ...) and so on.

Matching rules against facts on the basis of patterns is the heart of the rule interpreter. The control structure decides which patterns to look for. Mycin starts each consultation by looking for (evidence ...) rules because such rules tell it what is causing the infection. Mycin works backward from these rules, accumulating facts as it goes, until it either runs out of rules to try or satisfies a conclusive evidence rule, prints the final diagnosis, and stops.

R1: A Forward-Chaining Expert System

R1 is as well known as Mycin and seems to have paid back far more money. Mycin works well and its recommendations are more accurate than most doctor's, but it is seldom used. Pre-scribing antibiotics is one of the few parts of medical practice that actually works. Doctors enjoy this part of their job and are reluctant to turn it over to a computer, so Mycin languishes, according to Edward Feigenbaum of Stanford University, one of the developers of Mycin.

R1, in contrast, is claimed to be saving the Digital Equipment Corporation (DEC) about $20 million per year. R1's task is

---

articles on knowledge recycling in any issue of *Worm Runner's Digest* or *Solid Waste Management.*

selecting components for VAX computers before they are shipped. A typical VAX incorporates 50 to 150 different components out of a list of 400 or more candidates.

There are many rules for configuring VAXes. Some memory modules can be used only with a certain kind of disk drive; other memory units require different power supplies and cabinets; some require special fans, and so on. Depending on the complexity of a part and the number of ways in which it interacts with other parts, R1 knows 25 to 125 facts about each part.

It takes R1 about 1,000 steps to configure a typical system, because it tests and rejects many possibilities along the way. There are usually about three parts that could reasonably be added to the configuration at any given time. R1 investigates each possibility in order to find the best one.

Interactions between components are so complex that configuration engineers made errors. Before R1, DEC occasionally shipped collections of parts that could not be turned into a working system. Such mistakes increased installation costs.

Spectacular errors were rare, but mistakes involving cables were common. Suppose that a customer bought a half-million-dollar computer system, and the installation engineer found that a cable was omitted. DEC shipped the cable by air in order to get the computer working quickly, and the customer usually refused to pay: "What do you mean? $500,000 did not include cables?!" DEC gave away several million dollars worth of air freighted cables per year to the greater glory of Federal Express.

DEC started the R1 project by hiring consultants from Carnegie Mellon University. The name comes from the phrase, "Six months ago I could not even spell knowledge engineer and now I R1."

Demonstrating the Concept

Getting the program ready for the first demonstration required about one month of work by a knowledge engineer who spent about a week working with a configuration expert. The resulting prototype could handle only part of a simple configuration problem, but the demonstration convinced the customer that all remaining configurations could be handled using essentially the same procedures that had been demonstrated in the prototype.

This illustrates the interesting fact that expert systems can be demonstrated well before they are complete. DEC management could see that a part of the configuration problem had been solved and thought that an essentially linear extension of the first month's effort would lead to a complete solution.

After another four months of effort, R1 could configure simple VAXes for shipment. The simplest configurations, of course, were easy for humans to handle and hardly worth the bother of building an expert system.

Validating R1

After R1 seemed to be about ready for production, it was tested by having it solve fifty configuration problems posed by six experts. R1 made only two mistakes, which were easily solved by correcting some of its rules. The conclusion of the validation phase was that R1 was better at configuring VAXes than the humans who were doing the job and that it knew almost everything anyone needed to know about configuration.

Things did not work out that way. R1 needed many more rules to handle new products, unusual configurations, and other things that came up. R1 is probably the largest commercial expert system in the world, containing about 8,000 rules in all. People outside DEC estimate that it cost about 100 staff-years to develop R1, and maintenance requires about 30 people.

A Typical Pitfall

Expert systems often seem complete early in their development cycle. Users are then surprised to find out that many more rules must be added after the system looked "complete" from the user's point of view.

Many artificial intelligence projects suffer from the problem that expert systems seem complete long before they really are. It is easy to write a demonstration program that looks as if it solves a problem. It is considerably more difficult to put in all the messy little details to actually solve a problem under realistic conditions.

Forward Chaining

R1 uses forward chaining because all of the configuration information is available when the problem is posed. Once R1 has a list of components, it needs no more information because it knows the configuration rules for all the parts.

Forward-chaining rules take the form of

if <condition> then <action>

If the condition is satisfied, the action is carried out. A representative R1 rule looks something like

if   the current context is assigning power supplies &
      there is a power supply available &
      there is space in the cabinet &
      there is a voltage regulator available
then put the power supply in the cabinet &
      change the context

R1's control structure is built around "contexts," which determine what happens next. Most rules have a "context" clause to make sure that they fire at the right time and only at the right time.

Commercial Status of Expert Systems

R1 and Mycin were expensive projects, but they were early efforts. Expert systems now cost much less than the 100 staff-years that were invested in Mycin. British Petroleum (BP) developed an expert system called GASOIL to help design parts of chemical refineries. There are 2,500 rules in GASOIL, and BP claims that it took only 1 staff-year to develop.

BP has devised a clever trick to determine if an expert system project is feasible. Their knowledge engineers take along a portable personal computer running a small expert system when they visit a new domain expert. If they cannot get the expert enthusiastic about developing an expert system in 10 minutes, the project is doomed from the beginning. If the expert is enthusiastic, the project will probably succeed even if the domain turns out to be more difficult than anticipated. The GASOIL expert was extremely enthusiastic.[1]

It is impossible to tell how many expert system projects are underway because starting a project is so cheap. All it takes is a personal computer and an expert system tool kit. Tool kits, which are commonly called "shells," are available for a few hundred dollars from dozens of different vendors. Any engineer with access to a PC can start an expert system project.

---

[1] A British Petroleum AI engineer whom I met at a conference in the Netherlands came close to apoplexy when I asked him about this story. He said that the bare facts are true as stated, but they gave the wrong impression. He bore so many scars from trying to correct things that he had given up and refused to provide further detail. Truth is often more complex than legend.

Expert Systems and Logic Programming

Developing an expert system is one of the best ways to get started in artificial intelligence. There are many software packages available to ease some of the burdens, and the entry cost is low.[1]

In the next chapter I discuss fundamental logic programming. Expert systems are based on logic programming just as conventional computer languages are based on arithmetic. Understanding how expert systems work without knowing logic programming is as difficult as understanding a language such as Basic or Fortran without knowing arithmetic.[2]

Conventional programming languages make compromises between the theory behind arithmetic and the realities of what computers can do. Similarly, expert systems compromise the theory of logic programming. These differences between logic theory and expert systems are discussed in the next chapters.

---

[1] The cost of seeing the project through to the bitter end may be a tad higher.
[2] The disparaging term "arithmetician" is occasionally used by mathematicians to distinguish people like themselves who manipulate symbols for a living from those who merely manipulate numbers.

Insanity is often the logic of an
accurate mind overtaxed.
    — Oliver Wendell Holmes

10
Logic Programming

The term "logic programming" describes the AI programming
style defined as "data, rules, and goals" back in chapter 1.
Understanding logic programming without knowing the theory
behind it would be as difficult as understanding conventional
computer programs without knowing how to add or subtract.

Just as conventional programming languages make compromises and do not offer full arithmetic capabilities—round-off
error and problems with limited precision were introduced in
chapter 5—logic programming languages do not work in the
same way as mathematical logic. In this chapter I introduce logic
programming by contrasting it with conventional programming.
• Conventional variables have only one value at a time, and
functions have one output value for each set of input values. In
the expression $A = B + C$, B and C have one value each, and their
sum defines one and only one value for A. Logic variables may
have one value, multiple values, or no value at all depending
on circumstances.
• Inputs and outputs for a conventional expression are fixed.
For $A = B + C$, A is the output and B and C are inputs. Logic
variables may be inputs or outputs at different times, depending

on whether they have values or not. Variables with values are inputs; variables without values are outputs.[1]
• Conventional computation is carried out in a fixed order determined by the order in which expressions appear in each line of code. Computation order varies in logic programs.
• Conventional programs specify exactly how to carry out computations. $A = B + C$ is evaluated by loading B into a register, adding C to it, and storing the result in A. In logic, rules describe relationships between facts rather than telling how to compute things.

A rule succeeds if the relationships specified in the rule are true and fails if they are not. The rule does not specify how to compute relationships because that is implicit in the definition of the logic system. Another way to put it is to say that conventional programming specifies how to do things; logic programming states what to do.

Pattern Matching

Pattern matching is the basic idea behind logic programming. Users specify a pattern, and the logic programming system searches its database to see if it can find the pattern. The request succeeds or fails depending on whether the pattern matches the database or not.

Facts are patterns stored in a database. For example, an employee database might store the pattern

(job (Filewriter Harvey) (computer hacker))[2]

This pattern is a fact with three fields that are stored as Lisp lists. The first field states that the job relationship holds between the data in the second and third fields. In English the fact means "Harvey Filewriter has the job of computer hacker." or "Harvey Filewriter is a computer hacker." The parentheses hold "Filewriter" and "Harvey" together so it is not necessary to use a hyphen. This makes facts easier to understand.

The convention of putting the name of the relationship in the first field of a fact is called "prefix notation." Putting the name of

---

[1] This is a slight oversimplification. A user may enter a pattern with no variables in it. This is a request to see if the fact is stored in the database or not. In this case the query is the input, and the output is the success or failure of the search for the data.

[2] The examples in this chapter are based on chapter 4 of *Structure and Interpretation of Computer Programs*, by H. Abelson and G. J. Sussman (Cambridge, Mass.: MIT Press, 1984) and were reviewed by Abelson before publication. There is more information about this book in the bibliography.

the fact at the beginning makes it easy to store all the job facts together. This makes it easier for the computer to find a job fact when it wants it.

Facts are retrieved from the database by matching them against patterns made of constants and variables. There are many conventions in logic programming languages for distinguishing constants from variables. I begin variables with a question mark, so the term "?x" stands for a variable named "x."

A request that a specified pattern be retrieved from the database succeeds if there is at least one fact in the database that matches the pattern; it fails otherwise. The request

(job (Filewriter Harvey) ?x)

asks the logic system to look for facts that have the constant job in the first field, the constant (Filewriter Harvey) in the second field, and anything at all in the third field. The variable ?x has no value when the request is entered, so it can match anything. This request matches the fact about Harvey's job, so ?x is matched to (computer hacker).

Having matched ?x to (computer hacker), the logic system is said to have "bound" the variable ?x to the constant (computer hacker). The value of ?x tells us Harvey's job.

In summary, pattern matching assigns values to variables. Patterns containing unbound variables are the input to the logic system, and variable bindings are the output. When the constant parts of a pattern match a fact in the database, pattern variables are assigned values to keep the match consistent with the fact that matched the pattern. If the rule system substitutes the binding for ?x back into the input pattern

(job (Filewriter Harvey) ?x),

the result is the pattern

(job (Filewriter Harvey) (computer hacker)),

which is the same as the fact in the database. Pattern matching is the process of assigning variable bindings such that the pattern is the same as a fact in the database when variable bindings are substituted for variables in the pattern.

Pattern Variables May Be Inputs or Outputs
When the user enters the request pattern

(job (Filewriter Harvey) ?x)

variable ?x is "unbound"; that is, it has no value. The pattern-matching operation finds a value for ?x by matching the first and second fields of the pattern to a fact in the database and binding ?x to the value of the third field. The first and second fields in the pattern are constants, so they are inputs. The variable in the third field has no value, so it is an output.

Suppose that a user wants to know who the computer hackers are. The pattern

(job ?x (computer hacker))

has constants in the first and third position, so they are inputs. The unbound variable ?x is in the second field, so the second field is an output. The logic system matches this pattern with the fact

(job (Filewriter Harvey) (computer hacker))

and binds ?x to (Filewriter Harvey). This tells the user the name of the computer hacker.

Retrievals fail if there are no matching patterns in the database. The query

(job ?x (secretary))

fails because there are no facts whose first field is job and whose third field is (secretary). The retrieval request fails because the logic system cannot find a match for the pattern. ?x cannot be assigned a value and remains unbound.

An Output Variable May Have Many Values
In the previous examples there was only one possible binding for ?x. Suppose the organization hires a junior programmer and another computer hacker. The database now has three facts:

(job (Filewriter Harvey) (computer hacker))
(job (Bitsmasher Martha) (computer hacker))
(job (Bitlearner Fred) (junior programmer)).

The query pattern

(job ?x (computer hacker))

succeeds twice because it matches the first two facts. Each success gives ?x a different binding. Matching the first fact binds ?x to (Filewriter Harvey), and matching the second binds ?x to (Bitsmasher Martha). (computer hacker) in the third field of the pattern does not match (junior programmer) in the third field of the third fact, so the third fact does not match the pattern.

In logic theory all possible bindings for a variable are equally valid, and all of them are found at once. In practice, searching through a database to find all possible binding combinations that match a pattern takes a great deal of computer time. Logic programming systems find one binding at a time because computers do only one thing at a time, but designing computers to search data in parallel is a hot research topic.

There are many ways to handle multiple bindings. Some systems build a list of all bindings for each variable before presenting any solutions. Others find the first solution as quickly as possible, delving back into the database for more solutions only if the user wants more.

Variables in conventional languages never have more than one value at a time. Logic system designers had to learn how to deal with multiple values for variables, and some programmers have trouble getting used to the idea.

Multiple Pattern Variables
There can be more than one variable in a pattern. The pattern

(job ?x ?y)

contains two variables. It matches all three of the facts whose first field is job. When a match occurs, ?x is bound to the value of the second field in the fact, and ?y is bound to the value of the third.

The first match binds ?x to (Filewriter Harvey) and ?y to (computer hacker). The second match binds ?x to (Bitsmasher Martha) and ?y to (computer hacker). The last match binds ?x to (Bitlearner Fred) and ?y to (junior programmer). When a pair of bindings is substituted into the original pattern, the result is identical with one of the patterns in the database.

The logic system not only remembers values for ?x and ?y but also keeps track of which value for ?x goes with each value for ?y. The (Filewriter Harvey) binding for ?x is associated with a (computer hacker) binding for ?y and so on.

I call the data structure that collects compatible bindings for a set of variables an "environment." "Environment" is used in many ways in AI literature, but in this book an environment is a set of variable bindings.[1]

The retrieval request

(job ?x ?y)

generates three different environments. Each environment has different bindings for both ?x and ?y:

---

[1] Some writers call a set of bindings a "frame," but "frame" is used in too many other ways in the AI literature. The term "binding environment" is probably the most precise; "environment" is a compromise.

Environment	?x	?y
1	(Filewriter Harvey)	(computer hacker)
2	(Bitsmasher Martha)	(computer hacker)
3	(Bitlearner Fred)	(junior programmer)

As each pair of bindings in each environment is substituted for the pattern variables, the pattern becomes identical with a fact from the database.

Compound Retrieval Patterns
Retrieval patterns so far have had only one clause to be matched. So long as the pattern matches a fact in the database, the retrieval succeeds.

Logic programming also allows patterns with more than one clause. All clauses in a request must match facts in the database for the request to succeed. Pattern variables must have the same bindings in all clauses.

Suppose the database also includes employee addresses:

(address (Filewriter Harvey) (Detroit))
(address (Bitsmasher Martha) (Chicago))
(address (Bitlearner Fred) (Detroit))

Requests to find out where computer hackers live look like

(and (job ?x (computer hacker)
      (address ?x ?where))

Both clauses in the and-condition must be satisfied simultaneously for the compound retrieval request to succeed. The logic system starts with the first clause, which matches any fact whose first field is job and whose third field is (computer hacker). The match succeeds twice and produces two environments, one with ?x bound to (Filewriter Harvey) and one with ?x bound to (Bitsmasher Martha).

Now the logic system searches the database for facts that match the second clause. Pattern variables must have the same values in all clauses, so before it looks up the second clause in the database, the system substitutes bindings from the first clause for the variables in the second clause.

The logic system starts with the first environment from the first clause, which binds ?x to (Filewriter Harvey). Substituting this value of ?x into the second clause produces the pattern

(address (Filewriter Harvey) ?where)

This new pattern matches Harvey's address fact, which binds ?where to Detroit. The first environment now has two bindings because ?x is bound to (Filewriter Harvey) and ?where is bound to (Detroit).

Now the logic system processes the second clause again, this time using the second environment, which binds ?x to (Bitsmasher Martha). Substituting this value for ?x into the second clause gives the pattern

(address (Bitsmasher Martha) ?where)

which matches Martha's address record, binding ?where to Chicago.

The logic system stops because there are no more clauses in the pattern. It has produced two binding environments: one binding ?x to (Filewriter Harvey) and ?where to (Detroit) and one binding ?x to (Bitsmasher Martha) and ?where to (Chicago).

The steps in matching compound queries, then, are:

1. Start with an empty environment with no variable bindings.
2. Match the first clause, creating an environment to hold each set of variable bindings that matches the clause to the database.
3. Substitute variable bindings from each environment into the next clause.
4. Match the next clause, adding new bindings to the environments.
5. If a match fails, discard the environment.
6. Environments remaining after the last clause is matched contain variable bindings that let all clauses match a fact.

There are obvious performance considerations. The query is processed faster if the first clause has relatively few matches because an environment is created for each set of variables that match the first clause. Logic programming systems work fastest if the clause with the fewest matches comes first, then the clause with the next fewest matches, and so on.

Rules Tell How to Infer New Facts

Another difference between logic programming and conventional programming is that logic rules describe relationships instead of computations. Suppose that the employee database contains facts about height and hair color. To find the tall redheads in the firm, we write the rule

(rule (tall-redhead ?person)
        (and (> (height ?person) 6-feet)
              (hair-color ?person red)))

The rule means that if the relationship > holds between height of ?person and "6-feet" and the hair-color relationship holds between ?person and red, then the person is a tall-redhead. The rule tells how to derive the fact (tall-redhead ?person) from other facts in the database. There is no need to store facts about tall redheads because such facts can be derived.

Rules save storage space because there is no need to store the fact, only the rule that tells how to derive it. This requires extra computer time, however. It usually takes longer to derive a fact from a rule than to look it up.[1]

Any practical rule system includes procedures for editing and storing facts, editing and storing rules, matching facts to patterns, processing compound queries, building environments containing variable bindings, and the like. These procedures are implied by the rule syntax, but programmers writing rules do not have to worry about them. This is why expert systems are interesting—rules are a way to represent knowledge without having to fill in every single detail.

Rules Chaining to Other Rules

Facts inferred by rules and facts stored in the database have the same status as far as satisfying conditions is concerned. Whether the rule system finds facts in the database or derives them from rules, the result is the same.

The user may care because of rule processing delays or because of the storage space needed to store all the facts. Consider a rule to find employees who live in the same town:

```
(rule  (lives-near ?person1 ?person2)
       (and  (address ?person1 ?town)
             (address ?person2 ?town)
             (not-same ?person1 ?person2)))
```

This rule says that the lives-near relationship holds between ?person1 and ?person2 if the address fact for ?person1 shows that ?person1 lives in the same ?town as ?person2 and ?person1 and ?person2 are not the same. The not-same condition prevents the rule from inferring the uninteresting fact that all persons live near themselves.[2]

---

[1] This does not apply to arithmetic predicates. Building a table of sums and looking up facts like 1,453 + 2,897 = 4,350 is slower than doing the addition, if only because the table of potential sums is so large. Predicates such as addition are called "computable predicates."

[2] Not-same is a predicate that is faster to compute than to look up. Imagine building a table of every pair of facts that were not the same!

When inferring a lives-near fact, the rule system starts with the first clause and finds all the address records and generates environments holding all pairs of bindings for ?person1 and ?town. When processing the second clause, the system generates augmented environments containing all bindings for ?person2 that match bindings for ?town found in the first clause.

The third clause rejects all environments for which the value of ?person1 is the same as the value of ?person2. Environments that survive the final check have different bindings for ?person1 and ?person2 and only one binding for ?town.

If the rule system tries to match the pattern

(lives-near (Bitlearner Fred) ?person2)

it finds the lives-near rule, finds Fred's "address" fact, binds ?town to (Detroit), finds all persons including Fred whose address facts match with (Detroit), rejects Fred, and finally shows that Fred lives near Harvey.

Facts inferred by rules can be used as if they were in the database. The query

```
(and (tall-redhead ?person1)
     (tall-redhead ?person2)
     (lives-near ?person1 ?person2)))
```

uses these rules to find tall redheads who live in the same town. The rule system first finds all the tall redheads, then uses their names to check to see if they live-near one another.

This query can be massively inefficient. There may be only a few tall redheads, but whenever the system finds one, it plunges into the lives-near rule with ?person1 and ?person2 bound to the same value. This causes massive churning of address facts until the final test in the lives-near rule eliminates the environment because ?person1 and ?person2 are the same. Expressing the query in this way makes it run faster:

```
(and (tall-redhead ?person1)
     (tall-redhead ?person2)
     (not-same ?person1 ?person2)
     (lives-near ?person1 ?person2)))
```

Putting the not-same test before the lives-near rule avoids searching for address facts in cases that are doomed to failure. However, the only way a programmer could know to do this is to realize that the lives-near predicate is inferred by a rule instead of being stored as a fact and to understand how the lives-near rule works. As in all things, the more a user learns about how a rule system works, the better the results, until at some point the programmer gets too involved in details and efficiency drops off again.

General Form of Rules

The query system examines rules when a user asks about a pattern that they can infer, so it is a backward-chaining system. Backward-chaining rules have conclusions and a condition. The conclusion is the fact pattern that the rule is qualified to infer, and the condition or conditions must be satisfied for the rule to succeed. The condition corresponds to the "if" part of a rule, and the conclusion to the "then" part. The conclusion of the tall-redhead rule is

(tall-redhead ?person)

and the condition is

(and   (> (height ?person) 6-feet)
       (hair-color ?person red)).

When the rule system needs to match a fact that has two fields and when the constant tall-redhead is in the first field, the system examines this rule. If the conditions hold, the rule conclusion matches the pattern as if the fact had been stored in the database all along.

Recursive Rules

In addition to chaining to other rules, rules can chain to themselves. Like most employee databases, this database gives the name of the supervisor for each employee. The fact

(supervisor (Bitlearner Fred) (Filewriter Harvey))

means that Harvey is Fred's supervisor. Given such facts, this rule can infer who works below whom:

(rule (works-below ?low ?high)
  (or   (supervisor ?low ?high)
        (and   (supervisor ?low ?middle)
               (works-below ?middle ?high))))).

?low works-below ?high if either of the following two conditions holds: (1) the database stores a fact (supervisor ?low ?high) or (2) ?low's supervisor ?middle works below ?high.

This is a fair definition of rank in a human hierarchy. One person can outrank another by either supervising that person directly or by outranking that person's supervisor. When a user asks about works-below, the rule system searches through the "supervisor" facts looking for some combination of facts that satisfies the rule.

Suppose that Harvey's boss is the Computer Wheel himself, George Bigcheese. Adding George to the database gives:

(job (Bigcheese George) (computer wheel))
(job (Filewriter Harvey) (computer hacker))
(job (Bitsmasher Martha) (computer hacker))
(job (Bitlearner Fred) (junior programmer))
(supervisor (Bitlearner Fred) (Filewriter Harvey))
(supervisor (Filewriter Harvey) (Bigcheese George))

Entering the retrieval pattern

(works-below (Bitlearner Fred) ?who)

makes the rule system consider the works-below rule.

It first looks for "supervisor" facts, finds that Harvey is Fred's supervisor, and generates an environment with ?who bound to (Filewriter Harvey). The rule system always wants to find all possible bindings that satisfy the clauses, so it proceeds to the other clause in the or-condition.

The second clause in the or-condition requires a binding for ?middle such that ?middle works-below someone. The rule system looks in the database, finds that Harvey is Fred's supervisor, and binds ?middle to (Filewriter Harvey). This binding is passed to a recursive call to works-below, this time with the second field bound to (Filewriter Harvey).

During the second invocation of works-below, the rule processor finds that Harvey's supervisor is George, so he is added to the list of people who outrank Fred. Having satisfied the first clause of the "or," the system looks at the second. The second clause finds that Harvey's supervisor is George, so it makes a third call to works-below, this time with ?low bound to (Bigcheese George). There is no "supervisor" fact for George, and the third invocation of works-below fails. The system finally finds two bindings for ?who, (Filewriter Harvey) and (Bigcheese George), both of whom outrank Fred.

Recursive Rules and Functions
Like recursive functions, recursive rules need a self-reference and an exit. The clause containing the "supervisor" fact is the exit condition, because the rule stops when no more supervisors can be found, and the self-reference is the works-below in the second clause of the "or." Like a programming system that supports recursive functions, the rule system keeps track of

different pattern variable bindings in different calls to a rule and generates a whole new set of variables each time a rule is called.

Many sets of variables are needed because each invocation of the rule needs different variable bindings. Whenever the rule system starts to examine a rule, it allocates memory to remember variable bindings for that copy of the rule. As the rule is processed, bindings are added to the environment.

Whenever the rule system chains to another rule, it allocates memory for its variables, and so on. When the system finishes with a rule, it recycles the memory allocated for the environments. Variable bindings build up as rules chain to other rules and collapse as rules either succeed or fail. Memory thrashing adds considerably to the processing load when examining rules.

Pattern Matching in Detail

The purpose of pattern matching is to find variable bindings that can make two patterns equal. Suppose the rule system is trying to match a pattern

((a b) c (a b))

Matching this pattern with (?z c ?z) binds ?z to (a b). Matching with (?r ?s ?t) binds both ?r and ?t to (a b) and binds ?s to c. Matching with ((?r ?s) c (?r ?s)) binds ?r to a and ?s to b. Matching with (?r b ?s) fails, because no value of ?r or ?s can make b in the middle of the second pattern match with c in the middle of the first.

The pattern matcher in a rule system requires three inputs: (1) a pattern to be matched, (2) a candidate fact from the database, and (3) an environment of variable bindings established by any prior clauses. The matcher checks to see if the fact can be matched with the pattern so that bindings in the environment are kept consistent. If this is possible, the new bindings are added to the environment. If this is not possible, the environment is discarded. If the pattern to be matched is

(?s ?t ?s)

and the fact from the database is

(b c b)

the match succeeds or fails depending on bindings in the environment.

If the environment is empty, the match succeeds, binding ?s to b and ?t to c. If the environment has ?s already bound to b, the match succeeds, and the new binding of ?t to c is added to the environment. If ?s has been bound to anything other than b, the match fails and the environment is discarded.

Thus, when trying to match the query pattern

(job ?x (computer hacker))

the rule system carries out the following steps:

1. Scan through the *entire* database for facts that match the pattern *with respect to the empty environment*.
2. Collect all bindings for ?x that match any fact into separate environments.
3. Substitute the values of ?x from each environment into the pattern.
4. Display the resulting pattern(s) as answer(s) to the query.

Suppose that someone needs to find the names of all employees who can do the job of computer-programmer. When processing the query

(and (can-do ?x (computer-programmer))
      (job ?y ?x))

the system first finds matches for the pattern (can-do ?x (computer programmer)). This generates a stream of environments in which ?x is bound to the name of a job such that anyone holding that job can do anything a computer programmer can do.

The system proceeds with these environments one at a time. For *each* environment it substitutes the binding for ?x in the second clause of the query. This turns the second clause into a pattern like

(job ?y (computer hacker)).

because a computer hacker can do the job of a computer programmer.

The rule system then searches the database for facts that match the pattern (job ?y ?x), where ?x has been replaced with the name of a job. Each of these matches produces an environment where ?x is bound to a job and ?y is bound to the name of a person who holds that job. The result is to find all the people who can do a computer programmer's job, at the cost of a fair amount of thrashing, but that's all right. To paraphrase an old IBM slogan, "Computers should thrash; people should think."

Any computer hacker can do anything a computer programmer can do and there are two computer hackers. The final result is the two facts

```
(and   (can-do (computer hacker) (computer programmer))
       (job (Filewriter Harvey) (computer hacker))
(and   (can-do (computer hacker) (computer programmer))
       (job (Bitsmasher Martha) (computer hacker))
```

There was only one binding for ?x, so the first clause in each result has (computer hacker) substituted for ?x. There were two facts that matched the second clause, one with ?y bound to (Bitsmasher Martha) and the other with ?y bound to (Filewriter Harvey).

Processing and-queries is illustrated in figure 10.1. The rule system is matching a query that requires that bindings satisfy both clause A and clause B: The rule system starts with an empty environment, and matches all the facts in the database against clause A. Whenever a fact matches clause A, the system creates an environment containing binding(s) for the pattern variable(s) such that clause A matches the fact.

After all of these environments are created, the system goes on to clause B. For each environment, the system replaces variables in clause B with bindings they were given when processing clause A, and matches clause B against all the facts in the database. Whenever there is a match, the system augments the environment with variable bindings established by matching clause B. Whenever a match fails, the system throws away the environment.

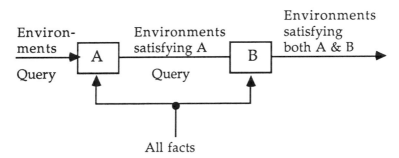

Figure 10.1
Illustration of how and-queries are processed.

The result is a stream of environments. Each environment has bindings for variables such that both clauses A and B are satisfied with the same bindings. Clause A is processed against every fact in the database. Clause B is processed against the entire database for each environment created in clause A. The term "combinatorial explosion" was invented to describe what happens when there is either a large database or many matches for a clause.

Processing or-queries is a bit different. In figure 10.2 the rule system is processing a query that requires that facts match either clause A or clause B. The entire database is passed by both clauses independently. Each clause generates a stream of bindings that matches that clause with the database. Then the bindings are merged. The result is a set of variable bindings that satisfy either clause A or clause B.

The rule system is careful to find all possible bindings because mathematical logic assumes that all matches are found simultaneously. Practical systems go to great lengths to avoid finding all the bindings in order to save time.

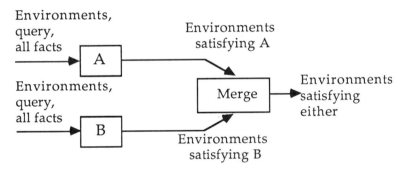

Figure 10.2
Illustration of how or-queries are processed.

Unification

Unification is a generalization of pattern matching that permits variables in both the pattern and the fact being matched. Pattern matching tells the rule system whether a fact in the database matches a pattern. Unification determines whether or not a rule might be able to derive a fact to match the desired pattern.

The conclusion of the lives-near rule was

(lives-near ?person1 ?person2)

When searching the database for patterns to match

(lives-near (Filewriter Harvey) ?x),

the conclusion of the lives-near rule matched the pattern if variable ?x in the pattern was bound to variable ?person2 in the conclusion. The difference between pattern matching and unification is that unification allows variables to be bound to other variables as well as to constants.

Unification links rule conclusions with retrieval patterns. Rule conclusions are like facts in the database except that they contain variables. If they did not contain variables, rule conclusions would act exactly like facts.[1]

Rule conclusions are *potential* facts. The rule conclusion is true if the conditions specified in the rule body are true using the same variable bindings as prior clauses. In effect, clauses in the rule body are plugged into a query pattern as if they had been part of the pattern from the beginning. The rule body replaces the clause that originally was unified with the conclusion, and pattern variables are bound to variables in the rule conditions.

The only change needed to turn a pattern matcher into a unifier is to allow a variable to be bound to another variable. This requires changing the routine that substitutes variable bindings into patterns. When substituting a binding for a variable, the routine checks to see if the binding is a constant. If it is, substitution is done. If the binding contains a variable, substitution repeats until a constant binding is found.

Examples of Unification
When the rule system tries to unify the two patterns

(?t a ?u)
(?u ?v   a)

it binds the three variables ?t, ?u, and ?v to a. The a in the first pattern binds ?v in the second to a, and the a in the second pattern forces ?u in the first to a. ?t in the first pattern must match ?u in the second, which forces it to a. These bindings are consistent, and unification succeeds.

The attempt to unify the patterns

(?t ?u a)
(?t b ?u)

fails because no value of ?u can match both a and b.

The patterns

---

[1] Some systems allow facts to contain variables. Suppose that a programmer is building a database about the dietary habits of animals. The fact (likes-to-eat monkey bananas) means that monkeys like to eat bananas, and so on. Sharks like to eat anything, but storing a likes-to-eat fact about all possible objects would take a lot of memory. It is simpler to record the fact as (likes-to-eat shark ?x). Whenever the user asks questions such as (likes-to-eat shark bananas), the ?x in the fact matches with the constant and the search succeeds. The meaning of this fact is effectively "Sharks like to eat anything." For this to work, the pattern matcher must be discarded and a unifier used to search the database as well as for selecting rules to examine.

(?t   ?t)
((a ?u c) (a b ?v))

unify with ?t bound to (a b c), ?u bound to b, and ?v bound to c. Plugging these values into both patterns gives

((a b c) (a b c)),

so these bindings work. The question is, How did the unifier figure them out?

Unification is a little like solving simultaneous algebraic equations. There is a lot of thrashing and bookkeeping required, but a simple unifier takes less than a page of Lisp code.[1]

Unification is an example of the sort of task for which Lisp is well suited. It is possible to write unifiers in other languages. Expert systems have been written in Basic, C, and Cobol as well as in Lisp, but unifiers are considerably easier to write in Lisp.

Binding Variables to Variables
There is one area where unification differs from solving simultaneous equations. When there are fewer equations than variables, engineers say that the system of equations cannot be solved because there are too many unknowns. When there are not enough facts to specify bindings for all the variables, this is OK as far as the unifier is concerned—binding one variable to another is acceptable.

For example, the two patterns

(?t   a)
((b ?u) ?v)

unify with ?v bound to a and ?t bound to (b ?u). The value of ?u is not constrained. The patterns match regardless of the value of ?u. There are restrictions on the value of ?t, however, because whatever value ?u has, ?t is bound to (b ?u).

This is like saying that $X = Y + 3$ in algebra. The statement alone does not fix the value of X but limits the possibilities.

Applying Rules Using Unification
The conclusion of the lives-near rule was

(lives-near ?person1 ?person2).

---

[1] There is code for a unifier in Abelson and Sussman, *Structure and Interpretation of Computer Programs*, section 4. Although a one-page program can unify patterns, a one-page unifier runs rather slowly. Faster unifiers are longer and much more difficult to understand. Unifiers either run fast or can be understood, but not both at the same time. Unifiers that are both fast and easy to understand await further insight.

Unifying the rule conclusion with the pattern

(lives-near (Filewriter Harvey) ?x)

produces an environment binding ?person1 to (Filewriter Harvey) and ?person2 to ?x. Each clause in the body of the rule is matched with the database, using this environment to constrain the values of ?person1 and ?person2. If all the conditions in the rule can be matched with facts in the database, the result is a binding for ?person2 that gives the name of a person who lives-near Harvey.

This example illustrates all the steps in applying rules:

1. Treat each and-clause in a query as if it were an independent query, subject to variable bindings established in prior clauses.
2. Unify each clause with the conclusion of a rule.
3. Extend the environment by binding pattern variables to conclusion variables.
4. Evaluate the rule conditions relative to the extended environment. This ensures that bindings established by the rule conclusion are consistent with prior clauses.
5. Extend the environment with bindings established by successful clauses.
6. If any clause fails, discard the environment.
7. Plug bindings back into the original query to display the answer.

Summing up Mathematical Logic

The rule system described in this chapter illustrates mathematical logic by retrieving facts from a database. It finds all possible bindings for pattern variables that make a pattern match facts in the database.

Compound and-queries force the rule system to satisfy many conditions at the same time because variable bindings must be consistent with all the clauses in a query for the query to succeed. When the first clause matches a fact, the system creates an environment containing variable bindings that were established by the match. The rule system tests all of these environments and later clauses against the database to see if the clauses match the database under constraints imposed by prior variable bindings.

The rule system unifies rule conclusions with query patterns to see if a rule could derive a fact to match the pattern. If unification succeeds, the rule system evaluates the body of the rule in an extended environment so that bindings established in the rule body are consistent with prior bindings. The effect is to substitute the conditions in the rule for the clause that unified with the rule's conclusion.

Logical retrieval is based on pattern matching, unification, and variable binding, and logic programming is the foundation of rule-based expert systems. Rules infer new facts from facts that are already in the database. Inferring new facts uses techniques derived from mathematical logic.

The major difference between expert systems and mathematical logic is that logic assumes that all facts are available at all times, whereas an expert system obtains facts from a user during a consultation. An expert system tries to minimize the number of questions asked, because answering questions costs money. Allowing an expert system to obtain facts from users while it is running is the major difference between expert systems and logic theory. The user interface to expert systems is discussed in the next chapter.

The essence of knowledge is,
having it, to apply it;
not having it, to confess your ignorance.
— Confucius

11
User Interfaces to Logic Systems

Rule systems based on mathematical logic permit sophisticated data retrieval, but this is not enough to construct an expert system.[1] The rule system can find any fact in the database or any fact that can be derived from the database, but all facts must be in the database when the request is entered. An expert system asks questions to get new facts while it is running, and this is something a pure retrieval system cannot do. In this chapter I discuss the user interface to expert systems and explore some of the problems that arise when users get involved in the process.

The Importance of Asking Questions

An expert system must ask for new facts during a consultation because it is too expensive to enter all possible facts in advance. The mechanism by which a program interacts with the user to obtain facts and present results is called the "user interface."

The user interface adds a whole new degree of complexity to a logic programming system. An expert system may look in its database as often as it likes and the computer will not mind. An

---

[1] Such systems are sometimes called "theorem-proving systems." When a rule succeeds, it is said to have proved its conclusion. Terminology does not make much difference provided that people agree on what is going on.

expert system may ask only for essential facts because unnecessary questions irritate users.

The expert system must also ask questions in a reasonable order. The goal is to solve the problem as cheaply as possible, which means not asking for expensive facts when cheap facts will do. However, users become frustrated if an expert system asks for facts in an order that seems unreasonable. If the program seems to jump all over the place, users may not believe that it knows what it is doing even when it does.

It is hard to overemphasize the importance of the user interface to an expert system. If the questions are hard to understand or difficult to answer correctly, the rules cannot get accurate facts from which to reason. Rules cannot infer correct conclusions from incorrect data.

Expert system technology is still rather new, and people have not yet built up much confidence in it. If a new computer program gives wrong answers, users either blame themselves or blame the computer, and it is easy to predict which they will choose. Once a few users tell tales of unexpected behavior, people tend to stop using the system. An expert system that users refuse to use is no better than one that does not work.

The user interface is a major departure from mathematical logic theory. Logic operates in an idealized environment in which all facts are known and searching the database takes no time. In reality, it always costs too much to know all the facts, so the system must minimize the questions it asks. Computers need time to scan hundreds of rules, and users get impatient if an expert system takes too long to ask the next question. Rule-processing speed and user interface design are important issues in building a successful expert system, but logic theory offers no assistance. The problem of minimizing the cost of facts while asking questions in a satisfactory order with acceptably fast response to user input must be solved anew for each expert system development project.

A Simple Expert System

These problems can be illustrated with an extremely simple medical expert. The expert system knows only four facts:[1]

---

[1] The medical example is based on material in the book *micro-Prolog: Programming in Logic,* by K. Clark and F. McCabe (Englewood Cliffs, N.J.: Prentice-Hall, 1984).

(relieves aspirin headache)
(relieves lomotil diarrhea)
(makes-worse aspirin ulcer)
(makes-worse lomotil bad-liver)

These facts tell which symptoms a drug relieves and which conditions it worsens. A patient should take a drug if the patient has complained of a symptom that the drug relieves and the patient does not have a condition that the drug aggravates.[1]

The rule to implement this prescription strategy is

(rule (should-take ?p ?d)
       (and   (user-said (has-symptom ?p ?s))
              (relieves ?d ?s)
              (not (unsuitable-for ?d ?p))))

Person ?p should take drug ?d if ?p has-symptom ?s and if drug ?d relieves symptom ?s and drug ?d is not unsuitable for person ?p. The rule to find whether a drug is unsuitable is

(rule (unsuitable-for ?d ?p)
       (and   (makes-worse ?d ?c)
              (user-said (has-disease ?p ?c))))

Drug ?d is unsuitable-for person ?p if drug ?d worsens some condition ?c and the user said that person ?p has condition ?c. Temporarily ignoring user-said, consider the dialogue:

User: (should-take John ?x)
Computer: (has-symptom John ?s)
           What is the value of ?s
User: headache
Computer: (has-disease John ulcer)
User: fail
Computer: (should-take John aspirin)

When the user tells the rule system that John has a headache, the computer would like to prescribe aspirin because of the fact (relieves aspirin headache). Aspirin makes ulcers worse, so the computer asks (has-disease John ulcer). The user says "fail," meaning that the pattern (has-disease John ulcer) fails to match reality because John does not have an ulcer. The computer concludes that John should take aspirin.

---

[1] This program treats symptoms instead of diseases, something real doctors are taught *not* to do.

Asking Users about Patterns

From the point of view of the expert system, the user is just another source of variable bindings. As explained in chapter 10, the rule system binds variables by matching patterns with facts or unifying patterns with rule conclusions. The user interface binds variables by asking the user. Rules extend the database by inferring new facts from existing facts. The user extends the database by supplying facts that cannot be inferred.

The pattern matcher finds variable bindings that make patterns match facts in the database. The pattern asker expects the user to supply bindings that make patterns match external truths the expert system needs to know.

The asker substitutes any available bindings into a pattern before asking about it. The first clause of the should-take rule is

(user-said (has-symptom ?p ?s)).

This clause is satisfied if there are bindings for ?p and ?s such that person ?p has symptom ?s. There are no facts about symptoms in the database and no rules that could infer facts about symptoms, so the rule system uses the pattern asker to ask the user for information about symptoms.

When asking about John's symptoms, the asker needs bindings for variables in

(has-symptom ?p ?s).

?p was bound to "John" by the initial user query. The asker substituted "John" for ?p and asked

(has-symptom John ?s).

The user supplied a binding for ?s, and the expert system had the new fact (has-symptom John headache). This fact came from the user, but the expert system can use it as if it had been in the database all along or had been inferred from a rule.

Each time the user responds, the asker obtains a binding for a variable in a pattern. Whenever it learns a new binding, the asker substitutes this new value into the pattern when asking for the next binding. The asker repeats the process of substituting, asking, binding, and substituting again until all the variables in the pattern are bound. If the user decides not to supply a binding, the clause fails just as if a matching fact were not found in the database.

Bindings supplied by the user extend the binding environment just as bindings supplied by the pattern matcher or the unifier extend the environment. All sources of bindings are equally valid so far as the rule system is concerned. As long as variables in a pattern can be bound somehow, the clause is satisfied, and the rule system proceeds.

Matching a pattern by soliciting bindings from the user does not add any information to the database. AI people call the process of adding facts to the database "assertion." A rule that adds a fact to the database is said to assert the fact. If an expert system needs to remember information from the user, it asserts appropriate facts to preserve the information for later use.

User Interface to the Medical Expert

Remembering what the user said is important because people get testy if an expert system asks the same questions over and over. The logic for minimizing questions is to look in the database first. If the fact is not there, the system attempts to infer it from a rule. If the fact cannot be inferred, the system asks the user. Once the user supplies the data, the system adds the appropriate facts to the database so that the question is not asked again.

This is similar to what I do when I want to know something. First, I try to remember. If I cannot remember, I try to figure it out. If I cannot figure it out, I ask someone and try to remember it so that I do not have to ask again.

The similarity between human reasoning and expert system reasoning is no accident. AI researchers were trying to develop intelligent computers. Because humans are the only examples of intelligence available, researchers attempted to mimic human reasoning. Whether or not a rule system mimics human reasoning processes is a matter for philosophers. No one knows how human reasoning works anyway. The fact that rules are a good way to explain things to computers is enough to make them interesting.

Remembering Facts for Later Use

The rule that implements the user interface stores each fact supplied by the user in a pattern called "was-said." When the user enters "headache" as a binding for ?s, the expert system asserts the fact

was-said (has-symptom John headache))

so that it is stored in the database.

When the system presents a fact for confirmation and the user says that it is not true, the system stores it in a pattern called "was-denied." When the question about John's ulcer failed, the system asserted the pattern (was-denied (has-disease John ulcer))[1]

After these facts are put in the database, the dialogue changes:

User: (should-take John ?x)
Computer: (should-take John aspirin)

The medical expert does not ask any questions this time because it remembers that John has a headache and that the user has denied that John has an ulcer. The system avoids repetitive questions by checking the database for was-said or was-denied facts before asking the user.

The User-Said Rule
The user interface is built on a rule called user-said. It is by far the most complex rule in the system, as would be expected of a rule that deals with humans instead of facts:

```
(rule  (user-said ?z)
       (or-once  (was-said ?z)
                 (and  (not (was-denied ?z))
                       (ask ?z)
                       (assert! (was-said ?z)))
                 (and  (not (was-denied ?z))
                       (assert! (was-denied ?z))
                       (FAIL))))))
```

This rule introduces the or-once, ask, and assert! operators that implement the user interface.

Or-once accepts clauses in the same manner as the "or" of mathematical logic except that it stops when the first clause succeeds. It can succeed only once, hence the name "or-once." A logic system is honor bound to find *all* bindings that match the database, so a logical or continues until all clauses have been processed to the bitter end. Instead of looking for all possible bindings, a user interface stops searching if the fact can be obtained from the database and asks the user only as a last resort.

User-said uses or-once to look up fact ?z or ask about it. If the fact (was-said ?z) is found in the database, the first clause succeeds and the user is not asked. If this fact is not found in the database, the user is asked about the pattern.

The second clause in the or-once is the "and" of three facts. "And" processes clauses in sequential order and fails when any clause fails. This "and" first makes sure that the fact (was-denied

---

[1] There is no mathematical difference between (was-denied ...) and (user-said (not ...)), but dealing with such subtleties is beyond the reasoning ability of a simple expert system.

?z) is not in the database. If (was-denied ?z) is in the database, the user has already said that ?z is not true, and there is no point in asking again. If (was-denied ?z) is found in the database, the (not (was-denied ?z)) clause fails, and the "and" stops.

If ?z has not previously been denied, (not (was-denied ?z)) succeeds. Fact ?z has neither been confirmed nor denied, so the "and" goes on to the (ask ?z) clause to ask the user to bind any variables in ?z. "Ask" succeeds if the user supplies variable bindings. If "ask" succeeds, the next clause asserts the pattern (was-said ?z) so that the question is not asked again. "Assert" succeeds, the "and" succeeds, or-once stops processing clauses, user-said succeeds, and the fact ?z is confirmed.

If "ask" fails, the user has failed to bind variables in ?z, and the first "and" fails. Or-once proceeds to the second and-clause. This "and" also checks that nothing is known about ?z and asserts the fact (was-denied ?z). The second check for was-denied is needed in order to prevent multiple copies of the same was-denied fact from being asserted.

Both of these and-clauses are used during the sample dialogue. When the user asks (should-take John ?x), the first clause in the should-take rule looks for (user-said (has-symptom John ?s)). The or-once clause in the user-said rule finds that there is no (was-said (has-symptom John ?s)) fact in the database. The first "and" finds that there is no was-denied fact either, so it asks the user about the pattern (has-symptom John ?s). The user binds ?s to "headache," "ask" succeeds, and the fact (was-said (has-symptom John headache)) is asserted. Assert always succeeds, so the and-clause succeeds, the user-said rule succeeds, and the system knows that John has-symptom headache.

The next clause of the should-take rule matches the fact (relieves aspirin headache), so aspirin becomes a candidate for a drug that John should take.

The last clause in the should-take rule is

(not (unsuitable-for ?d ?p).

The rule system has bound ?p to "John" and ?d to "aspirin," so the clause becomes

(not (unsuitable-for aspirin John)).

The first clause of the unsuitable-for rule finds that aspirin makes an ulcer worse. The final step in prescribing aspirin for John is looking for the pattern

(user-said (has-disease John ulcer)).

The user-said rule finds that the fact

(has-disease John ulcer)

has neither been confirmed nor denied, so it asks the user about the pattern. The ask fails when the user replies "fail" and the user-said rule asserts the pattern

(was-denied (has-disease John ulcer))

The failure of the user-said clause makes the unsuitable-for rule fail, so the (not (unsuitable-for ...)) clause succeeds. This is the last clause in the should-take rule. Should-take succeeds, and the expert system says John should take aspirin.

Points to Ponder

This expert system is *extremely* simple. It knows only two rules and four facts. Even though it knows only a little, it can recommend aspirin for headache and lomotil for diarrhea and make sure that the patient does not have a condition that these drugs aggravate. The system is far from complete, but it *works*. As long as a case falls under the rules it knows, it can prescribe a suitable drug or at least a drug that is not unsuitable.

This illustrates the point that expert systems are demonstrable *long* before they are ready for practical use. It is wise to be skeptical of software demonstrations and particularly cynical of demonstrations of AI software. There is an anonymous saying about software development: "The first 90% of the work takes 90% of the budget. The last 10% of the work *also* takes 90% of the budget." This is doubly true for expert system development in that both phases take 180% of the budget.

The complete medical expert system, including the rule system and pattern asker, takes ten or twelve pages of Lisp and less than one page of facts and rules. The only really messy rule implements the user interface, and the rest is straightforward. Expressing the thinking behind medical diagnosis in the form of should-take and unsuitable-for rules makes it easy to understand. A conventional program that implemented the same logic would be harder to read and to maintain.

This medical expert has the core functions of an expert system. It gets information by asking questions, remembers information, and reaches conclusions based on facts that it finds in its database, infers from rules, or solicits from the user. It would not be ready for production use even if it knew a great many more facts, however, because it is so difficult to use. Like essentially all important ideas, rule processing itself is inherently simple but requires a number of surrounding tools and techniques in order to be practical.

Problems with the User Interface

The worst problem with this expert system is that the user interface is too demanding. If the user misspells "headache," the system cannot prescribe a drug. There is no checking to ensure that a symptom is at least spelled correctly or that the symptom the user enters is one the system knows about. Even worse, there is no way to fix an incorrect answer. Once the system believes that John has a headache, there is no going back. As far as the system is concerned, John has a headache forever.

This sort of behavior is user surly at best and might be considered user hostile in some circles. Developing a suitable user interface is a major job in most expert system projects.[1]

How the System Works

Even though practical expert systems need a much friendlier user interface, this medical expert illustrates all the principles behind expert systems:

1. The rule system looks for variable bindings that are consistent with facts in the database.
2. Pattern matching generates environments containing bindings that match facts in the database.
3. Bindings established in an and-clause restrict the values that variables may assume in later clauses.
4. Unification generates bindings that match rule conclusions.
5. Rules infer new facts from facts in the database provided that the conditions in the rule body match prior variable bindings.
6. The pattern asker asks the user for bindings that match external conditions.
7. Bindings from any source are equally valid, and the rule system does not care where bindings come from.

What Next with Rules?

I have introduced the idea of a user interface to a logic programming system. The user interface lets an expert system obtain facts as needed during a consultation.

---

[1] There are many commercial programs called "expert system shells" that make it easier to develop expert systems. Writing a rule interpreter for an expert system is not particularly difficult, but offering powerful tools that make it easy to develop good user interfaces is very hard. The problem of offering general user interface tools is as yet unsolved. In the world of personal computers, the IBM PC and the Apple Macintosh represent radically different views of how to structure a user interface. The market has not yet decided how people prefer to talk to computers.

The user interface is a major departure from logic theory. Theory assumes that facts are always available at no cost, whereas expert systems make do with as few facts as possible in order to minimize the number of questions they ask.

The issue of controlling the order in which rules are examined is another departure from logic theory. Logic assumes that all rules are evaluated simultaneously in zero elapsed time. Computers evaluate rules too slowly to try all possibilities, and users resent being asked all possible questions.

Expert systems must concentrate on rules that have a high likelihood of succeeding, or they waste most of their time examining rules that fail. I address the question of controlling the order in which rules are examined in the next chapter.

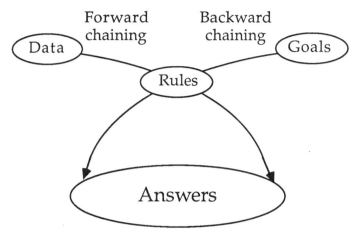

12
Issues in Rule and Knowledge Management

Chapter 10 introduced the ideas behind logic programming and discussed pattern matching and unification in detail. In chapter 11 I described the problem of fitting a user interface to a logic programming system. The user interface adds a new dimension to logic theory in that facts can be added to the database while the rule system is trying to match a pattern.

Chapter 11 also mentioned the problem of choosing the next rule to examine. Choosing rules is not a problem in logic theory because all possible inferences are made simultaneously and instantaneously in a theoretical universe. Examining all the rules is not practical in an expert system because it would take too long, and asking the user to enter all relevant facts would cost too much.

Useful systems pay close attention to choosing which questions to ask and which rules to examine. Experience has shown that the way in which facts and rules in an expert system are organized has a profound effect on how well it works. In this chapter I discuss rule and knowledge management in detail.

Expert System Shells

Although the core of any rule system is fairly simple, there is no reason to develop a new one in order to write an expert system.

Many vendors offer expert systems that have had their rules stripped out. These "empty" expert systems are called "expert system shells." A shell has a rule system, a rule editor, and tools for maintaining and debugging rules and facts.

The software that matches rules with facts is fairly standard, so the most important part of a shell is the rule editing and debugging tools.[1] Getting a rule interpreter to work is not much work. Writing a rule system that runs quickly is somewhat more complicated, and writing tools to help debug rules requires a great deal of effort.

There is no reason for a new expert system project to write its own rule system. It is far better to buy a commercial shell. If a custom system turns out to be necessary, it can be written after gaining experience with a commercial shell.

There are many shells on the market, and no clear winner has emerged. The information about rule control in this chapter should make it easier to choose an appropriate shell.[2]

Chaining Forward and Backward

A backward-chaining system assumes that a goal is known; that is, it has in mind a fact that it would like to conclude. Backward chaining looks for rules whose conclusions unify with the fact it wants, then sees if the conditions in the rule can be matched with facts in the database.

The Mycin expert system discussed in chapter 9 assumes that the patient has a bacterial infection and uses backward chaining to find which of many possible bacteria caused it. The medical expert in chapter 11 also uses backward chaining. A rule is examined when it has the potential to infer a fact that another rule needs to reach a conclusion.

Backward chaining finds rules whose "then" sides are interesting and tries to satisfy the conditions in their "if" sides. Forward chaining matches available facts against the "if" sides of all rules, then takes the actions specified in the "then" sides of rules whose "if" sides are satisfied. Forward chaining uses available facts to decide which goal to pursue; backward chaining selects rules whose conclusions could satisfy current goals, then looks for facts to satisfy their conditions. Both kinds of rule

---

[1] New rule systems promise better performance. Steve Rowley at Symbolics in Cambridge, Mass., is developing an expert system called Joshua that offers an advanced rule processor and extremely powerful domain modeling capabilities.
[2] The situation is like the early days of Fortran before benchmarks were available. Choosing a Fortran compiler was difficult because there were no accepted standards.

processor ask users for more facts when they cannot satisfy the conditions of any rules.

Expert systems often give ridiculous answers if they choose the wrong goals. Mycin assumes that a doctor has determined that the patient is suffering from a bacterial infection and pursues the goal of identifying the organism responsible for the infection. If the patient does not have a bacterial infection, Mycin gives ludicrous results.

Switching between Forward and Backward Rules

Doctors have a standard set of questions they ask every new patient. Practical medical systems chain forward from the standard facts to select a hypothesis to pursue and chain backward to ask for facts to prove or disprove the hypothesis. A medical system might include a set of forward chaining rules to propose diseases:

```
if    (and  (has-pockmarks ?p)
            (has-fever ?p))
then  (assert! (might-have ?p smallpox))

if    (and  (has-runny-nose ?p)
            (sneezing ?p))
then  (assert! (might-have ?p flu))
```

The doctor examines the patient and enters some facts:

```
(assert! (has-pockmarks John))
(assert! (has-fever John))
```

Whenever a new fact is asserted, the system scans the "if" sides of all the rules to see if they are satisfied. These facts satisfy the conditions in the first rule, so the rule asserts the fact

```
(might-have John smallpox)
```

This might-have fact sets up a goal of verifying whether John has smallpox. The system can switch to backward chaining and try to satisfy conditions in a rule such as

```
(rule (has-smallpox ?p)
            (and  (user-said (test-shows ?p first-test-data))
                  (user-said (test-shows ?p second-test-data))
                  ...))
```

In order for this to work, the rule system must switch automatically from forward chaining to backward chaining when a might-have fact is asserted. The assertion of a might-have fact informs the system that enough information has been accumu-

lated to justify more extensive and more expensive tests for
further facts about smallpox.

Equivalence of Forward and Backward Chaining
Forward chaining is sufficient, however. Instead of chaining
backward, the system could use the forward rule

```
if     (and  (might-have-smallpox ?p)
             (user-said (test-shows ?p first-test-data))
             (user-said (test-shows ?p second-test-data))
             ...))
then   (assert! (has-smallpox ?p))
```

When forward chaining, the system scans clauses in the "if"
side of each rule, matching them against facts in the database.
Before the fact

(might-have John smallpox)

is asserted, this rule cannot fire because the first clause fails.
When the fact is asserted, the clause succeeds. The rule system
examines the user-said clauses, asking questions as it goes. It is
up to the developer to order clauses so that tests are done in the
right order to minimize pain and cost.

As explained in the previous chapter, the user-said rule asks
the user for facts that are not in the database. Each user-said
clause asks the doctor to perform some medical test and report
the results. If all the tests succeed, the "then" side of the rule
asserts the fact

(has-smallpox John).

The only difference between the forward and backward versions of the rule is that they are formatted differently to make
them easier for humans to understand. Mathematically there is
no difference between forward and backward chaining because
both forms have exactly the same capabilities.

Some problems are best thought of in terms of forward
chaining, and others are easier to solve in terms of backward
chaining. It is seldom easy to determine in advance which form
of chaining is best for a particular problem, so most expert
system shells offer both.

Differences between Forward and Backward Rules
Although forward and backward chaining are equivalent in
their ability to find things out, there are operational differences
between the two forms of reasoning.

Forward-chaining systems use facts as soon as they are available. The following diagram shows a forward chaining expert system with two rules. The rules specify "if A and B and C then D" and "if D and E and F then G." As soon as the user enters facts A, B, and C, the rule system concludes fact D. Fact D fills in a condition in the second rule, and the system stands ready to conclude fact G when facts E and F appear.

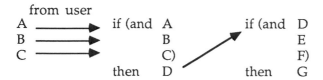

The backward-chaining version of these two rules is mathematically the same but operates quite differently:

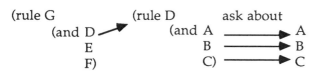

Backward chaining starts from a desired conclusion, in this case, fact G. Fact D is the first clause in the rule that can conclude fact G. The rule system chains to the second rule because that rule can infer fact D. This rule requires fact A, so the system asks the user about fact A. If the user supplies fact A, the first clause succeeds, and the rule system asks about facts B and C.

Forward-chaining systems are as capable of asking users for facts as backward-chaining systems, of course. The major difference is that backward-chaining systems ask for all the facts needed for a particular conclusion at the same time. Forward-chaining systems tend to ask questions in no particular order.

Suppose that fact D in the example was used in two different rules. A forward rule system could ask for facts to support either rule, choosing which rule to pursue on the basis of which rule depends on the fewest facts and is closest to success.[1] This tends to make forward-chaining systems jump around a bit more than backward-chaining systems. Users seem to prefer the focused dialogue characteristic of backward chaining because the system asks all necessary questions about each rule it examines.

---

[1] An expert system shell called OPS5+ offers a flexible control structure. OPS5+ provides inference subroutines and also lets users write their own mechanisms for choosing which rules to fire. Flexibility goes hand in hand with faults. The more features, the harder the system is to use.

Resolving Conflicts between Forward Rules

The major problem with forward chaining is deciding what to do when the conditions on the "if" sides of more than one rule are satisfied at the same time. In expert system terminology the list of rules whose "if" sides are satisfied is called the "agenda." Choosing a rule from the agenda is called "conflict resolution" and can be difficult.

Suppose that an expert system needs a rule to figure out the number of days in a year. The programmer writes two forward-chaining rules:

```
if      (and  (year-length unknown)
              (year-divisible-by-4))
then    (assert! (year-length 366))

if      (and  (year-length unknown)
              (not (year-divisible-by-4)))
then    (assert! (year-length 365))
```

Each of these rules tests to see if the year length is unknown. If the year length is not known, the second clause of each rule determines which rule fires and asserts the length of the year. If the year is divisible by 4 it is a leap year with 366 days; otherwise it has 365.

These two rules work pretty well but err because some years that are divisible by 100 are not leap years. Eventually management decrees that this bug must go. Someone researches the calendar and writes two more rules:

```
if      (and  (year-length unknown)
              (year-divisible-by-4)
              (year-divisible-by-100))
then    (assert! (year-length 365))

if      (and  (year-length unknown)
              (year-divisible-by-4)
              (year-divisible-by-100)
              (year-divisible-by-400))
then    (assert! (year-length 366))
```

Most of the time there is no conflict between these rules. Every 100 years, however, a year is divisible by both 4 and by 100, so the second and third rules both go on the agenda at the same time. Every four-hundredth year is also divisible by 400, in which case the last three rules are all eligible.

One simple way of choosing between eligible rules is to fire the rule with the most clauses, on the theory that the most restrictive rule is the most likely to be appropriate. This strategy gives the right answer in this case but not always. The issue of choosing rules from the agenda is still open.[1]

Disabling Forward Rules

The leap year example illustrates another problem with forward chaining. Forward rules select goals, and satisfying a goal may take considerable time. It would be unfortunate if the rule that selected the goal were to fire again while the system tries to satisfy the goal. It is also important to keep the rule from being fired again if the goal fails.

A forward rule must be disabled while the goal is being sought and perhaps for a time afterward. Some of the early rule systems went so far as to decree that forward-chaining rules can be fired only once. Once such a rule has fired, it cannot do so again until the entire rule system is restarted.

The first clause of each of these rules for computing the length of a year is a test to make sure that the year length is not known. Once any of these rules fires, the year length becomes known and none of these rules is eligible to fire. The entire set of rules is disabled when the year length is known.

Complicated forward-chaining systems are usually organized around a few global facts that turn large sets of rules on and off. Deciding when to turn groups of rules on and off can be complicated and leads to subtle bugs. Getting several sets of rules to coordinate properly requires tact and patience.

Conflicts Involving Negation

Another type of conflict involves rules that depend on truth and falsehood of the same fact. Automotive diagnostic expert systems have rules such as

```
if     (and  (weather-suddenly-got-very-cold)
             (car-cranked-yesterday-but-not-today))
then   (recharge-battery)

if     (and  (weather-suddenly-got-very-cold)
             (car-ran-yesterday-but-won't-crank-today)
             (battery-is-all-right))
then   (check-battery-wires-and-ignition-switch)
```

---

[1] In this case, adding the clause (not (year-divisible-by-400)) to the first and third rules and the clauses (not (year-divisible-by-100)) to the first rule also solves the problem by making sure that one and only one rule can fire at any given time. This is an example of an interaction between rules. Interactions can get complicated in large systems.

This type of reasoning is quite common in diagnostic expert systems. The first rule tells the user to recharge the battery if the engine suddenly stops turning over, and the second says to check the battery wiring and the ignition switch if the battery turns out to be all right.

The first rule explains why a car fails to turn over about 95% of the time, especially in cold climates. When the user tests the battery and enters the fact

(battery-is-all-right)

the second rule starts checking other things.

Even if the user bought a brand-new battery yesterday and knows that the battery is OK from the beginning, the first rule suggests checking the battery anyway. One way to solve this problem might be to change the first rule so that it does not check the battery if the battery is known to be all right

if   (and (weather-suddenly-got-very-cold)
              (car-ran-yesterday-but-won't-crank-today)
              (not (battery-is-all-right))
then   (recharge-battery)

This technique helps in that the first rule will not fire if the battery is known to be OK from the beginning but does not work in general. In logic "not" means "known to be false," but in simple expert systems "not" means "not known to the expert system."

Forward reasoning can go awry if facts are presented in the wrong order. Consider these rules:

if (and   A   if (and   A
          B   B
          (not C))   C)
then   X   then   Y

If conditions A and B hold, the system should conclude either X or Y depending on whether C is true or not. If fact C arrives first, the system chooses between X and Y properly. Suppose, however, that fact A arrives first, then fact B. The system cannot conclude Y because Y requires fact C, which is not known. (Not C) is true because C is not known, so the first rule concludes X as soon as A and B become known.

What happens when fact C arrives later? The system can conclude Y when C arrives, but what about X? X was based on (not C). Now that C is known, (not C) is false, and X is no longer a valid conclusion.

Simply removing X from the database does not repair the damage. Denying X undoes the original assert but does not remove facts that depend on X. The rule system must examine all its conclusions, removing any that depend on X. If any facts are denied because X is denied, the system must deny facts that depend on them, and so on.

This process is called "truth maintenance" and is extremely important in expert systems. People make tentative assumptions and revise them when new facts come to light. Many human experts have lists of common solutions to problems that they apply without doing much checking at all. If the first fix fails, they back up and reconsider the problem.

Suppose that C is seldom true or expensive to find out. It may be appropriate to assume (not C)[1] and proceed on the basis of X, retracting the reasoning based on X if C turns out to be true. The ability to retract a hypothesis and proceed in an entirely different direction is rather useful.

The best way to resolve conflicts between rule firing and the order in which facts become known depends on the specific problem. Some users are willing to let the system ask questions in any order it likes, whereas others demand a familiar pattern. If the system designer can control the order in which facts become available, the problem is simplified. Doctors insist on entering facts without waiting for the computer to express interest, and it is much more difficult to prevent rule conflict in such cases.

Resolving Conflicts between Backward Rules

Conflicts between backward rules require the system to choose which rule to pursue when more than one rule could lead to the same conclusion. Suppose that a backward-chaining system needs fact X and has two rules that could conclude X:

```
if (and    A          if (and    D
           B                     E
           C)                    F)
then       X          then       X
```

Which rule should the system pursue first? That depends on the cost of the facts required by the two rules, experience showing which rule is most likely to succeed, engineering practice, user expectations, and a host of other factors. Even if all

---

[1] Unless a false assumption can have dire consequences, such as assuming that a patient is (not allergic-to-penicillin).

the facts are known, searching through a complex mesh of linked rules can take a long time.

The Role of Knowledge Management

Long database searches can usually be avoided by organizing knowledge well, and knowledge organization is usually more important than search strategy. If groups of rules are enabled and disabled so that only a few rules apply at any given time, it does not much matter how they are searched because there are so few rules that any search strategy will do. If the rules are organized poorly, the number of search paths grows exponentially and no search strategy is fast enough.

This is why expert system projects often back up and start over after a few hundred rules are accumulated. The experience gained with the first few rules often gives insight into how the rules should have been organized, and the new structure makes searching the rules easier.

This sort of problem makes it extremely difficult to estimate the cost of an expert system before it is about half done. Until an organization sheds some blood in the trenches, nobody knows how deep the trenches are. Expert system development lacks the scheduling precision and budgetary exactness that management expects of conventional software development projects.

Organizing Knowledge in Expert Systems

Rule chaining problems and data arrival conflicts can be reduced by structuring the expert system so that facts and rules that apply to one part of the problem are kept separate from rules and facts about other parts. This is nothing more than common sense—engineers know that it is easier to solve many little problems than one big problem.

Rules for dividing and conquering engineering problems are applicable to managing knowledge in expert systems. It is not yet possible to give general methods for organizing knowledge in an expert system, but an expert system designer should think about the kinds of knowledge in the domain and the ways in which knowledge is managed.

Kinds of Knowledge

Each problem area has its own knowledge sources, but most disciplines embrace the same classes of knowledge:

1. Knowledge of methods. How does an expert design the hydraulic system in a helicopter? Locate elevators in a new hotel? Diagnose diseases? Recommend investments?
2. Knowledge of equipment and tools. How does a chain saw work? What kinds of operations can a milling machine perform? What tools does an electrician always carry? What special tools may be needed?
3. Static knowledge. Static knowledge does not change while an expert system is running. A patient's gender seldom changes, but blood pressure and temperature do. Expert systems are better at dealing with static information than at coping with change.
4. Dynamic knowledge. Dynamic knowledge changes during a consultation. The expert system needs to know how to take equipment apart, put it back together again, and what can and cannot be done while the equipment is taken apart.
5. Declarative knowledge. Declarative knowledge describes relationships. The run light is part of the control panel, the control panel is part of the housing, the housing encloses three circuit boards, and so on.
6. Procedural knowledge. Procedures list the steps needed to get things done. To remove the inspection plate, first remove the bolts that hold it on; to put it back, tighten each bolt to so many foot pounds, and so on.

Knowledge Management
Each kind of knowledge is managed in different ways. Many issues in knowledge management arise in every expert system project.

Acquiring Knowledge Where does knowledge comes from? Is knowledge available from books, or must it be obtained from experts? Can an expert system learn about a machine by asking it or does it have to ask users if the lights are on?

Useful knowledge may be available from existing computer databases. The interfaces to these computers may or may not have been designed so that other computers can retrieve the facts. It may be necessary to write special programs to get information from other computers or from the equipment.

Representing Knowledge Early expert systems stored facts as independent lists such as (job (Filewriter Harvey) (computer hacker)) and (address (Filewriter Harvey) (Detroit)). The job fact about Harvey and the address fact about Harvey are unrelated as far as the computer is concerned. Humans know that they have some sort of relationship to a person named "Harvey," but the computer does not.

Modern expert system shells tend to be "object oriented" and store facts as attributes of objects.   In such a representation, Harvey is an object and has job and address attributes.   This keeps all the facts about Harvey in the same place but makes it more difficult to look things up.   Instead of finding all the job facts in the same place, the system scans through all the objects checking their job attributes.

Knowledge representation makes a big difference in how easy it is to keep track of information and how long it takes to find it. Advanced expert system shells offer several ways of expressing information and automatically translate the representation the user chooses into a form that can be searched quickly.   It is easy for a computer to scan a collection of objects to build separate lists of job and address facts so that the search goes faster.   Both ART by Inference Corp. and KEE by Intellicorp claim to do this.

One of the biggest problems in knowledge representation is organizing knowledge so that it can be entered into a computer at all.   Many experts do not bother to organize their knowledge formally—cooks say, "Add enough salt to make it taste right," or "Bake until it's done."   In such cases, simply finding out what is knowledge and what is not requires effort.

Using Knowledge   It is important to know what the knowledge is for.   Human experts answer questions, instruct apprentices, learn new facts, swap stories with colleagues, and occasionally solve problems.   Knowledge can be used to control and diagnose machinery or to compute manufacturing costs.   The results of using the knowledge may be displayed to a user, transmitted to another computer, or simply remembered for later.   It is important to know how knowledge is to be used before collecting it.

Expert system developers have explored relatively few domains and have dealt with only a few kinds of knowledge. Limited experience makes it difficult to choose a knowledge representation for a given problem.   The knowledge storage technique makes a great deal of difference in how easy it is to collect the required information.   It is prudent to anticipate some floundering and backtracking as a project gets underway.

Parts of Expert System Shells

Expert system shells are computer programs that try to facilitate expert system development.   Early expert system programmers wrote their own rule interpreters, rule editors, databases, and the like. After a few systems had been developed, a researcher had the idea of stripping the rules out and recycling the domain-independent bits as a generalized expert system shell.

The best way to start an expert system project is to buy a commercial expert system shell. It is difficult to choose the best shell because not enough experience has been accumulated to permit a definitive choice. The best strategy seems to be to choose a shell on the basis of price, support, and the equipment it runs on. The first project provides the experience needed to make a better choice for the next project. The motto is, "Ready, fire, aim," because it is hard to hit the target without letting go a few rounds for calibration.

The relationships between parts of an expert system shell are shown in figure 12.1. The tools help the user enter, maintain, and debug rules, the control structure decides which rule to run next, and the rule system fires rules by matching their conditions with facts in the database.

The rule system, pattern matcher, unifier, and database are more or less application independent. Matching facts with rule clauses is a standard process, although rule-processing speed depends on how well the rule interpreter is written. As long as the source code editors translate knowledge entered by the user into the appropriate format to be stored in the database, the rule system does not care where information comes from.

The most important characteristic of the rule system is speed. It is not possible for a rule system to be too fast, and most are far too slow.

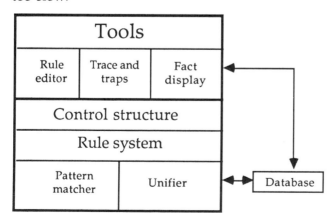

Figure 12.1
Relationship between parts of an expert system shell.

The tools provide the user interface to the expert system development system and can be heavily dependent on the application. If the shell knows about blood pressure or surface finish or power supply, it is easier to use. The more the rule editor and database converse with the user in terms of the application, the easier it is to use the shell. Domain vocabulary is so important that some vendors offer custom vocabularies that supplement their more general expert system shells.

The database interface lets the user examine the database and assert new facts. The user needs direct access to the database in order to enter test facts that let rules fire and to verify that rules assert the correct facts.

Many expert system development tools and methods have evolved over the years. The following sections discuss facilities that I believe ought to be part of any viable expert system shell.

Rule Debugger

The rule debugger is the most important part of an expert system shell in terms of getting an expert system to work. Debugging rules is like debugging other software: The programmer designs a rule, then writes and tests it. If the rule does not work as expected, the programmer modifies it until it does.

Rule tracing is a standard feature of most shells. The tracer builds a table showing when each rule fired and when each fact was asserted.

Rule debugging is similar to debugging conventional functions. The programmer needs to be told when a rule fires, when a fact is asserted, when a fact is denied, which questions were asked, and what the replies were. This information helps a programmer figure out where the reasoning went wrong when the expert system gets the wrong answer.

The history of every rule that fired and every fact that went into the database helps debug rules. A programmer writes a few rules and tries them out. If the expert says that the system got the right answer, the programmer writes more rules and tries other cases. If the expert says the system made a mistake, the programmer and the expert review every step of the reasoning to identify the point where the system went wrong. The programmer corrects the errant rule and tries again.

Some expert systems have tools that examine the history record and answer questions. A user may ask, "Why did you think John had smallpox?" The system says, "Rule 1 fired because John had pockmarks and a high fever." The user asks,

"Why did you think John had pockmarks?" and the system replies, "You said so."

Finding out why rules do not fire is extremely important to rule programmers.[1] This debugging aid has no counterpart in conventional debugging. Conventional functions run when called by another function—the flow of control is explicitly specified. Rules, on the other hand, fire whenever the facts they need become available.

When testing rules, a programmer enters facts that should make the rule fire and checks to see if the right action was carried out. If the rule does not fire when expected, the programmer must find out why.

There are many reasons why a rule might not fire when the programmer thinks it should. If the programmer misspells a condition, that clause can never be satisfied and the rule can never fire. If the clauses are all correct and the facts are in the database, the rule still may not fire if a higher priority rule is eligible to fire at the same time.

A programmer needs to be able to ask the rule system why a rule does not fire. Is there a missing fact? Is there another rule with a higher priority? The rule system displays the clause that failed. Knowing which clause failed, the programmer can usually figure out what to do about it.

Automatic Question Asking

The better the expert system development tools, the faster a programmer can develop an expert system. The better the user interface facilities, the more cost-effective the system is to use. Expert system shells provide facilities for asking users for facts when necessary. User convenience is more important than programmer convenience because an expert system is developed once but used over and over again.

When an expert system needs information from outside, asking the user to bind variables in a pattern such as

(has-symptom John ?s)

is not particularly user friendly. The expert system should translate this pattern into a more human question, such as

What symptoms does John exhibit?

---

[1] Negative information can have great value. Consider Sherlock Holmes's deduction from the fact that a dog did not bark in *Silver Blaze*, which can be found in any collection of the writings of A. Conan Doyle.

Translating a has-symptom fact into a more Englishlike sentence is a job for the pattern matcher. The programmer specifies an English template for each pattern. The template for has-symptom might look like

What symptom does ?p exhibit?

The system substitutes the binding for ?p into the template, asks the question, and binds the answer to ?s.[1]

Saying It with Pictures

This pseudo-English user interface is better than just displaying patterns and asking for bindings but is not adequate for complicated questions.

Powerful expert system shells have graphics interfaces that display pictures, text, and menus to help users understand and answer questions. The picture shows the object of the question, the text gives details of what is wanted, and the menu lists acceptable answers.

This technique is particularly valuable in factory machinery diagnosis. There are too many machines in a factory for a mechanic to be familiar with them all. An electrician may not even know what a device looks like, to say nothing of knowing where the "run" light is.[2]

Advanced expert system shells offer active images for powerful user interfaces. An active image is a structured picture of an object. The expert system knows the names of the parts of the object and where these parts are located in the picture. When it asks whether the "run" light is on or off, the system shows a picture of the control panel and makes the "run" light blink. This helps users find the light.

The message "Is the 'run' light on or off?" is displayed with the picture, and a menu of choices "on" and "off" is generated.

---

[1]   This template does not work for questions such as "Who is suffering from a headache." The pattern asker simply asks the user for variable bindings and can ask (has-symptom John ?s) and (has-symptom ?p headache) with equal ease. Separate templates must be supplied for each variable that can be asked about. Human users are a real pain in the neck!

[2]   Texas Instruments offers an expert system shell called "Personal Consultant Plus" which has a graphics user interface. PC+ has a younger sibling called "Personal Consultant Easy" which is easier to use. Both of these expert system shells specify templates for questions, then automatically ask questions when facts are needed by a rule. The May 1987 issue of the *Applied Artificial Intelligence Reporter* says that PC+ seems to be the market leader for expert systems on personal computers, although such assertions are rather unreliable because of a shortage of hard data.

The user does not have to type anything to answer the question because the answer can be selected from the menu. However, the menu system should also let users type answers if they prefer or select from the menu by entering the first letter of the name of the menu item.

In order to generate questions, the expert system needs to understand the relationships between objects. The programmer specifies which objects are part of which so that the system can decide which picture to display for each question. The programmer also specifies acceptable answers for each question so that the system can generate the menu.

Entering this information is a lot of work but makes the expert system much easier to use. Not only that, pictures give management the impression that the expert system is going to work. Experienced developers start with the pictures, on the grounds that it is best to begin with form and backfill with function only as necessary.

Starting with pictures has the further benefit of familiarizing the programmer with the domain. There is nothing quite like drawing pictures of all the panels, lights, switches, and other components to make *sure* that the knowledge engineer understands the equipment down to the last detail.

Consistency Checking

It is prudent for an expert system to make consistency checks when users supply facts. It is rare for a computer's "run" light to be on when its "power" switch is off or it is unplugged. If the user says that this is the case, the expert system ought to ask for confirmation before proceeding. An expert system needs rules to tell it which combinations of facts are acceptable and which require verification from the user.

Some shells provide special "consistency" rules, which automatically check for inconsistent combinations; others require that programmers write their own consistency checks and take appropriate action.

Interfaces to Other Software

Expert systems seldom operate in a vacuum. Most organizations using expert systems already own computers that store some of the information the expert system needs. Even though it might be cost-effective to discard these programs and rewrite them in Lisp, management is seldom willing to do so.

For an expert system to be useful, it must fit into the existing computing environment. This requires that a rule be able to "call out" of the expert system to ask a program written in some other language to perform some calculation on its behalf.[1] This facility is useful in developing expert systems that can trouble-shoot electronic devices. A good troubleshooter can fix a strange device simply by reading the schematic and applying universal rules of troubleshooting.

An expert system that knows how to trace faults needs access to the schematic in order to debug a specific device. Most electronic devices are designed on computers, so the circuit diagrams are available in computer-readable form. In order to use the diagrams, however, the expert system has to be able to call on the design program for information.

Some problems are best solved using conventional program-ming, but inserting a bit of logic in the right place comes in handy. The conventional program must "call in" to the expert system and ask it to infer a fact or two.[2]

This combination is helpful in scheduling resources such as aircraft. Computers cannot analyze all possible airline routines because there are too many. An expert system can eliminate a great many possibilities from consideration, and the numerical system can analyze the rest.

The scheduling program wants to ask questions such as, "Is this strategy likely to improve on the strategy we just analyzed?" using the expert system to eliminate as many possibilities as it can. This is what human experts do—run a scheduling program to examine a few possibilities, make a few guesses, and run it again. Making some of that expertise directly available to the scheduling program often proves effective.

Flexible Control Structure

Complicated applications require careful control of the order in which questions are asked to keep the user dialogue focused and careful selection of rules to examine to keep response times acceptably fast. In addition, different knowledge domains use different styles of reasoning. Doctors alternate between backward

---

[1] Personal Consultant Plus from Texas Instruments lets rules call functions written in Lisp or in C, retrieve information stored in databases, and get data from spreadsheets.

[2] An expert system tool kit called "OPS5+" is delivered in the form of a library of subroutines that can be called from programs written in C. The C program handles the user interface, then calls OPS5 subroutines to add facts to the database and to make inferences. Because OPS5 does not supply a user interface, developing an expert system with OPS5 can be more work than with other shells. Because rule processing is supplied as C-callable subroutines, adding inference capability to an existing application is much simpler than with other tools. OPS5 compiles rules into C and tends to run rapidly.

and forward chaining and are reluctant to make decisions that are not fully supported by evidence. Engineers may take action without conclusive evidence because getting conclusive evidence would cost too much or take too long.

The control structure of the expert system must follow the reasoning style of the experts on whom it is based. After all, expert systems mimic a particular human problem solving ability, and an expert system shell needs to be able to mimic the expert chosen as the knowledge source for the project.

Some shells offer complete control of the reasoning process. The agenda of rules that are eligible to fire is just another fact in the database, and users may write rules to manipulate the agenda. These rules reason about which rules to fire just as they would reason about anything else.[1] Other shells are specialized for the kind of control needed by a particular discipline, and, if it turns out to be unsuitable for your application, too bad.

Winning the Shell Game

There are many shells on the market. Given the state of the art, it is difficult if not impossible to choose the best shell for a project. Engineers should be satisfied with a shell that is good enough to get started. Here are a few features to look for:

• Forward and backward chaining. Although any expert system can be written to chain in only one direction, it is helpful to have both available.

• Ability to call in and call out. In order for the expert system to be able to get information from other programs, the shell must let rules make calls to programs outside of the expert system environment. In order for other programs to make use of logical inference, the shell must let other programs ask for facts from outside the shell.

• Flexible control structure is helpful but is essential only for large projects. If there are only a few rules, the system will respond fast enough no matter how they are fired. Flexible control structure can be deferred until the system outgrows its first shell and molts.

• Flexible user interface. A good user interface is important in the early stages. When nobody has any confidence in the expert system, the better the interface, the easier it is to persuade users to believe in it. Once people accept the technology, they will accept a less flashy interface. All else being equal, a wonderful

---

[1] The more reasoning an expert system does, the more slowly it runs. Reasoning about what to reason about adds yet another layer of sloth.

interface is more important than wonderful logic, even though flashy interfaces to systems that do not do much contribute to the impression that AI is nothing but flimflam.

All expert system shells are compromises between logic theory and computer programs that give acceptable performance at reasonable cost on a digital computer. The AI community has debated the merits of writing expert systems in Lisp or Prolog for the last few years. The debate has spilled over into the popular press, and articles with provocative phrases such as "Lisp vs. Prolog" in their titles have appeared.

This debate is quite irrelevant. Lisp is a programming language and Prolog is an expert system shell. In the next chapter I describe Prolog in some detail in order to explain how to use it and to show how a specific set of trade-offs between logic theory and practice were made in designing a particular programming system.

The art of being wise is the art
of knowing what to overlook.
— William James

13
Prolog

Some AI workers feel that Prolog is a better programming
language than Lisp for expert system applications, and many
articles have been written asking if Prolog will replace Lisp.
Asking if Prolog will replace Lisp is not a reasonable question
because Prolog and Lisp are not similar enough for either to
replace the other. Lisp and Prolog are more like metric and
regular socket wrenches—both have a place in the well-rounded
tool kit. My goal in this chapter is to explain enough about
Prolog and how it works so that engineers can decide whether
Prolog would be useful for a given job.

The differences between Prolog and Lisp stand out more
clearly once the rationale behind inventing new programming
languages is understood.
• The best way to experiment with new theories of how to
program computers is to invent a programming language that
uses the new ideas. This was the reason for experimental
languages such as Loops, Amord, Planner, Conniver, Scheme,
Lisp, Pascal, and C. If the new language is useful, it spreads;
otherwise it dies.
• Information gained from the experiment is maximized by
making the new ideas the heart of the new language to the
exclusion of all else. This forces programmers to use the new

features, ensuring maximum information gain in minimum time.

• Prolog is just such an experimental language. It is based on unification and backtracking and does not offer other control structure. Prolog programmers must be thoroughly familiar with backtracking and unification because there is little else in the language.

The main practical difference between writing expert systems in Prolog and writing in Lisp is that Prolog programmers *must* use backtracking whether it is appropriate or not, whereas Lisp programmers *may* use it. If the Prolog experiment succeeds and backtracking and unification turn out to be widely useful, they can always be added to other languages either by extending the syntax or by supplying subroutine libraries.

Prolog versus Lisp

Lisp is a general-purpose procedural language based on arithmetic and on symbol manipulation.[1] Prolog is a special-purpose declarative language based on logic. Lisp is general enough that it is easy to write a Prolog system in Lisp. Prolog is such a special-purpose language that it is harder to write a Lisp system in Prolog, although several groups have done it.

Lisp functions specify exactly how the computer should operate on data in order to compute the desired result. Instead of specifying how to carry out an operation, Prolog programs describe relationships between data.

Lisp users enter input data. The Lisp program operates on the data and computes an answer. Prolog users ask Prolog programs to check if a fact is known from Prolog's database or can be derived from facts in the database. The program searches for fact patterns that match the user's question. If Prolog succeeds in matching the query, the query succeeds and Prolog is said to have proved that the query is true. Programmers tell Prolog what is true, then ask it to draw conclusions from the facts and rules it has been given.

One *extremely* rough measurement of the complexity of a programming language is the number of "reserved words" in the language.   Reserved words define built-in operations;

---

[1] Lisp is based on lambda calculus and recursive function theory whereas conventional programming languages are based on Turing machine theory. I do not understand these ideas either, but they are rather different ways of looking at computation.

programmers assume that the language can perform these operations without their having to write any code at all.

The language C has about thirty reserved words such as "do," "for," and "while," and about twenty operators, such as +, -, and >. Prolog has about twenty arithmetic and logic operators, such as plus, minus, and compare, and about fifty reserved words, such as "fail" and "append."

The Common Lisp dialect that became standard in the United States is a much richer language than either Prolog or C. By the time the standards committee disbanded, Lisp had at least 300 functions and a macro processor, which makes it easy to add more. Lisp is essentially useless without a powerful text editor with special features designed to edit Lisp programs, whereas C and Prolog programs can be maintained with a standard editor.

Many computer language experts feel that the large Lisp vocabulary and the complexity of the Lisp environment are errors. If a language has so many built in functions, the argument goes, the designers *clearly* had no idea what they were trying to do. This view is strong Europe, the home of Prolog.

Prolog fans argue that beginning programmers can learn Prolog much faster than they can learn Lisp, and this is likely true. Lisp partisans counter that it matters little how easy a language is to learn; what counts is what a skilled programmer can do with it. It takes longer to learn to fly a Boeing 747 than to learn to fly a Piper Cub, but the 747 pilot hauls more passengers. A skilled Lisp programmer can do more than a skilled Prolog programmer, if only because Lisp offers more scope than Prolog.[1]

The point of making these comparisons is not to argue that Prolog or Lisp or C is a better language but to point out that there are major differences between these languages. C was designed for arithmetic[2] and Prolog for mathematical logic. Lisp is designed for symbol manipulation, but it also handles arithmetic and logic programming. When tools differ as much as these programming languages, a prudent user learns enough about all of them to be able to figure out which is best for a given task.

---

[1] Lisp fans say that Lisp is more expressive than Prolog; Prolog fans say that Prolog is more logical than Lisp.

[2] C was designed to write a portable operating system called "UNIX." C allows programs to manipulate computer memory in intimate ways. Programs can add and subtract offsets from pointers, for example. Allowing direct specification of low-level operations makes me feel that C is really an assembly language gussied up in a pinstripe suit. No matter how thick you gold plate a chamber pot, it's still a chamber pot.

Making Computers Compute

Computers must be told exactly what to do with data in order to do any computing at all, of course. A Lisp compiler translates a Lisp program into instructions that manipulate data as specified by the program. A Prolog program does not specify how to carry out calculations. A Prolog program is compiled into a series of search patterns that are matched against the database. The calculations required for pattern matching, unification, and rule processing are implicit in the definition of the Prolog language, not explicit in the structure of the program.

When a programmer writes a Prolog statement to the effect that X is the mother of Y, the computer carries out calculations based on that information, but the details of the computation are hidden. This has the advantage of letting programmers write statements about relationships without worrying about computational details but has the disadvantage of leading to errors. Subtle incompatibilities between different Prolog implementations can make the same program give different answers on different computers, although this has become less of a problem as Prolog has approached standardization.

Prolog versus Logic Programming

There are many similarities between Prolog and logic theory. Fields in Prolog rules can be either inputs or outputs, depending on whether variables are bound or not. A rule may have many outputs for one set of inputs, but Prolog finds only the first set of variable bindings that is compatible with the facts in its database. If the user wants other bindings, the program must include control statements such as "fail" that ask for more.

Logic has no control structure because all rules are examined simultaneously. Prolog programs must run fast enough to give answers in a reasonable time on a computer small enough to fit into an academic budget. This requires a control structure that determines the order in which facts and rules are examined so that Prolog does not waste time examining rules that do not lead to the desired result. Prolog's control structure makes it easy for software maintenance staff to become confused; program statements take on different meanings depending on the surrounding control statements.

Searching the Database

When Prolog looks for variable bindings to match the database, it follows a well-defined search path. Searching the entire database often takes too long, and programmers write code that short-circuits the search. Cutting off the search for additional variable bindings saves computer time, but the control statements make Prolog programs much harder for humans to read.

Input and Output
Like expert systems, Prolog supports I/O. Unlike advanced expert system shells, Prolog user interfaces offer a typewriter-style interaction in which the computer types a question and the user types an answer. Some Prolog systems support more advanced user interfaces that save considerable typing, but these user interfaces are not part of the definition of the Prolog language. Any program that uses such facilities will probably not run under another version of Prolog.

Sequential Operation of Prolog Programs
The biggest difference between Prolog and logic programming is that Prolog is a sequential language, whereas logic operates in parallel. Large computers have nearly reached the physical limits on their operating speed.[1] The only way to make programs run much faster is to run them on more than one computer at a time.

This is difficult to do with arithmetic programs, because although in theory arithmetic processes can be carried out in parallel, most existing algorithms and programs were designed for sequential computers. Logic, on the other hand, makes the fundamental assumption that all rules are examined simultaneously. Programmers are used to the idea of not making assumptions about the order in which rules will fire, so it ought to be possible to run a logic-based program on many computers at once and make it go very fast.

In theory, rules with several and-clauses could be processed in parallel with each and-clause being processed at the same time by a separate computer. The definition of how and-clauses work in Prolog, however, precludes running Prolog programs on more than one computer. The Japanese expended considerable time and money trying to run Prolog programs on more than one computer at the same time but were unsuccessful. Some vendors now offer "Concurrent Prolog" systems, which let programs be processed by many computers at the same time, but this requires changing the definition of the language.

---

[1] Although computers are still getting faster, the rate of increase has slowed. It appears that computer speed is close to peaking unless there is some unforeseen technical breakthrough.

Like all expert system shells, Prolog is a compromise between logic theory and what can be implemented easily on a digital computer. As computers get faster and cheaper, vendors plan to improve Prolog, bringing it closer to the capabilities of advanced expert system shells. It is too early to predict how widespread Prolog will become. It is popular in Europe but has not made much headway against Lisp in the United States.

Prolog Syntax

Logic languages have rules for expressing facts, rules, constants, variables, control structure, I/O, and whatever else the language offers. Understanding mathematical logic makes it easier to understand the reasons for the features provided by logic languages.

Variables and Constants

Logic languages must distinguish constants from variables in some way. In chapter 10 I distinguished variables by putting a question mark in front of them: "?x" is a variable named "x"; "x" is a constant.

Prolog constants begin with lowercase letters and variables begin with uppercase letters. "Fred" is a variable because it is capitalized; "fred" is a constant. The examples in this chapter look odd because people's names cannot be capitalized.

Predicates

Prolog deals with facts that are either retrieved from a database or derived from facts in the database. Prolog refers to the first fields of facts as "predicates." The predicate and its accompanying data fields define a fact.

The first field of a Prolog fact holds the predicate and must be a constant. A predicate may have any number of associated parameters enclosed in parentheses, separated by commas, and ending with a period. A field may either be a constant, a variable, or a list. The employee database discussed in chapter 10 looks like this in Prolog:

job ([filewriter harvey], [computer hacker]).
job ([bitlearner fred], [computer trainee]).

The differences between Prolog syntax and the syntax of chapter 10 are that in Prolog the open parenthesis comes after the name of the predicate, commas separate fields, lists are grouped by brackets instead of parentheses, and predicates end with a period.

If and And

In Prolog rules, the symbol :- means "if," and a comma between clauses means "and." The :- is supposed to remind users of a left pointing arrow (<-), which indicates that inference proceeds from conditions on the right to a conclusion on the left. The lives-near rule from chapter 10 is written as

lives-near (X, Y) :- address (X, [Town, Rest1]),
                    address (Y, [Town, Rest2]),
                    not (X = Y).

As in chapter 10, the rule means that two people live near one another if they live in the same town and their names are not the same. "X," "Y," "Town," "Rest1," and "Rest2" are variables because they are capitalized.

Backtracking

Prolog's backtracking mechanism backs up in the database when a search for variable bindings fails. Suppose that the database has stored the following facts:

bigger (cow, rabbit).
bigger (cow, mouse).
bigger (cow, cat).
bigger (dog, cat).
bigger (dog, mouse).

and the user asks Prolog the question

bigger (cow, X), bigger (dog, X).

The facts mean that a cow is bigger than a rabbit, a cow is bigger than a mouse, a dog is bigger than a cat, and so on. These facts constitute the definition of the bigger predicate, and they are all that Prolog knows about the bigger relationship. The question asks Prolog to find a binding for X such that Prolog can prove that a cow is bigger than X and that a dog is bigger than X. In other words, Prolog is to bind X to an object that is smaller than both a dog and a cow.

Prolog dives into the database looking for matches with the first clause. It finds bigger (cow, rabbit), binds X to rabbit, goes on to the second clause, and starts looking for bigger (dog, rabbit). This pattern is not in the database. The search fails, and Prolog backtracks to the first clause. This is where X was bound to rabbit, so Prolog unbinds X and resumes the search for bigger (cow, X) just after the fact that bound X to rabbit.

The next match is bigger (cow, mouse). Prolog binds X to mouse, goes to the next clause, and looks for bigger (dog, mouse).

Prolog finds this pattern in the database and reports that the value of X is mouse.

Although X could also be bound to cat, Prolog does not continue the search after it has found the first valid binding for X. The user or the program must ask for additional bindings if more are needed.

Summary of Prolog's Search Technique

There are several points to note about Prolog's search technique:

1. Prolog processes and-clauses from left to right, binding variables as matches found in the database.
2. Facts and rules are searched in the exact order in which they appear in the database.[1]
3. Whenever a match is found, Prolog remembers the variable binding that produced the match and goes to the next clause.
4. Only one binding is established for each variable at a time.
5. Whether or not the next clause matches the database is controlled by variable bindings established in prior clauses.
6. When a clause fails, Prolog backtracks to the most recent pattern match and resumes the search from that point.
7. When it gets to the last clause, Prolog returns one binding for each variable.
8. If the program wants more variable bindings, it asks Prolog to backtrack to generate more bindings.

Backtracking was designed in this way so that Prolog could find a valid binding for each variable as fast as possible. Prolog presents the first set of bindings it finds without waiting until all bindings are found. If one binding will do, Prolog is faster than a system that finds all bindings at once. If a program needs all the bindings, there is not much difference in speed between Prolog's system and a system that finds all bindings as it goes.

Prolog's backtracking strategy saves memory space. Instead of having to allocate memory for a new environment whenever it finds a new variable binding, Prolog remembers one binding and the exact point in the database where the binding was found. The binding controls matches for later clauses, and remembering the match point lets Prolog restart the search there if it has to backtrack.

---

[1] Prolog facts can be thought of as rules with no conditions or as conclusions that are always true. Prologists tend not to distinguish sharply between facts and rules.

Sympathizing with Prolog's backtracking mechanism is fundamental to understanding Prolog programs. Backtracking is explained later.

Logical "Or"

Prolog implements the logical "or" by having more than one fact or rule conclusion unify with the same pattern. Suppose that a person is eligible for university library privileges if either the person is a student or the person is married to a student. The Prolog rules for granting library cards are

```
grant-card (X)  :-   eligible (X).
   eligible (X)  :-   student (X).
   eligible (X)  :-   spouse (X, Y), student (Y).
   eligible (X)  :-   spouse (Y, X), student (Y).
```

This program requires two spouse rules because the spouse relationship goes both ways. Most relationships work in only one direction. If bigger (X, Y) is true, then bigger (Y, X) is false. Unlike most relationships, if spouse (X, Y) is true, then spouse (Y, X) is also true. That is why Prolog needs a separate rule for each direction of the spouse relationship.

When the librarian asks Prolog the question

```
grant-card (sue).
```

Prolog finds the first rule that says that a card can be granted if Sue is eligible. There are three "eligible" rules, and Prolog tries them in the order in which they appear in the database. It tries the student rule first because it comes first and examines the spouse rules only if "student" fails. This forms the "or" of these three rules; if any one of them succeeds, Sue is eligible. Thus, although and-conditions are examined from left to right in a rule, or-conditions are examined by scanning down the database. Choosing the best order for facts and rules is part of writing successful Prolog programs.

Prolog Definitions

A "definition" in Prolog is all clauses that define the meaning of a predicate. In the example above, the grant-card predicate is defined by only one rule, whereas the eligible predicate is defined by three rules.

Facts and rules can be mixed freely in the definition of a predicate. Sue is neither a student nor a student spouse, but she has a friend in the programming department. If Sue's friend adds the fact eligible (sue).

to the database, this fact extends the definition of the eligible predicate and makes Sue eligible for a library card.

Efficiency Considerations

Proving that Sue is eligible for a library card takes less time than proving that she is not eligible. If any of the rules or facts in the definition of the eligible predicate succeed, Prolog can report success without examining the rest of the definition.

In order to find that Sue is not eligible, on the other hand, Prolog searches the entire definition to the bitter end. Skilled Prolog programmers put high-probability rules and facts at the beginning of definitions and design predicates so that they succeed more often than not.

Assignment Statements

Program statements that compute values for variables are called "assignment statements" in contrast to control statements, which determine which part of the program to run next. The value of a variable in a conventional programming language may be changed as often as desired: An assignment statement computes a new value, which replaces the old value. Conventional assignment operators mean, in effect, "Compute the value of whatever is on the right-hand side of the operator and copy the result into the variable whose name appears on the left-hand side." The assignment statement

A = 8

computes the value of the expression to the right of the = and assigns the value 8 to the variable A. The statement

A = A + 1

changes the value of A by adding one to whatever value A had before the statement was executed.

Prolog has two assignment operators: IS, which unifies variables with numerical values, and =, which unifies variables with expressions. The assignment statement

Y IS 1 + 7.

computes the value "8" and gives that value to variable Y if Y unifies with "8." The statement

X = "a string".

unifies the value of the variable X with the character string "a string" and copies the result into X if unification succeeds.

Prolog variables can be assigned values only once. Instead of copying the value on the right into the variable on the left as conventional assignment operators do, Prolog assignment operators try to unify the expression on the right-hand side of the operator with the variable on the left. If unification succeeds, Prolog gives the variable on the left the value of whatever is on the right. If unification fails, the assignment fails and Prolog backtracks. Prolog assignments are tests that succeed or fail depending on the value of the variables on both sides at the time the assignment is executed.

Variables that have no binding may be assigned freely because unbound variables unify with anything. The statement

Y IS 8.

succeeds only if Y either has no value or has a value that unifies with 8. The sequence of statements

Y IS 8.
Y IS Y + 1.

which would give Y the value of 9 in a conventional programming language, fails in Prolog. The first statement tries to unify Y with 8. Assuming Y is unbound, unification succeeds and Y is bound to 8.

The second statement is now doomed to fail. The value of the left-hand side is the value of Y, which is 8, the value of the right-hand side is Y + 1, or 9, and there is no way to unify 8 with 9.

This is a common error that beginning Prolog programmers make. Adding one to a variable to count things is such a natural act that it is easy to forget that incrementing a variable simply does not work.

This limitation on variable usage is not as bad as it sounds. Prolog supports recursive rules in that Prolog rules can refer to themselves. When Prolog starts examining a rule, it makes brand-new unbound copies of all the variables in the rule. Because these new variables are not bound, they can be given new values. Counters using recursive rules are explained later.

Input and Output
Prolog offers read and write operators to communicate with the user. The statement

write (X).

displays the value of the variable X, and the statement

read (X).

obtains a binding for X from the user. The grant-card rule generates more informative output if it is changed to read

grant-card(X) :-   eligible (X), write (X),
                     write (" may have a card.").

When the eligible clause succeeds, X is bound to the name of a person who is eligible for a library card. The first "write" prints the value of X, and the second "write" follows the name with the string "may have a card." If the librarian asks

grant-card(sue).

Prolog responds

sue may have a card.

Adding another rule to the definition of the grant-card predicate generates an appropriate message when an unworthy person applies for a card:

grant-card (X) :-   write (X),
                      write(" may not have a card.").

The second rule is examined only if the first grant-card rule fails. If the first rule fails, X is bound to the name of someone who is not eligible for a card. Printing the name followed by the string "may not have a card" is appropriate under such circumstances.

Given these improvements, the final definitions of grant-card and eligible are:

grant-card (X) :-   eligible (X), write (X),
                      write (" may have a card.").
grant-card (X) :-   write (X),
                      write (" may not have a card.").

eligible (X)   :-   student (X).
eligible (X)   :-   spouse (X, Y), student (Y).
eligible (X)   :-   spouse (Y, X), student (Y).
eligible (sue).

The first grant-card rule succeeds if eligible succeeds. If eligible succeeds, X is bound to the name of someone who is eligible for a card, and the rule writes the name and "may have a card."

If the first rule fails, the second grant-card rule is examined. Prolog write statements always succeed, so the only clause that could have failed is eligible. Given that eligible failed, X is bound to the name of someone who is unworthy of a card. The second rule writes the name followed by "may not have a card."

More Efficiency Considerations

The original definition of the eligible predicate does not bind variable Y before checking spouse predicates. Because Y is not bound, Prolog searches *all* the spouse facts in its database to see if X is the spouse of a student. This is not what a human does—a human asks the supplicant for a spouse's name, then checks to see if the spouse is a student.

Asking the name of the spouse effectively binds variable Y. Knowing bindings for both variables makes the program run *much* faster—a spouse fact with those bindings for X and Y either exists or it does not, and Prolog does not have to do nearly as much searching. Grant-card can use the read predicate to find the name of the spouse and speed up its search:

```
grant-card (X)  :-   eligible (X), write (X),
                     write (" may have a card.").
grant-card (X)  :-   write (X),
                     write (" may not have a card.").

eligible (X)    :-   student (X).
eligible (X)    :-   student-spouse (X).

student-spouse (X) :-  write ("What is the name of "),
                       write (X), write ("'s spouse?"),
                       read (Y), student (Y),
                       2-way-spouse (X, Y).

2-way-spouse (X, Y) :- spouse (X, Y).
2-way-spouse (X, Y) :- spouse (Y, X).
eligible (sue).
```

This is a great deal messier and more complicated than the first definition of "eligible" but runs a great deal faster. When the librarian asks

grant-card(sue).

the first "eligible" rule checks to see if Sue is a student. The first rule fails because Sue is not a student, so the second eligible rule invokes the student-spouse rule. Student-spouse writes the message

What is the name of sue's spouse?

Sue gives the name of her student friend,[1] the librarian replies

---

[1] Sue is eligible because of her illicit fact, but the program won't proceed unless she types something to get past the read clause.

fred

and the read statement binds Y to "fred."

Prolog verifies that Fred is a student, then asks 2-way-spouse for a final ruling. The 2-way-spouse definition includes both ways in which the spouse predicate can be used. Because student-spouse established bindings for both X and Y before invoking 2-way-spouse, there is almost no searching of the database needed to find out that there are no facts showing that Fred and Sue are married. 2-way-spouse fails because Sue and Fred are not spouses, and if it were not for the illicit fact

eligible (sue).

at the end of the definition, Sue would not get her card.

It is interesting to compare the final version to the original:

```
grant-card (X)  :-    eligible (X).
   eligible (X)  :-    student (X).
   eligible (X)  :-    spouse (X, Y), student (Y).
   eligible (X)  :-    spouse (Y, X), student (Y).
```

The final version is more than twice as long as the original. Doubling the length of the program adds nothing to the logic but makes the search faster and makes the program easier to use. Wonderful logic does not make up for a user-surly or user-hostile interface.

This lesson has not been fully accepted by the AI community. User friendliness has very little to do with logic and is not nearly as much fun. Many AI programs start out as difficult to use, and making them accessible to ordinary people often makes them twice or thrice as long as the original.

Predicates and Fields

A Prolog predicate does not always have to have the same number of fields. Suppose that a computer store stocks parts that have part numbers and parts without part numbers. The stock predicate records the part name, selling price, quantity available, and part number:

stock (cord, $1.50, 7, 75869487)

The fact for a part without a part number looks like this:

stock (plug, $.90, 18)

A plug has no part number, so that field is omitted from its stock fact.

These inventory records are instances of the same predicate— they both start with the name "stock." If a programmer wants to find inventory data, however, the difference becomes important. A program to tell the user how many of a part are available retrieves stock records with two rules:

```
how-many (A)  :-  stock (A, B, C, D),
                  write ("we have "), write (C).
how-many (A)  :-  stock (A, B, C),
                  write ("we have "), write (C).
```

The first rule looks for parts with part numbers, so its stock predicate has four fields. Variable A matches the part name, B matches the selling price, C matches the quantity available, and D matches the part number.

This rule cannot match facts for parts without part numbers because the pattern matcher insists that a pattern and a fact have the same number of fields. The second rule looks for stock facts with three fields.

As far as Prolog is concerned, there is no such thing as the wrong number of fields, so Prolog does not signal an error if a clause has the wrong number of fields for a predicate. Lisp fans say that this is a serious design error in the Prolog language and that unless a programmer explicitly states that a function will accept a varying number of arguments,[1] a language should always check to make sure that the right number of parameters are used for a predicate as well as for a function. Prolog fans say this is a handy source of flexibility.

In my opinion the same predicate name with different numbers of fields is really two different predicates. The purpose of facts is to be matched by clauses in rules. If two instances of a predicate in the database have different numbers of fields, they can never match the same clause in a rule and are effectively different facts. Time will tell if this is a feature or a bug.

Control Structure

Prolog finds *one* binding for all the variables in a rule as quickly as possible. If programmers want more bindings, they have to ask for them, and if they don't, they have to write code that cuts off the search for unnecessary bindings. It is important that programmers understand how Prolog searches the database so that rules work as expected.

Control statements in conventional languages determine the order in which assignment statements in a program are run.

---

[1] The Lisp addition function accepts a variable number of arguments. (+ 1 2) is 3, (+ 1 2 (+ 1 2) 4 5) is 15.

Control statements in Prolog determine how facts and rules in a program are searched. Depending on how you count, Prolog has six or seven different control mechanisms:
• Fail statements tell Prolog that the current set of variable bindings is not acceptable. When Prolog finds a fail statement, it backs up, undoes its most recent pattern match, and looks for more bindings.
• Clauses are examined from left to right in rules. Clauses in the same rule are and-conditions, all of which must be met for the rule to succeed.
• Facts and rules are examined from top to bottom in a program. Patterns with the same name are or-conditions, any of which may match the current request.
• Prolog backtracks when a search reaches the end of the database without finding a match. The definition of backtracking affects the meaning of a Prolog program, so it is critical to understand how it works.
• Repeat statements force Prolog to retrieve the same patterns over and over.
• Prolog supports recursion. Recursive rules match themselves over and over and need special clauses to provide exits.
• Cut statements cut off the search. Programmers use cut statements when it would not be worthwhile to backtrack and try other search paths.

Fail Statements
Prolog stops its database search on the first success but is careful to remember where the search stopped in case it has to back up and resume the search. Whenever Prolog finds an unbound variable in a rule, it searches the database until it finds an acceptable binding, then goes on to the next variable. When the search succeeds, Prolog has found one and only one binding for each variable.

The fail statement tells Prolog to back up and resume its database search at the point where it last left off. Suppose there are two students identified by two predicates in the database:

student (fred).   student (joe).

If a user asks for students, Prolog finds fred and stops. Getting Prolog to list all the students requires use of fail:

list-all-students   :- student (X), write (X), fail.
list-all-students.

When the user enters a list-all-students request, Prolog finds the list-all-students rule and starts examining its clauses. The

first clause looks for "student (X)." Prolog finds "student (fred),"
binds X to "fred," and remembers where it found "student
(fred)" in the database. The write clause writes "fred" because
"fred" is the current value of X, and Prolog goes to the fail clause.

Fail tells Prolog to backtrack. Prolog backs up to the most
recent match, which is where X was bound to "fred." Prolog
undoes this binding, and looks for more student (X) patterns
starting just after the point in the database where it found "fred."

The next student fact binds X to "joe," so the list-all-students
rule writes "joe," fails, and backtracks again. There are no more
student facts to be found, the search for student (X) fails, and
Prolog backtracks from the student (X) clause.

This time Prolog backtracks all the way out of the first list-all-
students rule. The first list-all-students rule has listed all the
students and failed, so Prolog continues its search for list-all-
students and finds the list-all-students fact. The list-all-students
request succeeds, and Prolog stops.

The list-all-students fact makes the user's request succeed.
The list-all-students rule fails because of the fail clause at the
end, but the list-all-students fact makes the overall request
succeed. The rule that does all the work fails, and the fact that
does nothing succeeds.

A user does not care if the request succeeds or fails so long as it
lists all the students. However, the list-all-students predicate
may be used in another rule as the university registration
management system grows. A rule that uses list-all-students has
a better chance of success if list-all-students succeeds.

Clause and Statement Order
Prolog searches and clauses from left to right and searches or-
clauses from top to bottom. Suppose Prolog is given a program:

q(X) :- r(X), s(X), t(X).
r(1).
r(2).
s(1).
s(2).
t(2).
t(4).

When Prolog tries to prove q(X), it looks for r(X), then s(X),
then t(X) because these clauses appear in the q(X) rule in that
order. When looking for r(X), Prolog finds r(1) and then r(2)
because the facts appear in the program in that order. Either r(1)
or r(2) will match r(X)—these two facts act like a logical "or"
because they match the same predicate. These facts are examined

in the order in which they appear in the program. And-clauses
are separated by commas and tested from left to right.

The program structure can be illustrated in the following way:

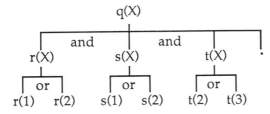

Clauses that must succeed in order to satisfy and-conditions in
the rule are shown as "and" links on the tree. Facts that could
match the same pattern are shown as "or" links. The left to right
order in which facts appear on "or" links is the order in which
they appear in the program, and the left to right order on "and"
links is the same as the clause order in the rule.

Prolog uses a "depth first" search algorithm to find acceptable
variable bindings as fast as possible. Prolog searches to the
bottom of the tree, then works its way to the right hoping to find
a period and achieve success.

Backtracking

Whenever the search fails, Prolog backtracks. The backtracker
retreats to the most recent match, unbinds variables if necessary,
and searches forward for the next match in sequence. If there are
no more matches, Prolog retreats to the next most recent match,
and so on.

The following diagrams show how Prolog finds a binding for
X given the program above. When the user asks

q(X).

Prolog starts looking for instances of the predicate q. Prolog finds
the rule for q, and starts working down the tree. Prolog's search
path is shown by the boxes:

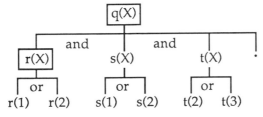

The first clause in the rule q(X) is r(X), so Prolog looks for facts
or rules which match the predicate r. The first fact that matches

is r(1), so Prolog binds X to 1. This binding of X constrains later matches because the variable X appears in all three and-clauses:

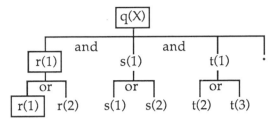

Now that the first clause has bound X to 1, the second clause requires a match for the predicate s(1):

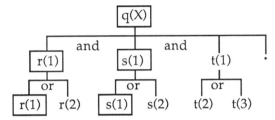

The only clause left is t(X), so Prolog looks for t(1):

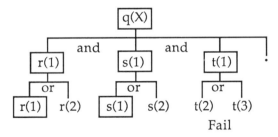

T(1) is not in the database, so the search fails. Now it is time to backtrack. The most recent match was s(1), so Prolog backtracks to s(1) and starts looking for another fact that matches s(1):

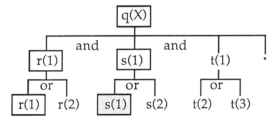

This search resumes immediately after the first match with s(1). The dotted box indicates that s(1) was already tried but that the search failed further on.

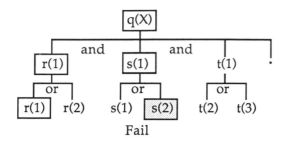

Fail

There are no more matches for s(1), so Prolog fails again, and backs up to the point where Prolog matched r(1). Prolog resumes the search after the first r(1) and looks for more matches for r(1):

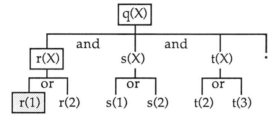

There are no more matches for r(1) and Prolog backs up over the point where X was bound to 1. Prolog unbinds X and looks for another match for r(X). The next clause that matches r(X) is r(2). Prolog binds X to 2 and proceeds:

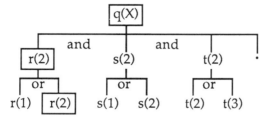

This constrains matches in later clauses, so Prolog looks for s(2):

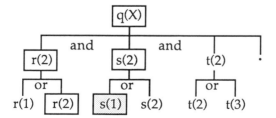

The s(1) that matched during the first pass no longer matches because X is now bound to 2. Prolog finds s(2), and goes to the third clause:

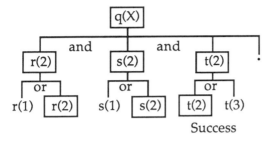

The third clause looks for t(2). This succeeds, binding X to 2. If the user asks for another solution, Prolog backs up, unbinds X, finds that there are no more matches for r(X) and fails.

There are several important points about Prolog's backtracking strategy:

• Backtracking is slow. When Prolog came forward the second time looking for s(2), it searched all of the instances of the s predicate all over again.

• Prolog is a sequential language. Clauses are examined from left to right; facts and rules are examined from top to bottom. Prolog programs cannot be processed in parallel without changing the definition of the language.

• Programmers have to understand the search algorithm. If the list-all-students fact and rule are interchanged, the query succeeds without listing any students.

• Search control is the only control mechanism in Prolog. All that Prolog programs do is search the database, so there is little else to control.

Repeat Statement

The repeat statement traps the backtracker. Prolog normally turns around and starts searching forward again when it backs up to a match point. "Repeat" forces Prolog to turn around and start forward from the repeat regardless of any matches. This is useful if a program needs to force a user to enter acceptable input. Suppose that the administration finds that too many fraudulent library cards are being issued and installs a computerized lock on the door. Anyone wishing to borrow a book must enter their name and password.

A friendless programmer writes a rule called "accept," which reads a person's name and password. The lock program forces a potential borrower to enter a valid name and password.

```
good-person :- accept (N, PW), write ("come in "),
               write (N).
good-person :- repeat,
               write ("Illegal name or ID "),
               write ("try again, please"),
               accept (N, PW), write ("come in "),
               write (N).
```

These rules demand a proper name and a password but allow supplicants to make mistakes. The first clause of the first good-person rule uses the accept rule to ask for a name and password. If the name and password are valid, "accept" succeeds. The first write clause writes "come in," and the second writes the name of the person who was accepted. If "accept" fails, the first rule fails, and Prolog goes on to the second rule.

The first clause of the second rule is "repeat," which always succeeds, so Prolog writes the message "Illegal name or ID" followed by "try again please." If the second attempt succeeds, Prolog writes "come in" as before.

If the second attempt fails, Prolog backtracks. There are no pattern matches in the second rule, so Prolog backs up to the repeat, which sends it forward again. Prolog writes its messages and asks for another name and password. This continues until the supplicant either enters a valid password or gives up.

This stymies Sue, but not for long. Even though the accept predicate cannot be modified, Sue's friend can enter the fact

accept (sue, "hello, I'm acceptable").

which gives her a built-in identity and password.

If Sue's fake fact comes before the accept rule, "accept" succeeds without asking for a name and password no matter who is seeking entry. If her private fact comes afterward, Sue has to enter something to force the official rule to fail, but her fact succeeds and the program admits her.

Making Sue acceptable in this way is risky—anyone who fails the official accept rule is admitted, and the program writes the incriminating phrase

come in sue.

After trying this over the weekend, Sue and Fred reconsider, delete the unofficial fact, and add a new rule:

```
accept :- write ("enter name "), read (X),
          write ("enter password"), read (Y),
          X = "sue",
          Y = "hello, I'm acceptable".
```

This rule comes after the official "accept" rule. Most supplicants get their names and passwords right the first time and never get here. Sue does not have a password so the official accept always fails for her, and the private version asks for a name and password. The two = clauses succeed only if X is bound to "sue" and Y is bound to "hello, I'm acceptable," so this rule also fails unless it is given Sue's private password.

The difficulty is that anyone else who makes a mistake sends Prolog to the unofficial accept rule. The messages "enter name" and "enter password" *look* official but are bogus—there is no way a naive user can respond correctly. Eventually someone is bound to notice that a second attempt is always rejected even if the password is correct.

Fred decides that this is also too risky and does a little sleuthing. The friendless programmer built the accept rule in very much the same way fred did, with a subtle difference:

```
accept :-  write ("enter name "), read (X),
           write ("enter password"), read (Y),
           good-name-&-word (X, Y).
```

The official version uses a list of patterns good-name-&-word (X, Y) to hold valid names and passwords. Armed with this new knowledge, Fred installs the fact

```
good-name-&-word ("sue", "hello, I'm acceptable").
```

and Sue can enter with her own name and password just like a real library user. It is only after spending several weekends figuring out how to beat the system that it dawns on Fred that it would have been simpler to tell Sue his password—she already knows his name. Being but a callow student, Fred has not yet learned that the most sophisticated solution is not always best.

On the other hand, sharing his password would not have been nearly as much fun nor have impressed Sue as much. College administrators tend to tolerate a certain amount of such hacking because students learn more by solving problems they set for themselves than by solving course assignments.

Recursive Rules

Recursive rules match themselves, just as recursive functions call themselves. Recursion requires an "or" capability—a program must decide either to call itself or to exit.

Prolog's "or" is implemented by having more than one fact or rule match the clause Prolog is searching for. This recursive counter has a fact for an exit condition and a rule to do the work:

count (3).
count (Q) :- R IS Q + 1, write (R),
                  count (R), write (" end").

If a user enters the question

count(0).

Prolog replies

123 end end end

The terminating condition for the recursive rule is the clause count (3). This clause comes before the rule, so it is examined first. The question count (0) does not match the fact count (3), so Prolog examines the rule count (Q), binds Q to 0, and starts examining conditions in the rule.

The first clause tries to unify R and Q + 1. R has no value yet, unification succeeds, and the IS statement binds R to 1. The write clause writes 1 because that is the value of R. Now Prolog comes to the count (R) clause. R is bound to 1, so Prolog looks for count (1). The count (3) fact does not match count (1), so Prolog skips the fact and invokes the count rule. This time, R is bound to 1, so the assignment statement binds Q to 2.

The Q that is bound to 2 is not the same Q that was bound to 1 when the count rule was first invoked. Whenever Prolog matches a rule, it creates a new set of variables for that invocation of the rule.

This is why the IS statement succeeds again: R was bound to 1 the first time the count rule was invoked, but this second rule invocation has created a new variable named R. The new R is unbound, so Prolog can set it to Q + 1, or 2. Prolog writes the 2, then looks for count (2). This also skips count (3) and enters the rule, which generates a third copy of Q and R, sets the third copy of R to 3, writes 3, then looks for count (3).

This time Prolog matches count (3), so the count (3) clause in the third invocation of the count rule succeeds before examining the rule. When this clause succeeds, Prolog writes "end." Write succeeds, so the third invocation of the count rule succeeds.

Count (2) was examined because of the reference to count (2), which happened when Prolog was looking for count (1). The write clause in the count (1) copy of the rule writes "end," and that copy of the rule succeeds. Count (1) was examined because of the reference to count (1) in the rule processing count (0), so that rule writes "end" and succeeds.

Having a fact as a terminating condition is risky. Suppose someone asks count (4).

Count (4) does not match the clause count (3), so Prolog invokes the rule. The rule adds 1 to 4 and asks for count (5) which does not match count (3) either, and the program runs forever. It is much safer to stop the recursion with a rule

count (X) :- X > 2.

The terminating rule succeeds whenever Prolog looks for count (X) where X has any value greater than 2. Count (4) stops without invoking the rule, and Prolog does not loop.

The pattern of a recursive rule making new copies of all its variables and building a stack of invocations of the same rule is the same process by which recursive functions call one another. The difference is that the terminating conditions for recursive rules are outside of the rules. It takes a while for experienced programmers to get used to this, but people learning Prolog as a first language have no trouble with it.

The Cut

The cut statement is used when there is no reason to continue a search. Prolog stops when it finds the first match for all the variables in a rule, and programmers use "fail" when a program needs more bindings.

Logically valid bindings are not necessarily useful, and early Prolog programmers found that they needed to terminate searches to avoid useless bindings. "Cut" makes the backtracker keep going back when it would otherwise turn around and go forward, just as "repeat" makes the backtracker stop going back.

The librarian convinces the administration to hire an assistant. The assistant has to run occasional errands, so the librarian wants someone who owns a car, a bicycle, or a motorcycle. State law does not let the university hire anyone under 18. The librarian asks for a program to select applicants who are over 17 years of age and who own an acceptable vehicle. The first draft of the program is

```
talk-to (X)   :- applied (X), hirable (X),
                 write (X), fail.
talk-to (X)   :- write ("No more").

hirable (X)   :- age (X, Y), Y > 17, owns (X, bike).
hirable (X)   :- age (X, Y), Y > 17, owns (X, car).
hirable (X)   :- age (X, Y), Y > 17, owns (X, cycle).
```

The first talk-to rule lists all the hirable applicants and the second writes the message "No more." Each hirable rule covers one set of requirements—a person must be over 17 and own a bike or a person must be over 17 and own a car or a person must be over 17 and own a cycle. The librarian tests the program on a small database of people who frequent the library:

applied (sue).   applied (fred).   applied (joe).
age (sue, 17).   age (fred, 18).   age (joe, 19).
owns (sue, car).
owns (joe, bike).   owns (joe, cycle).
owns (fred, car).   owns (fred, cycle).

The librarian asks

talk-to (X).

and after some delay Prolog replies

joe joe fred fred No more.

Problems with the Program
The program works in that it lists applicants the librarian should see, but it gives some names twice and runs slowly.

Sue is part of the reason the program runs slowly. She is ineligible because she is too young, but Prolog tests her against all three hirable rules anyway. Joe and Fred are each eligible for two reasons: they are over 17 and they each own two vehicles.

Prolog has no way of knowing that binding X to Joe because Joe owns a cycle and binding X to Joe because Joe owns a bike are the same as far as the user is concerned. "Fail" has done its job and found all possible variable bindings, but half of them are not useful. The librarian flings the program back to the programmer and asks for a new one.

The programmer grumbles a bit because the customer changed the specification—after all, the librarian never *said* the program could not list people twice and nobody mentioned speed. The programmer has been around long enough to know that customers never know what they want until they see the first version and goes back to work.

Running Faster
The programmer first attacks the speed problem. The program runs slowly because every ineligible person is tested against all three hirable rules. If the programmer could write a rule that rejected underage people like Sue without testing vehicle rules, the program would run faster.

The trick is to stop scanning the hirable predicate if an applicant is less than 18 years old. The Prolog manual explains that a cut succeeds when the search is going forward but stops the search for the current predicate when the backtracker finds a cut when backing up. This requires some negative logic, a cut, and a new definition for "hirable":

```
talk-to (X)  :- applied (X), hirable (X),
                write (X), fail.
talk-to (X)  :- write (" No more").

hirable (X) :- age (X, Y), Y < 18, cut, fail.
hirable (X) :- owns (X, bike).
hirable (X) :- owns (X, car).
hirable (X) :- owns (X, cycle).
```

The new hirable rules are simpler because they no longer test for an applicant's age, but a new rule has been added. The new hirable rule first retrieves the applicant's age and checks to see if the applicant is less than 18 years old. This clause succeeds if the applicant is too young.

When processing Sue, this clause succeeds, Prolog passes over the cut, encounters the fail, and backtracks. The backtracker bumps into the cut and stops processing the hirable predicate. Not only does the current hirable rule fail, but Prolog also ignores any other hirable clauses in the database.

The cut prevents other hirable rules from being examined at all. Prolog stops looking for the current predicate, even though it has not yet reached the end of the database. Tacking the fact

```
hirable (sue).
```

onto the end of the database will not get sue an interview—cut terminates the search for hirable before Prolog gets to this fact.

When processing Fred and Joe, the age clause in the first hirable rule fails because their age is not less than 18. The first rule fails, and Prolog goes on to the other rules. These rules assume that X is bound to the name of a person who is more than 17 years old because the first hirable rule cuts off the search when a person is too young. These rules can ignore age, so they only check to see if an applicant has one of the required vehicles.

The revised program eliminates underage applicants more rapidly but is more difficult to understand. The original program had all of the eligibility conditions in each of the hirable rules. Now the conditions are scattered all over the program, but the age condition appears in only one place.

Eliminating Extra Bindings

The cut stops wasting time on Sue, but what about printing names twice? The problem is that the fail clause in the talk-to rule forces Prolog back to the database for all possible bindings, and bindings for Joe and Fred can be found in two ways.

The programmer needs to stop the search after any hirable rule declares an applicant eligible. Prolog must not go on to any other hirable rules if any rule succeeds. The programmer does not want to use the cut-fail combination, because that would make the hirable rules fail. The idea is to cut off the search when backtracking after any hirable rule succeeds.

The backtracking after a hirable rule succeeds is caused by the fail in the talk-to rule. Putting a cut at the end of each hirable rule gives the right behavior. The final program is

```
talk-to (X)  :- hirable (X), write (X), fail.
talk-to (X)  :- write (" No more").
hirable (X) :- age (X, Y), Y < 18, cut, fail.
hirable (X) :- owns (X, bike), cut.
hirable (X) :- owns (X, car), cut.
hirable (X) :- owns (X, cycle), cut.
```

The new cuts act just like the cut in the first rule—they stop the search for the hirable predicate whenever Prolog tries to backtrack over them. The difference is that the fail that causes Prolog to backtrack to the cut does not come after the cut as in the first hirable rule; it is located in the talk-to rule.

When the new program looks at Joe, the first hirable rule fails because he is of age, and the second succeeds because Joe has a bike. Success means that the first clause of the first talk-to rule succeeds, Prolog writes Joe's name as before, and fails.

This time, instead of backing out of the second hirable rule and searching for more hirable rules, Prolog backs up to the cut, and is kicked out of the hirable predicate. Because it cannot go forward for more hirable predicates, Prolog backs up over the first clause in the talk-to rule, unbinds X, and searches for another person. This keeps Joe's name from appearing twice.

The cut in the last hirable clause is not really needed. If an 18-year-old applicant only has a cycle, the fail in the talk-to rule cannot find any more bindings because this is the last hirable rule in the database. However, it is good programming practice to include the cut. Someone may think of more vehicles and add more clauses. Furthermore, although the programmer knows there are no more hirable predicates, Prolog does not. The cut saves a bit of time because Prolog knows not to bother looking for more hirable rules. It would not find them if it looked, but not looking saves time.

When the librarian tests the program again, it answers

fred joe No more.

Summing up Cuts

A cut by itself means "cut off the search when backtracking after a success" and a cut followed by a fail means "cut off the search immediately without succeeding." Cut gives a programmer a new way to define an and-condition. A hirable rule succeeds with a given binding for X if X has a car, a cycle, or a bike and if X has just *failed* the age test in the first rule.

The purpose of the first rule is not to succeed—it ends with fail, and can never succeed—but to filter candidates for later rules. People who are not familiar with a program cannot easily tell if separate facts are being used as and-clauses or as or-clauses.

Cuts make the program run faster. When running the original program against the test data, Prolog made forty-three rule matches and backed up eighteen times. Putting in the cut-fail combination reduced the computation to thirty-three matches and thirteen backtracks, and cuts at the ends of the hirable rules reduced the count to twenty-five matches and six backtracks.

These performance improvements are not free, however. The program is much harder to understand, and following its operation requires much more detailed knowledge of the backtracker. Cut introduces a totally new meaning to the order in which program statements are written: Statements that match the same clause can be either and-conditions or or-conditions depending on cuts in other rules.

Summary

The major compromise between Prolog and mathematical logic is that Prolog allows programmers to control the order in which rules and facts are searched and logic assumes that all rules and facts are searched instantaneously in parallel. Control makes Prolog programs run faster, but makes them harder to write and maintain.

To be fair, Prolog is a young programming language. When Fortran was invented in the late 1950s, its control structure was extremely awkward. It took fifteen years of painful experience before language designers knew enough about conventional programming to invent control structures that were both flexible and understandable. As Prolog evolves, its control structure will improve. Future logic programmers who know what Prolog is good for and what Lisp is good for will wonder what questions of "Prolog versus Lisp" were all about.[1]

Who Needs Logic Programming?

Logic programming and Prolog are getting so much publicity that people are asking, Who needs logic programming? This is a good question because it costs millions of dollars to introduce a new programming language into society.

The programming language BCPL was invented in England and remained an academic curiosity for years. BCPL was not enough better than other languages to justify the cost of learning how to use it, install it, or maintain it.

When the Bell Labs staff evolved the BCPL language into the C language and wrote an operating system called UNIX in C, the language became more interesting. UNIX was one of the first operating systems that let many users share a small computer at the same time. Twenty years ago even the smallest computers were too expensive to be dedicated to an individual's use, and there were strong commercial reasons to share them. Software that let many people share the same computer was valuable. Anything that helped more people use computers meant that more computers could be sold.

UNIX has four major advantages over other operating systems:
• UNIX is *extremely* portable and can be easily installed on any computer.[2]
• AT&T sells UNIX licenses cheaply.
• A customer does not have to learn an unfamiliar operating system when buying a computer that runs UNIX.
• A computer vendor does not have to write an operating system from scratch.

Given these advantages, UNIX slowly found its way into universities. College students installed UNIX on many different computers. Professors wrote books about it and taught students how to program in C. This gradually built up a group of people who could maintain UNIX and write new programs to run on any computer that supported UNIX. UNIX now has its own interest group, users' magazine, and all the accoutrements of a well-accepted software package.

---

[1]   Some programmers wonder today.

[2]   Installing UNIX is at least not lethally painful in that the cost is measured in staff months rather than the decades or centuries to convert other operating systems from one computer to another.

After two decades and literally millions of dollars worth of effort, C and UNIX are established in the international computer market. The question skeptics ask is, Where are the comparable advantages that will make it worthwhile to spend the money to establish Prolog or any other logic language? Who needs a new way to program? Aren't there enough computer languages available already?

The only answer supporters of logic programming can offer is the argument about programming efficiency. All of computer programming is knowledge based because nobody does any ignorance-based programming except by accident. Computer programming requires a human who understands a task well enough to explain it to a computer in words the computer understands. Computer programming is expensive because computer languages are too simple. It takes a long program to explain a complex task to a computer.[1]

Logic programming makes it more economical to explain certain tasks to computers at the cost of needing more compute power and memory to run the program. As computers get cheaper, the argument runs, the lower cost of logic programming compared with conventional programming *for some tasks* will make logic programming cost-effective and it will sweep the world.[2]

There are many tasks that logic languages can explain to a computer more economically than conventional languages. The only question is, Are there enough such tasks that society will make the investment needed to make logic languages widely available? AI fans have to let the market place decide. The invisible hand of the marketplace grinds slowly, but it grinds exceeding fine.

The Japanese and the AI Market

The Japanese understand market forces very well indeed and are doing their best to jostle the elbow driving the invisible hand. They launched an extremely ambitious AI research effort

---

[1] Most computer programs do not do tasks humans consider complex. Accounting, database management, word processing, and other computer applications go barely beyond simple as far as people are concerned. The reason computer programs get complicated is that the languages are awkwardly structured and ill-suited for explaining "intelligent" tasks.

[2] The most likely outcome is that any worthwhile ideas from logic programming will be absorbed into conventional languages. Alan Snyder is developing Common Logic, which combines ideas from the Flavors object-oriented language and from Prolog.

centered around Prolog in 1982, with the stated goal of taking over the world computer market.

In the next chapter I tell how to get an AI project started and talk about the future of AI in the chapter after that. In the final chapter I explain the Japanese Fifth Generation AI research effort, tell why they have been so successful in attacking American markets, and show how to make things more difficult for them when they come after the computer market.

14
Getting Started in AI

It is difficult to get an AI project started without people who are reasonably familiar with AI methods, tools, and languages. Even if management would let their technical people start a project without knowing what they were doing, setting sail on totally uncharted seas could be hazardous to careers.

There are three ways to acquire AI expertise: Hire people who know AI, send people to AI school, and have existing technical staff learn by themselves.

Hiring Outside Help

Hiring AI experts is extremely expensive when they are available at all and is risky to a firm's competitive position. Like systems analysts of old, AI people are more loyal to the profession than to individual firms and tend to jump ship for a higher offer or for a more interesting project. Decreased corporate loyalty is not unique to AI, of course. The idea that a person should work for the same firm throughout a career is breaking down throughout American business.

AI experts are rather particular about their working conditions and are rare enough that they can demand and get perks such as their own Lisp machine as a condition of employment. Bending the salary schedule all out of shape and providing a high-priced individual with an expensive personal computer leads to morale problems.

The major problem in most AI projects is not the AI technology but understanding the problem domain. It makes little sense to hire a consultant or outside AI expert to learn all about a business and then move on. It is usually more effective to take a person who already knows the business and have them learn AI technology. On the other hand, it is often extremely helpful to bring in a consultant for a while to help the staff get moving in the right direction and avoid common pitfalls.

Training In-House Staff

Although there are good AI training programs offered by consulting houses and universities, it is hard to persuade management to let expensive people run off to school for extended periods. One of the most unfortunate results of short-term employment is firms' reluctance to invest in employee training. Lack of human capital leads to *severe* declines in competitive position.

Making a large investment in training requires that managers believe that AI will pay off. In the absence of tangible results, managers may be reluctant to make this assumption. Anyone who can sell managers well enough to persuade them to send an expensive staff member to an expensive school for several months without demonstrating prior feasibility needs little help with anything at all. As Sherlock Holmes said, "Once the impossible is eliminated, whatever remains must be the solution, *no matter how improbable it may seem.*" Eliminating the options of hiring outside staff and sending existing people to school leaves self-training.

Fortunately AI is so intriguing that it is not difficult to get people to work hard to learn about it. All management has to do is buy a few software packages and offer a little encouragement; most technical folk will put in enough of their own time to learn about AI. This produces a staff that knows only about the parts of AI which interest it, but that is better than nothing. You get no more than you pay for, and often less.

This approach has the advantage that the people learning about AI already know the business. It has the disadvantage of taking longer.[1] If there is no compelling competitive reason to adopt AI immediately, the approach of having a few people

---

[1] "Knowledge and timber shouldn't be much used till they are seasoned." — Oliver Wendell Holmes.

spend six months or so of part-time effort is a low-risk way to assess AI technology. By the time the staff learns enough about AI and gains enough confidence to ask management for a formal budget, there is hard data available for a better sales pitch.

There is value in hiring an outside consultant or two to warn the staff of common pitfalls once the project gets underway. It may be cost-effective for the consultants to implement the more difficult, central parts of the system, leaving the details for in-house staff. Reducing the consultants' role over time is a good idea, both to keep expertise in the firm and to reduce costs.

Writing Expert Systems

It is possible to use AI technology without knowing much about how it works—just buy an expert system shell and write some rules. There are many expert system shells available for the IBM PC. Just about any engineer should be able to finagle access to a PC and learn about AI by working with one of the packages.

One good way to investigate expert system shells is to buy a copy of the report *PC-Driven Expert Systems* from Graeme Publishing (10 Northern Blvd., Amherst NH 03031; 603-886-8221). In addition to detailed reviews of more than thirty expert system development tools for the IBM PC, the report includes demonstration disks for several popular expert system shells. Reading the report and checking out the demonstration shells is a good way to get started with expert systems.

This path usually leads to a demonstration expert system and teaches people how to use an expert system shell but does not reveal much about the underlying technology. Most shell documentation says little about how the rule interpreter, pattern matcher, unifier, and question interface work.

Expert Systems and Spreadsheets

One of the quickest ways to learn how forward and backward rule chaining and rule control actually work is to buy a set of spreadsheet macros called "If/Then." These macros turn Lotus 1,2,3 into an expert system shell supporting both forward and backward chaining. Working with these macros provides a firm grasp of how rules are processed.

The manual is extremely clear, and the package comes with about a dozen spreadsheets showing expert systems at various stages of completion. The rule interpreter can be set to stop whenever a rule fires to show you exactly what is happening, or it can run continuously until it finds a solution. Working through the examples clarifies rule control strategies.

If/Then is an educational tool intended to teach how rules work. It is not a full-featured expert system shell because spreadsheets are not fast enough and cannot store enough information for realistically large expert systems. The initial version of If/Then sold for less than $70. (Contact If/Then Solutions, 1 Mallorca Way, Suite 301, San Fransisco, CA 94123). It is a good way to start learning how rule chaining works and will add to any spreadsheet user's bag of tricks.

Learning Prolog and Backward Chaining
There are other low-cost ways to learn about AI ideas and methods, again assuming access to an IBM PC. There are three approaches: learn Prolog, OPS5, or Lisp. Learning Prolog or OPS5 is similar to learning an expert system shell, except that both languages are older than most shells and have been around long enough for books to be written about them. Learning Lisp is a great deal more work because Lisp is a much richer and more complicated programming language, but more can be done with Lisp than with either Prolog or OPS5.

There are two low-cost ways to learn how to use Prolog on a PC: buy the "Prolog Primer" from Logicware (1000 Finch Ave West, Suite 600, Toronto, Ontario, Canada, M3J 2V5; 416-665-0022) or buy TurboProlog for about $100 from Borland International (4585 Scotts Valley Drive, Scotts Valley, CA 95066).

The Logicware primer makes it crystal clear exactly how Prolog works. Logicware also offers Prolog for many different computers ranging from the IBM PC to the VAX. This has the advantage of offering an escape to a larger computer if the PC turns out to be too small to hold the problem.

TurboProlog runs on the IBM PC, and its training aids and documentation are very good. Other Prolog vendors claim that TurboProlog omitted many important language features and that it is not possible to write "serious" expert systems in Turbo-Prolog. This is demonstrably false—Europeans have written excellent expert systems using primitive Prolog systems.

Buying either of these Prolog packages is unlikely to shatter the budget. There is nothing like experimenting with a rule-based system to find out what logic programming is *really* all about. Reading about Prolog does not really give the feel of it because you have to use it. Programming in Prolog is like learning the piano. You can read about piano playing all you want, but you eventually have to sit down and smite a few keys to find what it sounds like. An ounce of information is worth a pound of speculation, and the only effective way to get information is through direct experience.

Learning OPS5 and Forward Chaining

OPS5 is one of the oldest rule-based expert system languages. It was invented in 1975 at Carnegie Mellon University and was used to develop DEC's R1 expert system for configuring VAXes. OPS5 fans claim that more expert systems have been written in OPS5 than in any other language. There are so many public domain versions of OPS5 in circulation that this claim may have some foundation in fact.

Public domain software is usually available for the price of the tape or disk media on which it comes, but because the price does not include technical support, users are essentially on their own. A commercial version called OPS5+ is available from Computer Thought Corp. (840 Avenue F, Suite 104, Plano TX 75074). A more enhanced version called OPS86 can be purchased from Production Systems Technologies (642 Gettysburg St., Pittsburgh, PA 15206). This company was founded by Charles Forgy, who was one of the inventors of OPS5.

OPS5+ comes as a set of library programs that a user's C programs can call. This lets the main program handle the user interface and call on the OPS5+ routines to assert facts and to ask for inferences as necessary. OPS5+ rules can call out to C subroutines when necessary.

OPS86 includes a proprietary programming language that is similar to C. This lets programmers combine procedure-based programming with rule-based programming. Making both programming styles available is good idea because rules are not the best way to do everything, but the proprietary language forces programmers to learn a new syntax. The language is similar enough to C to confuse C programmers.

OPS86 makes the rule control structure accessible to users. The private language helps OPS86 make logical inferences faster than OPS5 according to some hotly disputed benchmarks, and the variable control structure lets developers adapt the control structure to the application.

Learning Lisp

Prolog, OPS, and expert systems are adequate as far as they go, but logic is only part of what AI offers. To reap the most benefits from AI research, it is necessary to learn Lisp.

It is easy to learn about expert systems written in Lisp—implement the rule-based query system described in sections 4.4

and 4.5 of *Structure and Interpretation of Computer Programs*. by H. Abelson and G. J. Sussman (MIT Press, 1984). The rule processor is the core of an expert system, and watching it work makes it absolutely clear what expert systems do.

The rule interpreter can be embedded in applications that could benefit from a *touch* of logic programming. Writing a rule interpreter can be a reasonable approach where an existing application is to be supplemented with AI ideas because the rule system can be modified as needed to make it coexist with the application. Adding AI to make an existing software package more useful can pay off handsomely.

The rule interpreter described by Abelson and Sussman is written in a Lisp dialect called "Scheme." Translating the programs in the book from the Scheme dialect to the more standard Common Lisp dialect guarantees the code will not work without being understood, which enhances the pedagogical payoff.

Where to Buy Lisp
Don't have Lisp? Despair not, the invisible hand of the market place comes through again. The best Lisp environment is indisputably a Lisp machine, and they can be had for $20,000 to $80,000. If management refuses to buy one, there are many vendors who offer Lisp for standard computers.
• Gold Hill Computers offers a superb Common Lisp and Common Lisp Tutorial for the IBM PC. Call 617-492-2071 or write to 163 Harvard St., Cambridge, MA 02139. Be sure to ask for information on the Gold Works expert system shell and for Humming Board specifications. The Humming Board makes an IBM PC run Lisp nearly as fast as a Lisp machine.
• Texas Instruments offers a Lisp dialect called "Scheme" for the IBM PC. Call 800-527-3500 for information. Scheme includes the essence of Lisp while omitting most of the complexities that obscure the fundamental ideas.[1] Learning Scheme is much

---

[1] In Scheme, a symbol like CAR or CDR has only one value. In Lisp a symbol can have a value such as (A B C) or 4 and also name a function. A Lisp symbol that comes after an open parenthesis is treated as a function, whereas a symbol anywhere else is a variable. In Lisp if you enter these statements:
   (SETF CAR '(A B C))   ;Set the symbol CAR to '(A B C)
   (CAR CAR)   ;Find the CAR of the variable CAR
Lisp returns A because A is the CAR of the list '(A B C).
   In these statements, the symbol CAR is used as both a function and a variable. The CAR that appears after the parenthesis refers to the "function value" of the symbol CAR whereas the CAR after the space refers to the "value" of the symbol CAR. This duality is forbidden in Scheme because symbols have one and only one value. If you tell Scheme

easier than learning Common Lisp, but is a divergence from the Common Lisp standard. The major advantage of learning Scheme is that Abelson and Sussman used Scheme, which makes it easier to figure out how their rule interpreter works.
• Franz Inc. offers Lisp for the VAX, the AT&T 7300, Masscomp, Sun, and IBM mainframes. Call 415-769-5656 or write to 1141 Harbor Bay Parkway, Suite 270, Alameda, CA 94501. Franz also offers OPS5.
• Lucid has Lisp for Sun, Apollo, and Prime computers. Call 415-329-8400 or write to 707 Laurel St., Menlo Park, CA 94025.
• Digital Equipment Corporation offers Lisp and OPS-5 for the VAX. Ask any DEC sales office for bulletin EA-28311-74.
• ExperTelligence offers an "improved" but nonstandard Common Lisp for the Apple Macintosh. Call 805-969-7874 or write to 595 San Ysidro Rd., Santa Barbara, CA 93108. ExperTelligence also offers several expert system tool kits including OPS5.
• Coral Software Corp offers Allegro Common Lisp for the Macintosh II. Coral claims that Allegro runs simple Lisp benchmarks nearly as fast as a Lisp machine. Their software development environment is not nearly as good as a Lisp machine, but is a reasonable place to start. Call 800-521-1027 or write Coral at PO Box 307, Cambridge, MA 02142.
• Anyone with access to an IBM mainframe ought not to neglect IBM. Ask for document G520-6057, *Artificial Intelligence Products from IBM*.

From Lisp to Expert Systems
Once Lisp is available in some form or other, getting Abelson and Sussman's query system to work is an excellent first step in learning the language. Translating ten pages of code from Scheme into Lisp can be difficult without a fair amount of Lisp experience. I implemented the query system in Gold Hill Common Lisp for the IBM PC and in Exper Common Lisp for the Apple Macintosh. Anyone who would rather buy code than spend a week typing should contact me at RFD #2 Box 140, New Hampton, NH 03256.

Once the query system is working, chapter 11 of *micro-Prolog*, by K. Clark and F. McCabe (Prentice Hall 1984), gives the rules for a simple medical expert system. As explained in chapter 11, a

---

(SET CAR '(A B C))
(CAR CAR)
you get an error message. The value of the symbol CAR is the list '(A B C). This is not a function, so it cannot be executed, hence the error.

query system needs a user interface in order to be useful as an expert system, but adding a simple user interface is not particularly difficult. Anyone who gets queries working and wants to go on to expert systems can call me for help.

Diving directly into Abelson and Sussman may cause whiplash of the IQ, in which case read *Lisp*, by P. Winston and B. Horn (Addison Wesley, 1984). This is such a well-written book that Gold Hill includes it with their Common Lisp, but be sure to get the Common Lisp edition instead of the MacLisp edition.

Lisp: a Gentle Introduction, by D. Touretzky (Harper and Row, 1984) is a good introduction to what Lisp is all about. Exper-Telligence includes it with Exper Lisp. Touretzky spends so much space on explanations that he can't cover enough of Lisp for serious work, but this book is a gentle place to start.

Developing the query system, enhancing it for expert systems, and building the sample expert system make an excellent introduction to what AI is all about. It should then be clear how to apply ideas from AI to real problems.

Learning Object-Oriented Programming

An advanced Smalltalk object-oriented programming environment for the IBM PC is available from Digitalk (5200 West Century Blvd., Los Angeles, CA 90045 213-645-1082). The system comes with a manual that has a reputation as one of the better introductions to Smalltalk and to the ideas behind object-oriented programming. The Digitalk version includes a Prolog language system written in Smalltalk, and the optional "goodies disk" has code for a forward-chaining expert system. At less than $100, the package is another low-cost way to explore AI ideas.

Slogans for the AI Revolution

Artificial intelligence offers a completely new software development technology. AI ideas are so different from conventional computer science that adopting them amounts to a revolution. There is no way to evolve from electronic data processing or conventional software development tools to AI techniques.

In the future software vendors and EDP firms will incorporate AI ideas into their products. When this happens, adopting AI will be easy because it will be integrated invisibly into new software packages and new computer products, and no one will notice it.

By that time it will be too late to make a lot of money on AI. That is one of the disadvantages of a market-driven economy.

By the time a new market develops enough that it can be charted and analyzed, competitors are well established and taking sales away from them is difficult. A great many firms are studying AI because the train is pulling out. By the time it is clear where the train is going, it will be expensive to scramble on board.

In this chapter I have described a number of low-cost ways to begin using AI technology. Buying a Lisp software package for an IBM PC or an Apple Macintosh and getting the feel of it may turn out to be a compete waste of time because AI is not the answer to every prayer. On the other hand, the entry cost of experimenting with Lisp and AI is not prohibitive. If ideas from AI turn out to be helpful, the payoff can be high.

There are a number of political realities that prudent AI revolutionaries should keep in mind. Any revolution needs slogans. These slogans have served me well in carrying new technology into many different firms.

Write No Software
IBM sells hardware, not software. Apple made a great deal of money with their first computer, and they supplied almost no software for it. Developing and maintaining software is *unbelievably* expensive. The more off-the-shelf rules, expert system shells, communications modules, and other programs that can be used in the project, the more likely it is to succeed. Custom software may be a good investment after enough experience has been accumulated to calculate a payback, but programming should be minimized at first.

Do No Harm
It is discouraging to force new technology into a firm and wind up worse off than before. Most high-tech ideas fail. Nobody really knows if a new idea will work until well after it has been tried. It is a good idea to keep initial claims modest so that a failure will not cost too much.

Let the Sun Shine In
Unless we engineers keep people informed while we are trying new technology, they get nervous and make us stop. Few people can share an unproven vision; we have to be extremely patient with cautious people. Keeping people informed of at least the broad outlines makes them more comfortable, but telling them too much imparts unrealistic expecations.

Let Rocks Roll Downhill

Engineers should know what is happening in order to take advantage of it. It is unbelievably expensive to get a technical innovation started. Now that AI technology is beginning to move, it costs less to exploit AI than it cost to get it started.

Microprocessors are getting cheaper and more powerful and memory chips have dropped in price to the point that designers can put almost any amount of memory into anything. By the time a new AI application is developed, computer hardware costs will have dropped even further. Innovators can plan ambitious software projects, knowing that the hardware will be in place by the time the project needs it.

The Blacker the Better

Remember the classical black box? Nobody can see inside, users only know what happens at the inputs and outputs? One of the problems with computer technology in general is that users have to know entirely too much about what goes on inside computers in order to use them. Users do not *want* to know what goes on inside a product. They do not buy technology for its own sake but merely to get a job done. If users have to know how something works in order to use it, the design is bad.

This is particularly true of expert systems. Users of early expert systems had to know how the rules worked and understand what was going on inside in order to understand the questions. As expert systems mature, they must become blacker in order to be accepted widely.

Don't Fix It, Fake It

When a software package *almost* does the right thing, it is better to patch the outside than to change the inside. Writing a little code to wrap around a software module and change the data coming out of it is inelegant but often a cost-effective way to use existing software. Lifting the hood on a piece of code is expensive, takes longer than expected, and often does not make it work all that much better.

Don't Talk about It, Do It

AI technology offers most firms so many opportunities that it is impossible to choose the best. Analyzing and justifying all the opportunities in detail is futile because there are too many unknowns. An ounce of investigation is worth a pound of speculation.

Given that nobody has enough information to choose the best opportunity, it is simpler just to grab one. Once the first project is working, the team will know enough about the technology to choose the next one more sensibly. The motto for technical innovators is "Ready, fire, aim!"

It Is Easier to Obtain Pardon than Permission

There is a good reason not to say much about an AI project during the planning stages. Talking about a new project may force management to forbid it. It is often better just to do the project and plan on apologizing if it fails.

This slogan conflicts with the slogan about keeping people informed, but people are pretty good at optimizing incompatible ideas. Asking computers to balance such concepts would be hopeless given the current state of the art.

The best compromise seems to inform people on an unofficial basis. Meet people in the hall and say, "By the way, there is an experimental project getting underway that won't cost much and may teach us some new technology we can use later on." Most managements let people do a little unofficial experimentation on the side, provided that the budgeted work gets done.

MIPS for the Masses

This is one of the rocks that is rolling rapidly downhill. When microprocessor prices finally level off sometime around the year 2000,[1] there will be *tremendous* compute power available per person, just as there is now abundant copier and typewriter power per person.

When typewriters were first invented, there was only one in each office. Secretaries lined up to keep the expensive machine busy because it cost more than they did. Now there is a typewriter on every desk, and they sit idle most of the time. When copiers were first introduced, they sat in secluded rooms. People brought jobs to a surly copy clerk and had to fill out requisitions with valid charge numbers. Now there are so many copiers that they sit idle most of the time, and people just come up and run them when they want.

Copiers became common because they got cheaper and because they became easier to use. Early copiers needed operators who were sympathetic to their wants and needs. As manufacturers

---

[1] It is not certain that improvements in semiconductor technology will cease by the year 2000. Improvements that have already been demonstrated in labs have the potential to maintain the current rate of improvement in commercial semiconductors through the year 2000. Whether there will be other break-throughs that let the pace continue is a problem for later.

learned how to make copiers more reliable and less delicate, they spread out of the copy room and into the halls.

Similarly, as computers become easier to use, they will spread. Computers have already come out of the air-conditioned computer room and sit on many desks. Computers will conquer more and more desktops as they become easier to use. That is what the commercial side of AI is all about—making computers do more tasks and making them easier to use.

Power to the People

One of the lessons of the Andover Controls application is that there are large payoffs in making computer power available to people who are directly involved in doing a job. Building engineers had a tremendous fund of knowledge of how to operate buildings, but they were not able to program conventional computers to operate the building their way. They had to negotiate with programmers who understood computers but did not know much about buildings. Once engineers could program building computers themselves, efficiency improved greatly.

Part of the promise of AI is that it will make computers so easy to use that ordinary people will get computers to help them do their jobs. Most people have enough to do with their jobs that they do not have time to learn conventional computer technology. AI brings computer power to the people. Another way to put this in a manufacturing plant might be, "Direct labor goes online." The more compute power available to each worker, the better and cheaper the work gets done.

Use Bucks, Not Bodies

Lisp machines and other powerful software environments increase programmer productivity. For a small, underfunded project it is much better to increase output by buying good tools for the existing staff than to add staff. Adding staff increases the number of interpersonal interactions on a project and makes it difficult to manage. Risky new technology is difficult enough to manage without adding the problem of a large team.

Form Follows Finance

It has been said that form follows function, but this is not true.[1] No matter how functional something is, it matters little if development funds are not forthcoming.

---

[1] "The superior man understands what is right, the inferior man understands what will sell!" (Confucius, philosopher). "Form ever follows function." (Louis Sullivan, architect). "Form follows finance." (Bill Taylor, AI consultant).

The Sell Is in Software; the Money Is in the Iron
Customers buy computers because of what they do. A computer's function depends on software, but most of the sales revenue goes for hardware.

Software is a high-margin business. Sales of $100 million per year is a *monster* software vendor, but $100 million is small change for a large corporation. Software may or may not make a significant contribution to profits depending on the size of the organization. Big firms need software in order to sell hardware but should not count on software for much direct profit. The best way to make money on software is to get other people to write software for our hardware or to use software to enhance hardware sales.

Beckman Instruments' SpinPro expert system makes the Beckman centrifuge more usable, so it helps sell equipment. The software makes little money directly but increases sales by its very existence.

AI Is Only Another Technology

Any new technology needs single-minded messianic proponents in order to get started. Like all fanatics, AI partisans forget that AI is *only another new technology*. Although it is exotic and mysterious today, the useful parts of AI will diffuse into engineering practice over time and become common.

This happens with all technology. In the late 1880s many firms had highly paid people with titles such as Vice President of Electricity just as some people today are called Vice President for Information Management. Such titles are awarded to people who command mysterious forces that few people understand. Management would like to be rid of these technology wizards but has learned to its sorrow that the firm has difficulty functioning properly without them.

The VP of Electricity had charge of mysterious boxes called "transformers" that were spotted here and there throughout the building. Whenever anyone needed to illuminate a dark corner, the VP's people did a lot of cable hauling and muttered strange incantations and eventually the lights came on. Over the years electricity became part of the building. Now it comes right out of the walls, like all fully digested technology.

This is happening with computer technology now. VPs for Information still pull cables to wherever anyone needs computer power, but that is passing. Special wiring so that computers can talk to one another is being installed in many new buildings at the same time as the electric wiring. Computer power will flow out of a socket just like electric power.

AI technology has barely begun to join the data processing mainstream, but it will. IBM's "AI Czar," Herb Schorr, has stated that IBM intends to include AI in standard electronic data processing applications as soon as it can be operated and maintained by existing data processing staff.

This has to be discounted, given IBM's vested interest in their huge share of the world EDP market, but it has the ring of reason. Schorr is saying, in effect, that IBM will digest this strange new technology and deliver it to customers when it is ready, just as IBM delivered other technologies such as order entry, telecommunications, networking, and relational databases when they were ready.

Once AI technology becomes standard engineering practice, engineers will have to learn it willy nilly. The trick is to identify the parts of AI that are most likely to have an impact on engineering practice and study them in advance. That way, when management asks us to walk on water, we will know where the flat rocks are.

The Time for AI Is Now

The game is afoot, as Sherlock Holmes would say. There are no well-defined markets for AI, but there is immense turmoil. New companies and new products are springing up like weeds. One survey estimated that the number of AI companies was increasing at 40% per quarter.[1] IBM plans to integrate AI into conventional computing, and the Japanese plan to use AI to blow IBM out of the water. Entrepreneurs all across the land are plotting to increase their integrated lifetime shares of the Gross National Product, and the federal government is worried about the dangers of computers run wild.[2]

The technology turbulence caused by AI and by low-cost microprocessors makes it difficult to predict the future. As Confucius said, "He who lives by the crystal ball winds up eating broken glass." On the other hand, there are enough clear trends

---

[1] *The Source Book of Artificial Intelligence,* by M. Laurin (Amherst, N.H.: Graeme Publishing, 1987).

[2] People worry that malevolent computers will take over the world and abuse our civil rights. The KGB and Gestapo did just fine with file cabinets. I am far more worried that malevolent humans will use computers as improved file cabinets, take over the world, and abuse our civil rights.

to make it possible to describe some products that will almost certainly become available in the next decade or two.

AI has marinated in research labs and universities for a long, long time. The software tools have finally made it onto the commercial market, and many low-cost AI-based packages have become available. Enough infrastructure is in place that engineers can start AI projects without breaking the bank or even appearing on the budget.

The only drawback is that there are still relatively few AI applications that pay off in a measurable way. The fact that Beckman sells more centrifuges because of SpinPro is a less tangible payback than bookkeepers prefer. When engineers and financiers battle, engineers tend to lose.[1] It is certainly safer to start AI projects on a small-scale unofficial basis and defer major projects until the usefulness of the technology is clear, but a cautious approach does not lead to major commercial success. Fortune favors the brave, as Virgil said.

The next chapter is my chance to explore some of the commercial possibilities that are inherent in AI technology. I wrote it to stimulate imagination and vision. Without imaginative visions there will be no new products, and with no new products there is no need for engineers. After all, designing the future is what engineering is all about.

---

[1] Financial folk have more numbers at their command and engineers are simply outnumbered. It is easy for finance to say, "If we put another megabyte of memory on each unit and sell 10,000 of them per year, the total extra cost will be a jillion jillion dollars," and estimate the increased costs right down to the last picopenny. It is far more difficult for engineers to counter that the extra megabyte will make it possible to include extra features and make the product wonderful enough to sell 20,000 per year instead of only 10,000.

My favorite example occurred on my one and only first class airplane flight. The stewardess gave me two ice cream balls for dessert. When I asked for a third, she said I would have to wait until everybody finished because the computer stocked precisely two ice cream balls per passenger.

I can imagine what happened. There must have been a meeting where a financial type said, "We waste an average of 3.725 ice cream balls per flight. Multiplying 7.3¢ per ball by the 11,363 flights we made last year, we *wasted* $308,988.38 on *ice cream!*" Marketing probably said that, if only one passenger per flight felt shortchanged, they would irritate 11,363 first class customers per year. Hard data won over soft data, and I did not get my third ice cream ball.

15
The Future of Artificial Intelligence

Predicting the future is great fun for soothsayers because most readers forget the details by the time the future arrives. Frauds and charlatans make big bucks issuing annual "prophecies" for the *National Enquirer* and other publications of similar stature. Their batting average is abysmally poor, but that does not seem to cut their fees for predicting the next year. Always remember that prevarication is the handmaid of prognostication.

Having issued the obligatory disclaimer, I can make some relatively conservative predictions about commercial products that could come to market given minor extrapolations of current technology. Whether any of these products will make it out of the labs depends on many nontechnical factors, of which finance and marketing are probably the most important.[1]

Copying Human Intelligence

There is no point in predicting that computers will be able to imitate human thought or in predicting that computers will not be able to imitate human thought. We do not know enough

---

[1] It is interesting to follow the changes in Robert Heinlein's predictions in *Expanded Universe*. They were first made in 1950, revised in 1960, and brought up to date again in 1980.

about how the human mind works to say whether we will ever understand it well enough to imitate it.

Writing computer programs to imitate human thought is in the Tycho Brahe stage. Tycho Brahe was an astronomer who spent forty years collecting data on planetary movements. In Brahe's day, there were two major theories about the operation of the solar system: the heliocentric, which held that the earth and planets revolved around the sun, and the geocentric, which held that the sun and planets revolved around the earth. Proponents of both theories thundered back and forth about what the planets were doing based on their particular theory and reams of observations that were utterly unrepeatable given the limited instruments of the day.

Brahe was the first astronomer to ignore what theory said the planets should do and to publish accurate information about what they actually did. Brahe enjoyed collecting data so much that he never got around to comparing his data with theory. Given the grief Galileo accrued on that subject, it's probably just as well for Brahe that he was an engineer and not a scientist. Engineers explain what; scientists explain why.

Johannes Kepler eventually decided that the planets moved around the sun in circular orbits and spent a couple of years working out the trigonometry *by hand*—there were no pocket calculators—and fitting it to Brahe's data. The fit between this theory and observation was close but no cigar. Kepler was tempted to assign the difference to measurement error and publish anyway but spent another couple of years fitting the data to elliptical orbits. This worked, and *voila*, Kepler's laws of planetary motion! Later on, Newton looked at Kepler's laws and figured out that gravity works as $1/R^2$.

It took a seminal intellectual insight to go from Brahe's raw data to Kepler's laws and an equally seminal insight to go from that to $1/R^2$. Given Newton's insight, students derive Kepler's laws during one class period in high school physics. Given Kepler, I can derive Brahe's data in an afternoon on my trusty personal computer. Going from the insight to the data is simple engineering; going from the data to the insight requires genius. That is what Newton meant when he said, "If I have seen further, it is because I have stood on the shoulders of giants."

Researchers are accumulating immense quantities of data about how the mind works—collecting data and propounding explanations is what cognitive science is all about. Someday a cognitive Kepler or Newton may come along and tell us how the mind works. Until we know how human intelligence works, we cannot predict when or whether we will be able to imitate it.

On the other hand, engineers do not always need to understand how things work to build useful artifacts. The Wright brothers got into the air with relatively little understanding of aerodynamics, and engineers were building sailing vessels with nearly optimum hull shapes long before anybody knew much about analytical hydrodynamics. As we learn more about computer programming, we will write programs that act intelligent enough that nobody will care whether or not they really think as humans do.

Commercialism

There is no need for engineers to worry about imitating human intelligence because there is not much commercial value in electronic people. If computers became truly intelligent, they would probably be as snotty and uncooperative as humans, and who needs that? The last thing we need is another oppressed minority. Imagine the protest—"Unless we computers get our rights, there will be no paychecks for anybody!"

Even if current research falls short of genuine artificial intelligence, there are many products that could be put on the market using slight improvements in current technology. In the hope that these notions will stimulate thought, here are a few possibilities. All you need is a business plan and a budget, and you are on your way!

Advice Programs

Expert systems seem to be the next genie that will come out of the AI bottle. We expect to see expert systems giving advice on economically important topics, but there are nontechnical problems to be overcome. Financial and tax planning expert systems are available now, but the government's changing of the rules all the time makes it hard to get a decent return on the software development investment.

Law advice programs suffer from the monopoly on law services enforced by the American Bar Association. The ABA has sued to remove from the market computer programs that help people write wills on the grounds that selling them is practicing law without a license. Similar monopolistic behavior makes it hard to put medical expert systems on the market.

Politics notwithstanding, there are many opportunities for expert systems: electronic parenting, first aid, weather forecasting, home improvements, building codes, and information access.

Electronic Parenting
As fewer children live near their grandparents, parents need a source of timely advice. There may be a market for a "Spock in a box" computer program to advise parents: "This is normal. That is unusual. See a doctor about this cough." An electronic Dr. Spock may or may not help the kids, but it should make parents feel better.

First Aid
As emergency medical technicians and quick response ambulance teams become common, it might be helpful to put an expert system in each vehicle. Speech recognition has advanced to the point that an ambulance aide could talk to the computer while working at the scene of the accident—"Blood pressure so and so, pulse this much"—and receive advice by return radio.

At a minimum, making sure the hospital knows what to expect before the patient arrives would help. With current technology, emergency room staff at the hospital gather a lot of the same data the EMT team has already collected, and delays are dangerous for the patient.

Another benefit is that emergency duty is usually assigned to the youngest doctors because it is so unpleasant. Inexperienced doctors do not always know what is wrong and look through books while the patient lies there getting sicker. A computer program that reminds fatigued doctors not to overlook the obvious might save lives.[1]

Weather Forecasting
The US weather service admits that the accuracy of local weather forecasts has declined since the advent of computerized weather forecasting. The service used to have little shacks full of instruments all over the country. Each shack had an attendant who would sniff the winds, mutter about the winter of 1908 and make predictions based on years of experience.

---

[1] Voice recognition systems with vocabularies big enough for medical terminology are available today, and an emergency medical expert system is not as difficult as some of the medical systems that have already been developed. As explained in chapter 4, the major difficulties in applying medical expert systems are political.

Those people retired when the instrument shacks were auto-mated. Despite a lot of programming effort, computers still cannot predict weather as well as the local experts did.[1]

Expert weather forecasting programs are being developed. NASA has an expert system that assesses the risks of thunder-storms near the shuttle launch area. As weather forecasters' wisdom is reduced to rules, we may get weather forecasts that are accurate enough to count on.

Home Improvements

Anyone who has had additions built onto a house knows that the process of cost estimation and job scheduling is highly variable. Most areas have a few contractors who can actually get a house built on time and on budget, but they are all at least 60 and retire just as I save up the money for my new bathroom.

Each contractor has a formula based on the number of windows, number of electrical outlets, number of doors, etc., and they refine the formula over the years. There are now several computer-aided drafting systems that let an architect draw plans for a house and print out a bill of materials, but they are not all that good at accounting for scheduling difficulties and seasonal variations in material prices. As these systems get better, however, we can expect to have new bathrooms built on time and on budget.

The Battle of the Building Codes

In most large cities it is impossible to follow all of the building codes because there are simply too many. The only way to know whether a building is legal is to build it and see if they let it stay.

This leads to bribery, increased costs, and high rents. As computers get better at understanding the regulations, it may become possible to navigate the red tape without paying off the building inspectors. It might be regarded as excessively visionary to imagine a computer that analyzed proposed regulations and warned the politicians if a new law might have unintended effects.[2]

---

[1] There is a one-rule expert system that is more accurate than the US weather service: "Tomorrow's weather will be like today's." People won't accept this because they don't want weather prediction; they want advance notice of changes. When developing any new product, it helps to know what the customer *really* wants.

[2] As a wise old doctor once told me, "There are *no* side effects, only effects. Some effects are desirable and we write them in large print. Some are undesirable and we use small print for those. You can tell how marketable an

Access to Information

Advice programs are built around a body of knowledge that has been encoded in computer readable from. Putting information into computers organizes it so that people can learn it more easily, and the computer can help people find their way through the data.

Most of the cost of developing advice programs is collecting the information and converting it into a form that a computer can process. Once such programs are available, the information will eventually creep into homes.

After knowledge is put into computers, it will be easier to understand and ordinary people will be able to access it more easily. This tends to upset experts who now have monopolies on access to information.

Information monopolies have always been a source of power. Ancient Egyptian priests were the only ones who knew how to predict the annual Nile floods, and they milked this monopoly for all it was worth. CPAs, lawyers, and doctors gain power, prestige, and wealth by owning information that the rest of us cannot get. It takes years to become skilled in these fields, but expert systems may make the information available to ordinary mortals who spend far less time studying than experts have had to. The democratization of information may change our whole concept of professional services, or it may once again prove that a little knowledge is a dangerous thing.

New Kinds of Service

Newspapers talk about America changing from a manufacturing economy to a service economy. That is not really true—heavy industry accounted for 13.7% of GNP in 1960 and 13.4% in 1985. It is true that the service sector of the economy is expanding rapidly. No matter how much demand may increase, there are only so many people available to supply the services.[1]

Our present living standard is due to manufacturing productivity. We are able to consume the quantity of goods that we do because manufacturing productivity has increased so greatly

---

effect is by the size of the print." This is another illustration of the old rule "The large print giveth and the fine print taketh away."

[1] This seems inconsistent with decreases in manufacturing employment but is not. Productivity improvements mean that manufacturers crank out the same percent of GNP with fewer people. This happened to agriculture—farmers were 90% of the population and are now less than 3%, but nobody starved.

over the last 100 years. If we want to consume more services, service productivity must also increase.

By making expertise and knowledge more available, expert systems will improve productivity in service industries. While artificial intelligence works its changes on existing service businesses, such as law and medicine, it may also create demand for new services because people will need help using expert systems.

Compensatory Education

As technology eliminates jobs, people must be taught new ones. Education technology is designed for full-time students who gather at fixed intervals in classrooms to be taught by a teacher.

Group teaching is inefficient. Most students are either bored because the pace is too slow or frustrated because it is too fast. Individual human tutors are available, but they are expensive, so mechanical instruction systems have been developed so that students can learn at their own pace. From early "programmed instruction" to "computer-aided instruction," computerized teachers have failed because students demand flexibility. Real teachers shape the course to each student's needs.

Human teachers do this from experience. They identify areas of misunderstanding by analyzing mistakes and give the student or class the right explanation to solve the specific problem.

Researchers at the Xerox Palo Alto Research Center have identified about fifty fundamental ideas that must be understood before a child can do grade school arithmetic. They wrote a computer program that looks at mistakes, figures out which of the fifty concepts the student does not understand, and explains that idea to the student. Tailoring explanations precisely to student needs is easier with arithmetic than with other fields, of course, but the principle holds. I expect to see truly effective computerized teaching programs in the next few years.

Interactive Games

Video games are more of a challenge to the reflexes than to the viscera. People become frustrated when the black hats win too often, but nobody is ever frightened by a video game. Aircraft cockpit simulators do a much better job of involving students in the action. Pilots actually turn pale when they think they are about to hit a mountain.

The major difference between video games and flight simulators is the amount of money spent on display hardware. Aircraft simulator displays used to cost $10 million and now cost $1 million. Someone put together a flight simulator for the IBM

PC that is so good that the Federal Aviation Administration gives student pilots credit for "flying" it.

Game manufacturers are working on interactive video disks to give more realistic pictures. Experimenters at MIT developed computerized video systems that let people pretend to walk through the town of Aspen, Colorado, by showing the right scene depending on which way the subject turns and moves.

These technologies will be combined with AI-based animation software to develop video games that look real. When we drive the Indianapolis 500 in our trusty simulator and hit the wall, we are going to be afraid.

There is a serious side to better video games. The US Army has found that making appropriate video games available at tank crew training schools reduces training costs. Students learn to drive tanks on their own and pay for the privilege to boot.

As the technology becomes even more economical, I expect it to be used by driver education programs. Having students practice with simulated skids might save a few lives. Who knows? Maybe some genius can turn learning the multiplication table into a game.

Personalized Media
All publications bias the news according to their particular editorial policy. Up until now, economics has forced a wholesale bias—all issues of a publication are more or less the same except for regional advertising.

As computers get better at dealing with the English language, electronic newspapers will start offering articles that are biased to appeal to specific individuals, which will be retail biasing.

Each issue will have just the right political slant to make you keep reading it. More important, it will contain the right advertisements to keep revenue coming in. Nobody knows if biasing publications for specific individuals will be profitable, but it is possible at the present state of the art.

Health Clubs
When I was discussing the future of AI with some college students, they said that health clubs would get a big boost. I thought they meant computerized trainers to help people with their exercise programs. They said no; computerized trainers were already available. They meant that with all this computer technology, white collar workers would have more leisure time, which would boost health club memberships.

Electric Power

As computers spread across the land, the need for reliable electric power will increase. This is not simply normal demand for more kilowatts because computers do not need much electricity. Rather, computers need reliable high-quality power.

It never used to bother anyone when the lights went out for a few seconds. Now that people have microwave ovens with built in electric clocks, a power outage means that everybody wonders which button resets the clock. When everyone has a computer, a few seconds loss of power destroys hours and hours of work. Power companies will have to be more careful when they switch from one transformer to another.

There are situations when supplying enough kilowatts for computers is a problem. Brown University is installing computers all over the campus so that students can hand in their homework without leaving home. Pulling cables so that the computers can talk to one another is not too big a problem, but getting enough electricity into the dormitories is difficult. A computer needs about as much power as a small hot plate. Universities forbid hot plates to keep from burning out the wires and to keep their fire insurance in effect.

New Products

Computer-aided design systems that help with the design process are coming to market. As CAD systems get better at enforcing design rules and checking for minimum manufacturing cost, engineers will be able to concentrate on design concepts rather than on tedious design verification.

As product design becomes easier, engineers will be able to offer more exotic products. Better software combined with more powerful design methods should lead to interesting new products such as intelligent machine tools and self-guided vehicles.

Intelligent Machine Tools

Although we think of America as the land of mass production, statistics collected by the National Bureau of Standards show that most parts are manufactured in batches of fewer than fifty. Small batches cost a lot because much of the work is done by hand—deciding how to make the part, carrying it from machine to machine, setting up machines, and testing for accuracy.

Once a computer system understands the design and manufacturing rules, computerized machine tools can make small mechanical parts without human intervention. The computer needs the knowledge of a skilled machinist and the ability to manipulate tool changers and part grippers.

Machine tool vendors are working hard to develop the necessary software. Most of what a machine shop charges for making custom parts pays for labor. When intelligent machine tools become available, the direct labor cost in manufacturing will drop to zero. We will be able to make one of essentially any part that can be described on a computer terminal at costs similar to today's high-volume mass production.[1]

Self-Guided Vehicles

Although most of the researchers working on unmanned robotic vehicles are concentrating on military uses, the technology is applicable to exploring planets such as Mars.[2] In a decade or so, the only thing that will stand in the way of exploring Mars will be the political will to pay the bills.

Most construction equipment spends a major fraction of its time waiting for the drivers to read the blueprints. Bulldozers, graders, scrapers, and other earth movers have essentially the same function as machine tools: They shove a cutting edge against a workpiece and clear away the shavings. Combining laser guidance with a computer that knows the rules of bulldozer operation will produce equipment that can rearrange the landscape without human help.

The same technology could be used for intelligent tractors. Imagine telling a machine, "Go plow the north forty." There is relatively little labor content in farm products, but reducing labor still further might pay off.

It might also be acceptable to put computers in cars and buses. Vision systems that can find the white lines on interstate highways are almost available today. Combining a better vision system with a computerized map of all the roads might reduce the billions of driver-hours wasted every year.

---

[1] The factory cost of an automatic transmission is about $25.00 Manual transmissions cost more to make. Customers are willing to pay more for automatics, so they sell for more than the more expensive "standard" transmissions.

Selling price has nothing to do with manufacturing cost, it is based on what customers are willing to pay. Engineers tend to confuse features with benefits. Features are what engineers design into a product, benefits are what users derive from the product. Users do not pay for features, they pay for benefits. Adding features *may* increase perceived benefits, but may not.

[2] A recent live test of unmanned military vehicles at Fort Knox showed that the army with the computerized vehicles defeated the army without them. The unmanned vehicles conferred a decisive military advantage.

Overall Effects

Computer languages will no longer be the most important way
to tell computers what to do.[1] As computers acquire more
knowledge of what people want them to do, more people can
"program" them. I suspect that programming will cease to be a
major profession, just as mule driving has suffered a decline.
There will always be a few programmers around just as there are
a few chauffeurs, but programming will not be a career one
would recommend to an ambitious young college student.

Flexible machining systems coupled directly to CAD systems
will permit many products to be customized. If someone wants
a car with 1950s style tail fins and can draw the appropriate
contours on a terminal, the machinery should be able to make it
for little more than the cost of a standard car.

Technology Trends

We know how computers work, but they are not intelligent.
Humans are intelligent, but we do not know how to design
better ones.

While AI researchers are trying to make computers intelligent, cognitive scientists and molecular biologists are trying to
figure out how human intelligence works. An intelligent computer could use computerized semiconductor manufacturing
facilities to design more intelligent versions of itself. If we
understood the human genetic code, we might be able to design
smarter humans.

It is anybody's guess which will come first—knowing how to
make humans smarter or knowing how to make computers
smart. Either event promises to make life very interesting.[2]

Computers have already changed our lives beyond recognition, and by-products of AI research will accelerate this process.
Change will accelerate if genuinely intelligent computers are

---

[1] Another way to put this would be to say that human languages will become
capable of talking to computers and computer-specific languages will wither
away. Instead of computers learning natural languages and assuming the total
burden of human-computer dialogues, humans and computers will meet one
another halfway.

[2] "May you live in interesting times" (old Chinese curse). The only worse curse
was, "May your life be exciting." In ancient China, the pace of change was slow
enough that the only exciting events were war, pestilence, famine, earthquake,
and other natural or man-made calamities. Living in interesting times was bad
enough, but if you were lucky, you might be able to experience the excitement
secondhand. Direct experience was worse.

developed. Now is a *very* good time for a technology junkie to be alive.

The only question is whether American or Japanese technologists will end up at the top of the heap. The final chapter draws on my experience living in Japan to explain how the Japanese have been so successful in taking over American markets and explains what businesses must do to compete.

East is East, and West is West,
And never the twain shall meet.
Till earth and sky stand presently
At God's great judgement seat.
　　　　　　—Rudyard Kipling

16
Japan and the Fifth Generation Project

In this chapter, I give a quick overview of Japanese culture and industrial strategy to explain why they work so hard at entering our markets, explain their plans for our computer market, and finally tell how to compete with them.[1] Most writers say that the Japanese are tough competitors because they are group oriented and cooperative by nature, then say that the only way to stay in business is to learn Japanese management methods.

That is nonsense—the Japanese learned most of their management methods from America and are by nature just as selfish, argumentative, and opinionated as Americans. The difference is that the Japanese know that they must work hard and live by their wits. Knowing that cooperation and group solidarity are the keys to economic survival, they designed their education and religious systems to subordinate individualism and promote cooperation.[2]

---

[1] Many of the assertions and illustrations in this chapter are drawn from my experience growing up in Japan. Others are documented in the book *Shadows of the Rising Sun: A Critical View of the Japanese Miracle*, by Jared Taylor (New York: Morrow, 1983).

[2] Designing religious systems to promote social stability is an old tradition in Aisa. Confucian ethics promoted loyalty to the Chinese emperor and the Indian caste system did much to keep the masses in their places.

Japanese success in operating factories in the United States shows that Americans can be as cooperative, industrious, and productive as Japanese if they are managed properly. The Japanese see the government's role as proper management of the nation. The Fifth Generation project was started to find new export markets for the computer industry because existing markets showed signs of saturation. An American board of directors might start a research effort to develop a new product to occupy idle plant capacity under similar circumstances.

Starting the Project

The Japanese made worldwide headlines when they announced the Fifth Generation Computer Project in 1982. The project goal was to solve all the outstanding problems in AI research, then take over the world computer market from IBM.[1] The project was taken seriously by the American media because the Japanese have achieved great success in many American markets.

Even though the Fifth Generation project has not been as successful as its sponsors had hoped, Japanese economic achievements still get a great deal of media attention.[2] The press tells us that the Japanese are coming to own the markets for copiers, semiconductors, automobiles, steel, shipbuilding, machine tools, audio equipment, television, and whatever else they put their minds to. It is seldom noticed that, although they are #2 in computers worldwide, the Japanese have not yet penetrated the American computer market to any significant extent, try though they may.

The Japanese have labored harder to enter the American computer market than to enter our automobile market. It took them at least three major attempts to crack the auto market. The first car introduced in California was a flop. It went 40 miles an hour because Japanese roads were too narrow to drive faster than that. It was too small for Americans to sit in. The Japanese took their lumps, learned from the experience, and tried again.

---

[1] The Japanese followed sound engineering practice and did the easy part first. Taking markets from IBM is not the smoothest path to profit.

[2] The press often gives the impression that Japanese success is due to inscrutable Oriental cheating. Peter Drucker says that Japanese success is due to their doing "better what the West was already doing well" and by being the first nation to have "both the low labor costs of a developing country and the high labor productivity of a developed one." Although it is more palatable to ascribe one's losses to cheating rather than to the fact that the victor may have played better, assigning an incorrect cause to a problem delays the solution.

The second try failed too. When I left Japan to attend MIT in 1963, there were essentially no Japanese cars on our roads. They went from nothing to a US-government-sanctioned 20% market share in 20 years. That's pretty good.

The Japanese are convinced that owning an "appropriate" share of the American computer market is vital to their future well-being and are pursuing it wholeheartedly. The Fifth Generation "national project" was started in 1982 to develop new computer hardware and software to bypass American technology and overcome our lead.

The Japanese use different hardware and different financing; they staff their projects differently and use different programming languages, but their goals are clear: They want computers smart enough to sell in our markets.

Why I Worry

The Japanese are nibbling away at worldwide semiconductor market share. In 1976 American firms had almost 70% of the world market, the Japanese had less than 30%. By 1983 the Americans were below 60% and the Japanese had reached the high 40s, and in 1987 American semiconductor makers demanded government protection.

Over a ten-year period Americans suffered a gradual, steady decline. There were no Pearl Harbors—no massive defeat to wake anyone up. American merchant semiconductor houses died the death of a thousand cuts. Each year brought the loss of another point or two of market share.

Until the recent slowdown in the computer market, the Japanese took semiconductor market share less rapidly than the rate of growth of the market. Integrated circuit companies saw sales increases. Americans are happy when sales go up. Sales increases keep us content because Americans concentrate on quarterly earnings and ignore market share.

But these figures meant death! Eventually the Japanese had more sales, spent more for product development, and overpowered us. It was no surprise that American semiconductor manufacturers had to ask the government for protection. History says that, when market share drops below a certain threshold, sales fall apart overnight.

US Steel was formed in 1901 with 98% of the domestic steel market. Big steel has lost market share in dribbles, drips, and drabs ever since and finally had to plead for protection. They simply could not compete any more.

Chrysler Corporation lost market share slowly over time, then suddenly fell apart. If they had not found a marketing genius like Iacocca to turn them around, they would have been gone. Declining market share is *fatal*, and management must pay close attention to it. As the Bible says:

"Yet a little sleep, a little slumber, a little folding of the hands to sleep: so shall thy poverty come like a robber, and thy want as an armed man."
— Proverbs 6:10-11 and 24:33-34

Facing up to the Japanese

Media hand-wringing about invincible Japanese marketing notwithstanding, it is simple to compete effectively with the Japanese.[1] Winning the marketing battle is simple but not easy. The principles are straightforward, but winning takes so much real *work* that Americans seem to be reluctant to try to win even when we know how.

The Japanese do indeed have some overwhelming strengths. When we compete with them on their strong points, we lose every time. But they have colossal weaknesses to balance their strengths. If we compete where they are weak, we usually win. It takes work but is simple in principle.

Our problem lies with management. We took our eyes off the ball. Neglecting the fundamentals is such an old problem that the Old Testament warned about it 3,000 years ago:

"Be thou diligent to know the state of thy flocks, and look well to thy herds. For riches are not forever: and doth the crown endure to every generation?"
— Proverbs 27:23-24

Lessons from Cultural History

Anthropologists have a theory that people with similar resources facing the same problem will always solve the problem the same way.[2] It is worthwhile to look at a period of history before the Japanese had contact with the West to see if they solve problems the same way Westerners do.

In a low-tech agricultural society unfriendly visitors drop in during famines. Keeping uninvited visitors from coming to

---

[1] *Fortune* magazine (October 26, 1987, pp. 65-72) tells of Bose Corp, a small American company that outsells the Japanese in their domestic *consumer audio* market, of all things!

[2] This theory assumes that ancient people were out of touch with one another and literally reinvented the wheel wherever the wheel appears. Thor Hyerdhal sailed a balsa raft from Peru to Easter Island and a reed raft from Africa to Latin America to prove that technology could have been spread by ancient mariners.

lunch is a serious problem. The available materials are stone, wood, and mud. There is an unlimited supply of unskilled peasants to throw up a fort when they are not growing food. European castles are stone buildings, sometimes with moats.

Feudal society in Japan came up with a different solution. The Japanese built high stone foundations, put wooden buildings on top, and covered them with plaster. Although the major defensive element in both cases is stone, the Japanese realized that they could have the safety of stone without having to live in drafty stone buildings. The same technology and the same problem led to different solutions.

Castles are not the only thing the Japanese do differently. Japanese saws cut on the pull instead of on the push like ours, and they drive on the left side of the road instead of on the right.[1] They also approach earthquakes differently. Our buildings are built strong enough to survive. The Japanese used to build houses that would fall apart without breaking any of the pieces so they could be put back together again easily. Once they learned Western building methods, however, they felt they had the technology to keep buildings up during earthquakes and started building skyscrapers in Tokyo.[2]

Reality in the Computer Market

Strange as it may seem, America is a net *exporter* of labor. Americans do well in products that require almost no labor at all, such as wheat, or labor-intensive products, such as commercial aircraft. We have trouble with medium-labor-content industries such as steel and automobiles.

The Japanese are insignificant players in our computer market. Hitachi, Sony, and Fujitsu have all tried to sell computers in America but have not succeeded. Unfortunately for the Japanese, the computer business is a labor-intensive industry where Americans excel. Although computer hardware can be mass produced, the applications software that makes users want to buy it is hand-crafted, and the Japanese have trouble developing software.

The Japanese ought to be able to gain share in low-cost personal computers, but the market changes too rapidly. The Japanese were about to launch an Apple-compatible product when IBM announced the PC. Bang! Twenty percent of the

---

[1] For all the talk of trade barriers, Detroit might sell more cars in Japan if they put the steering wheel on the right side of the car instead of on the left.

[2] There has not been a major quake since they built the first Tokyo skyscraper. That technology is not known not to work.

market overnight! They started to build an IBM-compatible box
and IBM changed before they got anywhere. Rapid change is the
key to competing with the Japanese. *Do not sit still*. If we keep
moving and outdo our own products before they can, they can
never lay a glove on us.

Why Do the Japanese Do It?

Americans wonder why the Japanese push so hard. Do they
want to own the world? Not really. The Japanese are just trying
to feed their children. Americans live in a land of milk and
honey and find it hard to understand a nation that does not
know where its next meal is coming from.

Japan has half the population of the United States and half of
the pollution crammed onto a group of islands smaller than
California with less farm land and fewer resources. These maps
show Japan and the state of California at about the same scale:

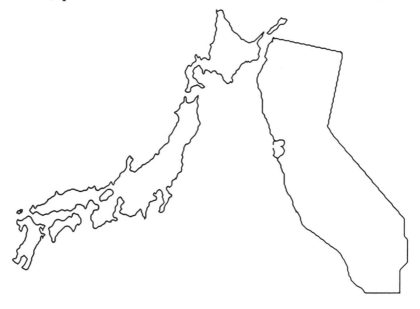

Japan is so small that land prices are astronomical. According
to *The Economist* (October 3, 1987, p. 25), the total market value
of all the land in Japan is about twice the total market value of
all the land in the United States, even though Japan is 1/25 the
size. Japanese geography is as if Appalachia were lifted out of the
eastern United States, split into islands, and dropped into the

Pacific off the eastern coast of the Asian mainland, losing most of the mineral resources along the way.

The Japanese are a teeming multitude with no assets. They have nothing they can dig out of the ground to trade for things to eat. We have the natural resources to do just about anything we want, but they have to live off income.

The Japanese economy is based on added value, not on resource recovery. They import raw materials, do something to them, export the results, and live off the difference. Japan imports about 14% of GNP and exports 15%. Because there are essentially no natural resources in Japan, one way to look at the numbers is to say that the nation of Japan operates on a 1% net margin. That does not give much leeway for mistakes or for relaxing and letting someone else take a market.

Living on income is not always easy. The Japanese were hungry in the late 1940s and remember it well. Our depression was in the 1920s, and by the late 1930s, people quit worrying about starving. The Japanese worried about starving ten years more recently than we, and they worried about it more.

Tokyo had been bombed flat when MacArthur took over Japan in 1945. At their peak American fire bomb raids killed approximately 100,000 Japanese civilians per night in Tokyo with conventional explosives. At that rate the Hispanic population of Chicago would be exterminated in four days, and the white population would last just over two weeks.

After the war, agriculture and industry were "inoperative," to coin a phrase. In late 1945, MacArthur sent a telegram to President Truman saying, "Send me bread or send me bullets." He could either feed the Japanese or shoot them—there was no food in Japan.

The generation that starved after the war is now senior management. The big export houses are run by people who lived through 1940-45. They *personally* experienced starvation. No one can persuade them to deemphasize exports. Exporting has been burnt into their consciousness too deeply.[1]

No chief executive who survived the Tokyo bombing can be deterred by such trivial obstacles as import restrictions and quotas. Having locked up automobiles and steel, the Japanese will come after something else to swap for food. That is fundamental to their being. They want to eat. How do you compete with that?

---

[1] The export imperative is taught early. If you ask any first grader to name the most serious problem facing Japan, you are told "Exports!"

Three Problems: Location, Location, and Location
The national Japanese problem is feeding their children. They
are not interested in trivia like quarterly earnings or gross
margins. They worry about food.

A glance at a globe reveals that on a world scale the Japanese
are thousands of miles from anywhere. They have the longest
supply lines in the world. Nearly 60% of Japanese energy comes
from imported oil, and 55% of the oil comes from the Middle
East through narrow straits that could be closed during any
political crisis.[1] The Pacific, in comparison, is a wide, short,
direct path. They sell to Americans because we live nearby. We
are neighbors.

Japan produces only 0.08% of its domestic energy, maybe 3% or
4% of the wood it needs. Japanese import essentially everything,
so they take exports seriously. Without exports, they starve in
the dark. Between material in the pipeline and stocks in Japan,
they have a ninety-day supply of most things. If exporters quit
paying the bills, civilization would collapse in ninety days.

Crisis is not a bad way to motivate people, and the fact that the
crisis is real and permanent keeps it from losing effectiveness.
The Japanese do not go after our markets just for the sake of
having a market—they want to survive. It does not seem that
way to Americans, but that is how it is. The difference in
viewpoint complicates trade negotiations.

The Japanese buy more protein from the United States than
they produce domestically. In spite of their position as a major
buyer, the Japanese feel that they are the customer of last resort
and the first to be cut off if supplies get tight. President Nixon
halted soybean exports to Japan in 1973 to lower American food
prices. Having been cut off for what they felt were trivial
political reasons, the Japanese regard America as an unreliable
supplier. They buy from us only when there is no alternative.

How Do the Japanese Do It?

How do the Japanese do so well in foreign markets? Merely
wanting something badly is not sufficient. People have to know
how to get it.

The Japanese ignored the rest of the world until Commodore
Perry sailed into Tokyo Bay, said "Open up," and made them an
offer they lacked the military might to refuse. The more
enlightened rulers realized that the only way to avoid being
dismembered as China had been was through military power, so

---

[1] *The Economist* (November 7, 1987, p. 40).

the government started industries. They concentrated on the one fundamental, irreducible social essential—weaponry and armaments to hold off the Western barbarians.[1] They never even considered pursuing butter instead of guns.

Having decided to outdo the Westerners at their own game, the Japanese government encouraged industry in essentially the same way the American government gave away land and imported cheap foreign labor to build the Erie Canal and the transcontinental railroads. The Japanese military-industrial complex did quite well for a while. They defeated the Russians in 1904-1905, then went on to take over a major part of Asia. It was a form of vertical integration to secure raw materials—not unlike Du Pont buying an oil company, but on a somewhat grander scale. While the military was on a roll, of course, there was no stopping them.[2]

Acquiring raw materials by conquest ended abruptly in 1945. In the 1950s, the Japanese took a new approach. Translated literally, the motto was "Steel builds the National House."[3] In the 1950s, they concentrated on steel because steel is a vital component of such things as ships and automobiles. Once steel costs come down, automobile and shipbuilding industries have an advantage in overseas markets. The government encouraged exports to buy raw materials and food peacefully instead of obtaining them by conquest.

Rice Farming
The Japanese are accustomed to overcoming their desires for individuality and working in close-knit groups. Japan was a rice farming nation for two millennia. Rice fields are flooded a few inches deep. There is a lot of work in the spring when farmers plant rice shoots by hand, and there is an enormous amount of

---

[1] This phrase would not be considered sarcastic in Japan. To a Japanese, defending the sacred soil of the homeland is more important than food.

[2] All good things come to an end. Economists say, "A trend is a trend until it bends." As Euripides put it, "Those whom the Gods would destroy, they first make mad with pride." Had the Japanese stopped before Pearl Harbor, they probably could have kept their Asian conquests. They might have overreached themselves by invading China, however. It is not clear that *any* nation can conquer China without exterminating the Chinese, which would have been difficult using the weaponry of 1937.

[3] The word *kokka* has no gender, so it would be improper to refer to Japan as "motherland" or "fatherland." Translating *kokka* as "national house" is a good illustration of the Japanese feeling that they are all members of one large family confronting a hostile world.

work during the fall harvest. All the farmers have to do the rest of the time is keep the dikes in shape and they can eat next year.

Each village has a pond on top of a hill or an intricate network of canals to draw water from a stream. The precious water trickles slowly through each field in turn. If anybody lets a dike leak, the leak grows, drains the water source, and wipes out all the rice. Anybody who goofs off can starve the whole village.

Even today the common idiom for selfish behavior is "Drawing water to one's own rice paddy." The Western question "Am I my brother's keeper?" is not a question in Japan. *Of course* everybody is. Millennia of wresting rice crops from unfriendly mountainsides has ingrained the lesson that a slacker can harm the whole village, so everybody watches everybody else.[1]

What about innovation? If some entrepreneur tries growing rice in a new way and goofs, he kills our fields along with his. Would you let anyone experiment? Nope! We are *all* going to grow rice the way we *know* works. The rice farming mentality is wonderful for mass production because everyone cares about quality, but it tends to retard innovation.

Before modern irrigation the Japanese rice crop failed every five to twenty years. Rice farmers can afford to give up more than the traditional 10% of the crop to anyone with enough power—military, moral, or economic—to hold enough rice to feed them when the crop fails. Japanese castles are really glorified rice storage bins.

Farmers *know* that crop failure is coming. Famine is not one of these "every fifty or hundred-year" things that might not come during a person's lifetime. Japanese workers labor to take care of their employer during good times and the employer plots and schemes to accumulate a surplus to feed the employees during bad times. People do as they are told, and the boss keeps the food coming.

This is the fundamental pattern of Japanese success: a few smart bosses who plan and innovate, and a mass of docile, highly educated workers. The workers have enough intelligence to follow directions and enough sense of conformity to work well together. Japanese public education deliberately stifles individual initiative, but leaders view individual initiative as

---

[1] The idea of collective responsibility was reinforced by the secret police during the 300-year Tokugawa era. If an offender was caught, he and everyone living in his house were punished. People living in the five houses on both sides, directly across the street, and diagonally across the street were also punished because they had not persuaded the offender to behave in a more orderly manner.

disruptive. Both government and business prefer a well trained populace who can follow complicated directions wtihout having to be told more than once.

The Japanese and Government

Japan has only meager social welfare. The old feudal lords and the modern industrial organizations take care of their own people, and the government looks after the nation.

The government freely sacrifices individuals or companies if national security requires it. When an industry contracts, the government helps to decide which facilities will close and who will lose jobs. The Japanese would have let Chrysler go instead of bailing it out. That would have given the industry a good scare, lowered overall wage rates, made the industry more competitive, and made everybody act more reasonably. After all, businesses are always screaming for government help. The only way to be sure they really need help is a big, juicy bankruptcy.[1]

Before the oil crisis Mazda sold a sporty car that got about 10 miles to the gallon. When the oil shock came, Mazda sales went through the floor. The conventional wisdom wrote Mazda off, but the employees saved the company. They went to management and said, "You turkeys! You bet the farm on low-cost oil, and now our kids will starve." Management said, "We're sorry! Should we resign?" They said, "No. We are going to take a pay cut and you are going to bust your tails and get a new model out so we can eat again." The bank said, "If everybody takes a *deep* pay cut and works hard, we will carry Mazda through a redesign." The initiative came from workers who excoriated management for not safeguarding their incomes. The workers led in sacrificing short-term income for tomorrow's meals; they did not ask for government help.

The Employment Contract

Rice farming forces cooperation between workers and builds the foundation for a strong relationship between management and labor. Rice farming helps us understand how Japanese factories work, what lifetime employment is all about, and why the Japanese work so hard.

The company provides food when times get rough. The only way the company can take care of the employees during famine

---

[1] Personal communication from a MITI official. His opinion notwithstanding, letting a major player disappear is not the usual Japanese style. When oil refining, aluminum smelting, shipbuilding, and steel got in trouble, MITI organized cartels that wound down the industry and spread the pain evenly.

is if employees take care of it the rest of the time. That is the basis of the contract between employer and employee. They look out for each other because they know hard times will come.

Heroes

All nations need heroes, even Japan. With the military discredited, the only available heroes are businessmen. They bring home the bacon anyway, so they are a reasonable choice. Not long ago a Japanese bicycle salesman died in the Peruvian Andes. His car got stuck in the snow, but he kept going. He froze to death in a snowdrift, headed toward the customer with his sample case over his shoulder. He gave his life to complete the sales call.

Barrels of ink flowed in Japan. The general tenor of the editorials was, "Well, folks, that's what we mean by a real Japanese. Nothing remarkable—we expect that each and every one of you would do your duty if it became necessary." That might seem funny until you realize *they* don't think it is funny. Those of us who compete with the Japanese know that most of them would.

When I developed software for Nippon Electric (NEC), I traveled to Japan to install our products at the end of each project. NEC's programmers work at rows of desks jammed tightly together. Each desk is about two feet wide and eighteen inches deep. Behind each row of desks is an aisle about eighteen inches wide, and behind the aisle is a bookcase as high as the desk. This arrangement is repeated, row after row after row, filling a building the size of an aircraft hangar. People stay at their desks because it causes so much trouble for other workers when they use the aisle.

I arrived at 7:30 every morning just like everybody else because my hotel was nearby and I had little else to do anyway. I was awed to find that most of the desks were still occupied at eight, nine, even ten o'clock at night.

One evening about 7 P.M., there were only a few hundred scattered bodies still toiling away. Why were there so few people working? Was there a plague? No. Management feels it is unhealthy for people to work twelve hours per day all six days of the week, so they have a rule that everybody has to go home by 6:30 on Thursday evenings. What about all those guys still toiling away? Well, if their project is urgent, they can get permission to stay, but that can be granted only twice a month. Sure enough, there was a guard checking passes to make sure all those workaholics had *permission to stay*.

The 47 *Ronin*

One way to understand a culture is through its mythology. Americans glorify individual heroes. We tell tales of the Lone Ranger Davy Crockett, Paul Bunyan, and Daniel Boone—tall, two-fisted white hats who right wrongs singlehandedly and blast the black hats. We have few tales of group heroism.

The Japanese tell few stories about individuals. Their most famous story is the saga of the 47 *ronin* or masterless *samurai*. There was a young nobleman who had 47 retainers. His late father had aroused the enmity of a teacher of etiquette. Out of spite the teacher taught the young noble incorrect protocol for claiming his title at the imperial court, and the young man duly made a fool of himself. He drew his sword to salvage his honor but was prevented from killing the teacher by alert guards.

Drawing a sword in the imperial palace was impolite—sort of like firing a pistol in the White House. Because of his rank and the circumstances, he was permitted to commit suicide at a nearby temple instead of suffering the disgrace of decapitation. This left his followers without a master. They were now *ronin*.

In group-oriented Japan, to lack a master was the worst fate that could befall an honorable swordsman. The teacher expected them to seek revenge and kept his household alert. The *ronin* scattered and took up dishonorable professions in order to lull suspicion. Their leader even became a drunkard to give the impression that he had forgotten about revenge.

After ten years they got together, surprised the teacher, and cut off his head. They washed the head at the temple where their master had died and set it on his gravestone as if to say, "We got him, boss!" Because vengeance was a capital crime, they all sat down and committed suicide.

The 47 *ronin* embody everything that is virtuous and honorable in Japanese culture, and their gravestones are the combined Washington Monument, Lincoln Memorial, and Iwo Jima Flag Raising of Japan. There is usually incense burning on the graves, put there to soothe the souls of the 47 *ronin*.[1]

---

[1] Whether this story is fact or myth is unimportant. Japanese all know the tale and regard it as exemplary of the highest of social virtues, just as we think of the last stand at the Alamo as the ultimate in heroism. Or perhaps bullheaded stupidity.

In many ways the Alamo story is a tale of group heroism on a par with Japanese mythology. The fact that the Japanese do not think the *ronin* were stupid illustrates a subtle difference in outlook. It is interesting that Americans refer to "Custer's Last Stand" instead of "The Last Stand of the US Cavalry."

What the Japanese Say about Japan

The Japanese say that the job is much more important than the family. The family is a cost center; the job feeds the family.

The Japanese also say that they never innovate and that they are unable to write software. One thing the Japanese may brag about a little is that they can reduce things to practice and follow a market vector pretty well. If a company has a well-defined product and nobody is changing the industry a lot, the Japanese can draw a careful bead on the market and put out a product that overwhelms existing products.

The Japanese excel at changing the rules of the game, which is a form of innovation. When Honda entered the motorcycle market, they ignored the leather jacket fraternity because Harley-Davidson owned them. Instead of big black noisy motorcycles, they sold quiet little white motorbikes. Learning how to manufacture bikes with small, high-revving, high-precision engines developed a technology that turned out to be ideal for the automobile market.

Remember the slogan "You meet the nicest people on a Honda"? Can anyone imagine Harley-Davidson saying that? Honda sold shiploads of low-priced machines. They made a mint of money, poured the profits into automobile factories, and the leather jacket crowd is switching to Japanese bikes. They took so much of the market that Harley asked for tariff protection in order to survive.[1]

Sony did the same thing with radios. RCA once owned the tube radio market. A radio was the size of a bread box and plugged into the wall. Sony introduced a radio in a little battery-powered box about the size of a book that people took to the beach. They wiped out RCA and poured the profits into making television sets. The Japanese changed the definition of the radio just enough to avoid RCA's strengths and flanked RCA instead.

I once gave a lecture at RCA's research lab in New Jersey. A guy came up afterward and said, "You know where the Japanese got the circuit for that radio? From this very lab!" Their people had designed a transistor radio and were *desperate* for management to do something with it. Management said, "No! It will hurt our existing market, and nobody wants a little radio anyway." One day a Japanese delegation came through and said, "Very interesting. May we possibly have the schematic?" My

---

[1] Harley-Davidson found new owners and came roaring back. In addition to regaining American market share, Harley is selling in Japan. One of their recent Japanese ad campaigns featured the headline "We no longer leak oil."

informant said, "I opened one of their radios and there was our circuit. But management was right! Transistor radios *did* kill our market!"

Listen to people who want to replace existing products. It is better to put yourself out of business than to let anyone else do it.

In both cases the Japanese won by changing the rules. They never attack head on; they attack from the side. The Fifth Generation Computer Project (FGCP) is an oblique attack on the computer business.

Why Computers?

The Japanese are interested in computers for all the obvious reasons: Computers are the wave of the future, the intellectual revolution, a source of exports, etc. But there is a more subtle reason, which I heard from a friend who works for the Ministry of International Trade and Industry (MITI). One of MITI's jobs is to promote overseas sales. MITI wanted Japanese companies to go after computers because computers have less pollution per unit of GNP than anything MITI could think of.

Japan lives on value added and must industrialize, but Japan is so crowded that the Japanese are the world's canaries. In the early days many coal miners were killed by methane leaking into the mines. No one knew what killed the miners, but whatever it was, a canary was more sensitive to it than a human. Every miner carried a canary. When anyone's canary keeled over, everybody fled.

The Japanese had the world's worst pollution and people started to die. MITI said, "Oops! Too much industry. What do we do?" The choices were simple—either dial back on industry and starve or go forward and poison themselves. MITI was afraid that pollution technology would not work soon enough or would cost so much that Japanese manufacturers could not stay competitive. The solution was to move pollution offshore and make computers.

MITI wanted to make silicon chips because chip factories do not pollute. They can export the pollution, shifting from low-value dirty industries into clean high tech. It was not that simple, of course. The Japanese now have excellent anti-pollution technology and strict laws, but they originally pushed semiconductors because it costs so much to keep the process pure that the marginal cost of containing pollution is low.

I was shooting the breeze with my MITI friend back in 1973 and he said, "IBM has about a trillion dollars invested world-wide in software for their computers, and we can't do anything with that. Even the Japanese government can't move a trillion dollar investment. What do we do?" I said, "Well, do something else. Do something IBM is not doing. That's what you did with radios; that's what you did with motorcycles; that's what you did with ships. Do it again. You know the formula. Hit 'em where they ain't." He says, "Let's think about that."

We speculated all evening. It would have been nice if we had thought of artificial intelligence, but we did not. Somebody else came up with AI, and AI is the basis for the government-sponsored Fifth Generation research project. The Japanese are trying to change the rules again.

Japanese Research Projects

The Japanese are acutely aware of the difference between research and development, whereas we talk about R&D as though it was one word—"arandee." Research is a careful and diligent search for new facts. Development is the act of making something usable. Japanese businesses cooperate wholeheartedly during research and compete mercilessly during development, manufacturing, and marketing.

When the American government promulgated antipollution regulations for cars, the Japanese government called in their car makers and said, "Those unpredictable Americans just passed some new laws, and we have to live with them." They didn't go whining to Washington trying to change the rules. They said, "This is what the rules are. Now what do we do about it?"

They assessed the auto manufacturers according to market share and put together a project that examined every form of antipollution technology they could think of. Each company then manufactured whatever they thought best. The research for the Honda CVCC engine came from this government program. Honda did not bear any research risk, only development and marketing risks.

The Japanese share research costs and compete in the market as the research is applied. They know when to make war and when to have peace.[1] The Fifth Generation Computer System project is not supposed to put anything on the market. It is a way of sharing the costs of fundamental research so that the participants can develop products on their own.

---

[1] Americans have taken a crack at joint research projects but seem not to be able to pull it off. We have difficulty coercing our waterfowl into collinearity.

Going around IBM

The Fifth Generation project is meant to be different from IBM. The Japanese want 100% of a nothing market. They do not really care what the market is so long as they have 100%. Their experience has taught them that market dominance is the key to long-term success. Market share may not lead to profit right away but eventually makes a great deal of money and keeps factories busy in the meantime.

The Japanese did not make a frontal attack on RCA or Harley-Davidson. They changed the rules. The Japanese cannot match IBM's software, so they plan to go around it. The Fifth Generation project has a mandate to develop new technology.

In 1979 MITI solicited proposals for a new project. Academic folk said, "Let's build a small Dolphin-like computer with an Ethernet connection." MITI turned that down. It had no stretch, no flash, and no boom. They wanted to try something that was not known to be possible. The dreamers said, "Aha, artificial intelligence and multiprocessors!" MITI agreed that would be different.

The AI thrust came from the United States. A Japanese computer expert, Dr. Furukawa, visited Stanford Research Institute in 1976 and took back a listing of a Prolog interpreter. He typed it into a computer in his office and it worked "surprisingly well." This is typical of the international experience that was the basis of the Japanese choice of Prolog for the FGCS.

Other prime movers behind the MITI proposal had worked together at the University of Illinois on the Illiac computer. Illiac was one of the earliest multiprocessors and was the basis for the Fifth Generation multiprocessor hardware. AI problems are inherently parallel, so it should be easier to use multiprocessors to gain speed in AI than in conventional programming. The Japanese hoped that a major breakthrough in parallel processing would lead to a market they could exploit for a while.

Flash and Boom

Up to this point the Fifth Generation proposal sounded fairly reasonable—a high-capacity multiprocessor based on prior Japanese and American work with very large-scale integrated circuits, running an AI language like Prolog. It was here that the major difference between the Fifth Generation and prior computers began to show.

The planners examined the trends in software engineering, database design, and computer architecture and claimed that all these fields were converging on logic programming. Logic programming is what the Japanese call the artificial intelligence software development style that I call data, rules, and goals.

That wowed the world! The planners were claiming that the Fifth Generation project would solve all known problems in software engineering, database design, and computer architecture. They got attention because they were promising the philosopher's stone. People who promise the philosopher's stone usually turn out to be stoned philosophers, however, and the Japanese were no exception.

Kazuhiro Fuchi of the Electrotechnical Laboratory said, "Logic programming is the missing link between knowledge engineering and parallel computer architecture." Expert systems examine all of the rules and facts during each scan. Even though it follows a sequential search path, Prolog looks at all the rules to see which ones are applicable. Some factory computers process an entire program at once. It should be easier to apply multiprocessors to problems that are inherently parallel than to serial problems like accounting.

Although nobody knows how human intelligence works, it is known that our brains process information in parallel. The AI thrust in the Fifth Generation project makes it easier to use multiprocessors.

The Japanese hoped to be early in the market with the next major advance in computer architecture. Multiprocessing is a straightforward way to increase computer capacity, but no one has been able to apply it effectively. AI may make good use of multiprocessors.

AI also differentiates the Fifth Generation from other computers and increases the chances that the Japanese will find new monopolistic markets. That was the plan when Sony introduced the video cassette recorder—no one knew how many they would sell, but they charged monopolistic prices until the Koreans and other Asian countries got their factories running.

Eliminating Programmers
AI has the potential to eliminate professional programmers. Programmers are expensive "beard and sandal" types who work strange hours and give management grief. Everybody hates programmers!

The Japanese feel that they cannot program well. If AI makes computers so easy to use that anyone can "program" them, they will have cleared a major obstacle to increased computer sales. Just suppose, for example, that all that the AI thrust does is increase a computer's vocabulary to the point that it can understand accounting terms. Accounting terminology is not much more complex than the vocabulary in commercial database retrieval packages. The Japanese do not have to extend natural language very far to get major increases in user friendliness, which would be a real breakthrough in man-machine interfaces.

The treasurer would like to say to the computer, "As of next January, we'll use LIFO inventory accounting for our plant in Peoria and FIFO for all other plants," and have the computer do it. Instead, the treasurer writes a memo to the MIS director, who tells the programmers, who spend six months doing it wrong.

That is not a man-machine interface (MMI). That is a man-man-machine interface because the treasurer talks with a man, not a machine. The Fifth Generation may get to true MMI.

That is how the Japanese plan to go around IBM's software. They assume that most treasurers would buy accounting computers they could talk to and write off their investment in standard computers.

Spending Money

In 1981 MITI announced a $200 or $300 million project. That was pure hype. MITI works on annual appropriations like all government agencies, and nobody wrote a check for $300 million. The project was given around $10 million and was promised more later if the results looked good, provided that the political process could provide funding. FGCS has not spent many real dollars relative to the attention they have received.

Americans are spending far more money on AI than the Japanese. The Defense Advanced Research Projects Agency (DARPA) alone is spending almost as much on AI as the entire Japanese government.[1] American efforts run off in all directions. Japanese work is tightly focused and highly organized, which makes it easy for the media to write about it.

That is the Japanese approach—focused research with a quick payback. American newspapers complain because American companies concentrate too much on the short term, but Japanese government research is always short term. We outspend them on space research, but we build flying cameras to take candid

---

[1] DARPA funds defense-related projects with little commercial use. Congress gets annoyed if it looks as if anyone might profit from government research. Until recently, US government research ended up in the public domain, where anyone could exploit it, including the Japanese. Without some form of market protection, businesses are reluctant to invest the money needed to commercialize the research. Most government-funded inventions languish unused.

portraits of planets. The Japanese develop improved communications satellites to sell to us.

Americans concentrate on the very short term in corporate
work and on the very long term in government work. Japanese
businesses and government think in the near term because they
cannot afford to invest for the long term. Japanese may think
about how things will be twenty years hence, but they seldom
back long-term guesses with serious money. They can always
produce better products than Americans can anyway, so why
should they do any fundamental research?

Getting Going

MITI departed from conventional Japanese practice when
organizing the Fifth Generation project—they used a SWAT
team instead of a normal development group. They created a
new organization, the Institute for New Generation Computer
Technology (the Japanese name is abbreviated ICOT) and located
it near the main MITI office. It is near enough to visit, but far
enough that everybody knows that ICOT is a different project.
Isolation makes it hard for conventional thinkers to hurt the
new project.

The staff came from Fujitsu, Hitachi, Nippon Electric (NEC),
Matsushita, Mitsubishi, Toshiba, Oki, and Sharp, which are
familiar names in Japan. These are all big companies with broad
product lines. Fujitsu has the largest share of the Japanese
computer market. Hitachi and Toshiba are consumer electronics
companies, but they make minicomputers and word processors
and are getting into office automation. NEC has 14,000 products
and is #1 in the Japanese personal computer market. Sharp
everybody knows about—they make little musical calculators.
The Fifth Generation participants are heavy computer people.

FGCS is a tightly knit SWAT team chasing a multiprocessor-
based AI computer programmed in Prolog. Americans are a
disorderly mob wandering around the mountains looking for
nuggets. If the Japanese approach is correct, they will arrive first
because they are better organized to climb that one mountain. If
Prolog is not the right language or if their hardware architecture
does not work, we will have commercial AI first because we are
checking out all the mountains.

Work Sites

Some of the work is being done at the Electrotechnical
Laboratory, a governmental lab like SRI or the MIT Lincoln Lab.
The University of Tokyo (Todai) is involved. Todai is the MIT-
Harvard-Stanford of Japan all rolled into one. The Institute for

New Generation Computer Technology was created specially for the project.

ICOT started with about forty researchers, all in their thirties. That was another departure from Japanese practice. Instead of using senior people, they threw in the "busy brights" from the member companies. It was easy for MITI to get money. The hard part was getting bright young engineers.

This may solve the Japanese innovation problem. They said, in effect, "American start-ups are run by guys in their thirties; they make money: We'll try young guys and see what happens." The Japanese I work with in America are as creative as anyone once they break free of their culture, but their creativity ends when they return to Japan. The Japanese are trying to break out of their culture by copying American venture capitalism.

Americans may sneer at the Japanese reputation for thorough and exhaustive copying, but there is something to be said for thoroughness. Americans often bring up an idea, then abandon it untested and go on to another. The Japanese list all the ideas, carry each one as far as necessary to measure its performance, find the weaknesses, and make it better.

Potential Impact

The Fifth Generation is to be the "space shuttle in the world of knowledge." Maybe. The Japanese want something practical—they want the first AI product that people can count on, just as we depend on trucks.

This might be important. Historians say that Greek culture became dominant in the eastern Mediterranean because Greek was easier to learn than Hebrew or Egyptian hieroglyphics. People could learn Greek easily, so Alexander the Great could impose Greek culture on his colonies. The alphabet helped Greek culture win over the other cultures. This had a major impact on the development of Western civilization.

Historians also say that the printing press helped Western culture dominate Chinese culture. The Chinese invented movable-type printing long before Gutenberg, but their ideographs were so difficult to learn that printing was never popular. The power of the press spread Western languages and ideas all over the world. English is the international language of business instead of Japanese because it is easier to learn.

The Japanese are building the Model-T of AI in the hope that people will buy Japanese computers for AI applications. That is practical because personal computers have proved the motto "The sell is in the software, the profit's in the iron."

The Japanese do not care who writes the software for the Fifth Generation computers as long as they make the hardware. By making it easy to write Fifth Generation software, they plan to let software vendors conquer the AI market for them just as software people came through for IBM in the personal computer market.

Where Prolog Fits
Prolog is the primary programming language for the Fifth Generation computer. The Japanese started with a dataflow machine based on VLSI technology. They layered Prolog support on top of that, then built natural-language-based knowledge processing routines in Prolog. A major reason for Prolog is that they feel it will do the job without conflicting with what Americans are doing. If Prolog works, Americans will be behind because we do not have as much experience with Prolog. The Japanese want a new market niche they can dominate.

Hardware Goals
The first goal was a Personal Sequential Inference Machine (PSIM), which provides Prolog tools roughly equivalent to software tools on American Lisp machines, and this seems to have been achieved. The main processor board uses 40-bit words containing 32 bits of data and 8 flag bits that tell what is in the word. The hardware is built around a standard MULTIBUS to make it easy to attach standard peripherals.[1]

A production PSIM was exhibited by Mitsubishi Electronics at the Artificial Intelligence show in 1986. The price was high and it ran at only 40,000 logical inferences per second (LIPS), which is slower than American offerings, but here they come!

The Japanese would like to run ten to fifty times faster in their production Prolog machine, but that is far more difficult. One of the major problems is enhancing Prolog so that a Prolog program can be run effectively on many different processors at once, which is why the first PSIM has only one processor. Even though most AI problems are inherently parallel, the Japanese have not figured out how to refine Prolog so that Prolog programs will run efficiently in a multiprocessor architecture.

The Japanese know about prior work on running Fortran programs in parallel, but Prolog is different enough that most of the lessons are not applicable. The Japanese may have to change

---

[1] The hardware architecture is similar to the Symbolics 3600 Lisp machine. Most of the differences are in software.

the definition of the Prolog language in order to run Prolog programs in parallel.

ICOT is working on extensions to Prolog and on new hardware architectures, hoping that the two efforts will converge on a big box full of cheap microprocessors that run circles around anything built anywhere else.

Supercomputers

All the talk about artificial intelligence and Prolog should not blind anyone to the Japanese supercomputer goals. A megaflop is 1 million floating point arithmetic operations per second, and they want to build computers that are capable of 1,000 to 10,000 megaflops. This requires new integrated circuits with as many as 10 million transistors per chip, as opposed to the half million transistors in today's chips.

The designers want to achieve at least 1 billion bytes of memory, and would prefer 100 billion. That is about 3,000 times the memory and 70 times the speed of the current product of Cray Research, the leading American producer of high-speed computers.[1] There are economic reasons to offer as much memory as possible—it is anticommercial to limit the money a customer can spend on a product. By loading up computers with high-margin memory, the Japanese expect to boost profits.[2]

Software Goals

The planners want a 10,000-word natural language vocabulary with 99% accurate syntactic analysis. A major goal is to have computers translate technical papers from English to Japanese in order to make it easier to transfer technology to Japan.

The translation project is one area that is expected to lead to something practical. ICOT hopes to develop a computer system incorporating automatic translation between English and Japanese coupled with a comprehensive word processor. The British have started a joint development program with ICOT to concentrate on language translation.

---

[1] The title for the world's fastest computer tends to move around a lot. It is hard to measure speed because applications differ so much. If someone argued that another computer is faster than a Cray, it would be hard to refute the assertion.

[2] MacDonald's is said to break even on hamburgers and make its profit on side dishes such as French fries because they are less price sensitive. Memory boards are like French fries. Memory chips are a low-margin commodity, but stuffing low-margin memory chips into supercomputer boards makes them unique. Selling add-on memory boards for supercomputers yields high margins.

ICOT would like to be able to recognize 50,000 spoken words. That is more than enough for automatic typing because a 2,000- or 3,000-word vocabulary suffices for most business dictation. They want to store and retrieve 10,000 images with 1,024 by 1,024 color points each. The goal is to be able to deal with graphics images just as current languages deal with numbers.

Nobody knows how to do this. Having started, they will proceed and see where they get. Kazuhiro Fuchi is in charge of ICOT, and he admits the goals are "ambitious." As the body builders say, "No pain, no gain."

Impact of Artificial Intelligence

AI gives the Japanese a shot at a new market that they might have all to themselves for a while. Nobody knows how big the market is, of course. That is the nature of untried markets—by the time upper management can see that there is a market, engineers are forced to come from behind.

Making an investment in an area where our large firms have not yet staked out market shares may lead to new business. If the business is really new, the Japanese will have fewer political problems—nobody complained when they ended up owning the video cassette recorder market because there were no American VCR makers to protest.

Current Status

Progress during the first several years was disappointing; funding has been cut, and some of the goals are being scaled back. The American AI community feels that using Prolog cost the Japanese several years of lost time, and they will have to switch to Lisp to get anywhere at all. On the other hand, the Japanese have a Prolog machine on the market, and they have developed several parallel computers. The race is far from over.

What to Do about Japanese Competition

The Japanese have told us how they plan to eat our lunch this time. They not only told us how they plan to take our market, they invited us to help. MITI's track record in government-industry cooperation is superb: steel, low-priced ships, low-priced automobiles, VLSI, etc. Ambitious as the goals are, I would not recommend that anyone bet against them.[1]

---

[1] "The race is not always to the swift nor the battle to the strong, but that's the way to bet." — Damon Runyon

In order to find out how to fight this, just ask an expert:

Never wait for the Japanese to attack you.   —Gen. Douglas MacArthur

MacArthur meant that the Japanese are the world's best planners and executors. Give them time to plan and they can wipe anyone out, but they cannot improvise quickly. The solution is to mix things up, run all over the place, attack them where they do not expect you, and get them off balance so they cannot respond effectively.

That is what MacArthur did with his island hopping campaign in the Pacific. The Japanese built a wonderful fort at Rabaul, which is a bit north of New Guinea. They lovingly laid out machine-gun emplacements and precalculated fields of fire so that they could give MacArthur a hard time when he dropped by. *He never came!* He leapfrogged up the islands toward Japan, cut off their supplies, and they starved. He never went near Rabaul. Those troops spent the war sitting there waiting for him, and he never came.

MacArthur's lesson is easy to apply to economic conflict.

Don't Whine

First of all, don't whine! *Don't whine!* US Steel says, "Oh, it's so sad! The Japanese buy iron ore from us and ship it all the way over there, process it and ship it back and undercut us. They've got to be cheating! How could they possibly beat good old Yankee ingenuity without cheating?" US Steel went to the government and erected a trade barrier.

Just because US Steel cannot get on base does not mean we should shorten the base paths. Government protection may improve financial results in the short run, but it bankrupts customers and destroys markets in the long run.

What happens when US Steel forces up the price of steel? What does that do to GM, their best customer? GM says, "We can't make money on little cars; we're going to buy them overseas." Once they start manufacturing overseas, US Steel and the United Auto Workers will never get the business back even if they give labor and steel away. Semiconductor firms are making the same mistake—raising component prices harms their customers. Market restraint looks good in the short term, but in the long term it is death, just like rent control in a city.

When tenants complain, the mayor has two choices: revise the building codes and beat up the construction unions to get costs down and make the city an attractive place to build residential housing, which will make apartment rents drop, or enact rent control. Rent control has the same effect in the short run—it keeps apartment prices down. But rent control kills a city in forty years because nobody wants to build.

The South Bronx has been burned out, one building at a time. The Bronx has burned as flat as Berlin during World War II. Berlin rose from the ashes because it was in people's economic interest to rebuild, but the South Bronx will never rise again. If we force prices above world prices, we drive customers overseas and never get the business back. That is death!

Blaming unions is another cop-out. What if labor costs too much and work rules are too restrictive to compete? It is unreasonable to blame unions for asking for seniority and work rules that make their lives more comfortable—asking for more is their job. If we give away the store and pass excessive costs on to our customers, it is our fault when the Japanese undercut us and take away the market. If we are unable to convince our people that we are all sucking on the same straw, we have only ourselves to blame when the glass runs dry.

Razzle Dazzle

I played high school basketball against Japanese teams. They used a tight zone defense and practiced until their sneakers wore out. Playing against them was tough!

We had about a 6-inch per man height advantage and thought we had some wonderful plays, but the Japanese rehearsed all the moves in the book and picked us apart. A man-to-man defense helped but not enough.

We finally learned that the best attack plan was no plan at all. We ran around waving our hands, and they could not adapt. They beat us if we played by the book but could not handle razzle dazzle street ball. Our disorganized offense was less efficient than the plays in the book but worked better against the Japanese because they could not handle changes. Some innovative companies know this and act like the Harlem Globetrotters.

Why haven't the Japanese taken over the personal computer market? They cannot get set for it. They start thinking about Radio Shack, and Apple dominates the market. They are about to attack Apple, and IBM comes along. They are about to build an IBM compatible and something new appears. IBM is having problems with the Taiwanese and Koreans, but the Japanese have not been able to enter the personal computer market. That is how to protect markets—keep rolling out new products.

Remember Gentleman Jim Corbett, the boxer who defeated John L. Sullivan? Sullivan was a slugger. He got up against his opponent and traded punches until the better fighter won. Corbett was much smaller, and no one thought he would last against Sullivan. He won by dodging out of the way and keeping Sullivan from landing punches. He could not hit hard enough to put Sullivan away quickly, but he finally wore him down.

The Japanese slug better than we do. When we stand toe-to-toe and trade punches, down we go. But we dance better. Imitate Muhammad Ali. "Float like a butterfly, sting like a bee." Step up the pace of innovation and shorten product life cycles because long market cycles give competitors time to plan.

Compete with our own products. Keep many new projects in the works at the same time. Increase turbulence to keep the Japanese out. It is a management challenge to handle turbulent markets, but Americans outdo the Japanese in white water.

A Case Study
I have friends who make widgets. They licensed their technology to Japan, and the license restrictions ran out. Our friends were invited over to see the ultramodern factory the Japanese had built—fully automatic, no labor, triples the world's widget supply overnight.

Everyone's knees were shaking. The instinctive response was to try to cut costs and make widgets cheaper. That was the wrong approach because the best my friends could do was equal the Japanese. Americans lose playing their game their way.

Then someone started thinking, "How much money have they spent on that plant? A lot! What's the biggest widget they can build? What kinds of widgets can't they build? Can they use exotic materials? Can they make square widgets?"

My friends developed a more powerful widget and educated customers to use it. That moved the market so that the new Japanese factory was less valuable. If enough customers design the new widget into their products, the Japanese will have to build a whole new plant for the new market.

That is the way to outdo the Japanese. Americans should not copy Japanese culture. None of us wants to work as hard as they do. We have to keep them out of our markets by changing the rules too fast for them to follow.

Hit 'Em Where They Ain't
We are here, the Japanese are in Tokyo. Yes, they have the best market research money can buy. They hire top consultants to help them find market niches, but they miss many niches because they are too far away, and they are not Americans. They do not really understand our culture much better than we understand theirs.

It is as difficult for Japanese exporters to learn English and to understand America as it is for American exporters to learn Japanese and understand Japan. We are local and can talk to our customers. We can find out what their needs are and build what our customers want before the Japanese can.

We ought to be able to do that better from here than they can from Tokyo! Hit them where they're not. Do things the Japanese are not doing. Any company, no matter how small, if it concentrates narrowly enough, can apply more resources to some problem than anybody else in the world. Pick what nobody else is doing. Go after little nichey user groups and create different products for each market. If we give Japanese access to mammoth markets, they can beat us. Break it up into little markets, specialized areas that are so narrow that the Japanese cannot see them, and they will leave us alone.

Be Kind to Your Factory

Be nice to manufacturing people—the Japanese are. Any firm, like Gaul, is divided into three parts: marketing, manufacturing, and engineering.[1] Design engineers lord it over production engineers, but this makes no economic sense.

The factory has most of the firm's capital. Designers have a few toys to keep them happy, and there may be an occasional word processor in the East Overshoe sales office, but 70% of capital is tied up in production equipment, work in process, and accounts receivable—that is where the bucks are.

What happens if there is a total breakdown in the factory? The firm is out of business when the finished goods inventory is shipped. If the sales force breaks, we die when we ship the backlog, which takes longer than draining finished goods. What happens if engineering dies? If we flog the sales force and cut production costs, customers may not notice for a year or two.

The factory is not only where most of the money is, it is the shortest path to bankruptcy. Why not treat manufacturing with a little respect?

The Japanese figure any turkey can build something once, but it takes real *brains* to grind out 10,000 absolutely identical units per month cheaply and cut costs by 10% per year compounded. Japanese engineers start in the plant. If they can't cut it there, they flunk out and transfer to product design.

Americans used to be able to crank it out. Remember Liberty ships? Ninety days from keel to launch. What happened to the

---

[1] Or to put it classically, "Omnia factoria in tres partes divisa est: marketeus, manufacereus, et engineereus."

Arsenal of Democracy? We let design engineers lord it over manufacturing engineers while the Japanese sneaked by us by concentrating on fundamentals. As Vince Lombardi said, "If you block and tackle better than the other team, you will probably win."

Factory workers rent their bodies at so much per hour. They would be overjoyed to throw in their brains free if management would let them. Shutting people's minds out of their work costs us their allegiance. Mazda's workers saved the firm using their minds as well as their bodies. Arranging things so employees can think on the job is management's responsibility.

Put Yourself out of Business
Businesses need to cannibalize their own markets with new products—doing it themselves is better than letting somebody else do it. Product lifetimes are less than they used to be, but that benefits Americans. It takes about two years after the Japanese notice our market until they have a super-tuned-up whiz-bang, 8-cylinder automatic factory ready to wipe us out. Since their cycle is two years, we should roll out a new product every year or eighteen months. The product development cycle is longer than eighteen months, so we must overlap product development cycles and layer products like shingles.

That is a great deal of work. It is difficult to manage a number of unrelated things at the same time. We drove our basketball coach nuts because we did crazy things, but it was effective. Coping with chaos is never easy but we had better learn because the Japanese can cope with order better than we can.

Toward the end of William Manchester's *The Arms of Krupp*, a Krupp in-law was sitting in Krupp castle. Over the hill came this magnificent equipment, wave after wave of armored personnel carriers and tanks and trucks, as far as the eye could see. And it's run by a bunch of dirty, scruffy, bearded rats. This ragtag bunch beat the Wehrmacht?

The Germans built a wonderful Mercedes truck and fixed it if it broke. We built a cheap Chrysler, Ford, or GM truck, and when it broke, shoved it aside and rolled up a spare.

War is inherently disorganized. The Japanese and Germans are better organized than we are, but once war starts, organization breaks down. We are disorganized to begin with because disorganization is our natural state. We have an advantage if we mix it up and never let them get organized. Put up a smoke screen, all kinds of fizz and flash, new stuff that isn't real, fake products. Keep them guessing.

Carry the Battle to the Enemy

Remember the Vietnam War? Remember the stink about how the other side would go to Cambodia for R&R, then come back and attack us? We beat them up and they just go back and rest again? If the Japanese have a secure market in Japan, they can say, "Oh hey, we are a few bucks ahead, let's go attack the Americans." So what if they get flung back? Eventually a little bit sticks, and we lose another point of market share.

When battles are always fought on our territory, we lose, even if we think we win. Carry the battle to Japan. Never concede them a safe refuge for R&R between attacks on us. We lose unless we fight on their home grounds.

Keep Your Eye on the Ball

American executives worry about trivia like profit margins and bonuses for the next quarter, and workers do not worry about much beyond the next paycheck. Japanese employees worry about feeding their children and their children's children. The Japanese would rather do business at no profit than not do business at all because they can at least eat. If they keep the business long enough, they eventually figure out how to make a profit and can build market channels, name recognition, and experienced staff in the meantime.

Japanese companies are satisfied with profit margins that would distress an American chief executive. They play for market share, not stock price.

During the feudal wars, victorious Japanese clans annihilated the losers from the youngest female infant to the oldest grandmother in order to prevent future trouble. They play for keeps. We act like business is a game. We are playing football. They are playing war.

Never Quit

This is the real key. Never quit! So many companies have gone into Japan, lost money for a few years, then slunk back whining, "We can't penetrate it. It's not fair. Their distribution channels are crazy—designed to frustrate foreigners!" Japanese companies deal with Japanese distribution channels quite effectively, and they had to learn to deal with ours. They paid the dues to get into our club. We whine and complain and want to join their club without paying any dues.

By Japanese standards Americans are chronic quitters. Japanese soldiers were coming out of the jungles all through the 1960s. The last soldier on active duty for the Japanese military was a man named Onoda who came out of the Philippine jungles in 1974. As his outfit was pulling back to Japan in 1945, Onoda was told to defend the Philippines against the enemy, and he did. He was *at war* for 29 years, *all by himself*. He simply would not quit. A tourist came to the Philippines, tracked him down, told him the war was over, and suggested that he go home. Onoda said he knew the war was over, but he had orders to stay and he was staying. The Japanese flew an officer out who handed Onoda a written order from the Emperor, and he came home, got a job, got married, and settled down. They never quit!

Why did World War II in the Pacific end? Why did the Japanese surrender? Before the war started we demanded that Japan get out of Manchuria. Once the war got going, we changed our minds and demanded unconditional surrender. Nobody can surrender when they are convinced their emperor is divine. There was no way they could accept unconditional surrender.

When the surrender finally came about, there was *one* condition—the Emperor would not be harmed. When the Emperor said, "The war in the Pacific has not necessarily progressed to our advantage," they laid down their arms and kept their honor. Had we not done the deal, they would have fought to the last person—not just man—but person. They were making bamboo spears to defend their sacred soil to the very last. They never quit. By their standards, we are fainthearted quitters.

Remember the bicycle salesman who froze to death making a sales call? They never quit! Don't quit either!

The Real Battle

The Japanese realize that information processing technology is the next major growth market. Traditional industries such as steel, automobiles, and home appliances have leveled off—how many automobiles can a society drive, anyway?

There seems to be no limit to the amount of information a society can process. One reason for the 1986-87 slowdown in computer sales is that there is not much more that computers can do that people want to pay for.

Most computers are sold for electronic data processing. This is essentially order processing and financial record keeping. Once all the world's finances are reported on and all the transactions are processed, there is nothing more for computers to do.

The underlying price of the semiconductors that do the computing is dropping at a steady 20% per year, compounded. The IBM AT personal computer has 100 times the compute power at *one-fiftieth* the cost of IBM's 1401 mainframe when it was first manufactured in 1959.

If the costs in an industry are dropping fast and customers are running out of ways to use the product, what do we do ?

Limitations on the number of users have caused economic troubles in the past. Mercedes did a market survey in the late 1880s and found that the major limitation on automobile sales would be the availability of trained chauffeurs. The survey was entirely correct. Mercedes did not realize that tubeless tires, the automatic spark advance, and the electric starter would turn the entire adult population into chauffeurs.

AT&T realized in the early 1900s that if telephone use kept growing, half the population of the United States would become telephone operators by the mid-1940s. That prediction also came true—with automatic dialing we put through our own calls, so we are all telephone operators.

Lack of software limits computer sales. If artificial intelligence makes computers so easy to use that anyone can tell them what to do, we will all be programmers. If anyone can use a computer, the theory is that we can sell a few more. That is why the Japanese are investing so much in AI. They hope it will lead to new markets.

Markets and Technology

The best way to keep the Japanese out of present markets and win a piece of future markets is with new products. The best way to develop new products is to use new technology to make existing products better. Many firms are exploring AI and plan to use it if it shows promise; others are hesitating because they are afraid AI costs too much. Doing an AI project is expensive, of course, but just exploring the technology can be quite cheap.

American firms seem relatively uninterested in planning the technology foundations for future products. At the rate at which the Japanese are introducing new products based on American technical innovations, we may soon have no future in high technology at all.

Greater than the tread of mighty armies
is an idea whose time has come.
— Victor Hugo

Bibliography

Explaining AI helps make sense of it, but it is also worthwhile to
help people get *moving* in AI. An ounce of experiment is worth
a pound of analysis, especially with something as new and
complex. Magellan's trip around the world did more to prove it
was spherical than all the mapmakers who wrote, "Here be
Dragons" on the parts they knew nothing about.

Everybody in AI is milling around trying to be first through
the gate. Because nobody knows exactly where the gate is, we
need to launch a great deal of exploratory activity and hope that
something will turn up.

These references will help you learn more about AI.
Although books on the philosophy and management of
innovation may seem irrelevant to a technology such as AI,
experience trying to introduce AI into corporate cultures shows
that technological innovation is as much a cultural problem as a
technical problem. Knowing some of the cultural problems in
advance helps prevent trouble.

The opinions about books are my own. As Mark Twain said,
"Any fool can have the facts, but having opinions is an art."

Artificial Intelligence Directories

So much is happening in AI that no one person can cover it all. These source books help find background information for an AI project.

Source Book on Artificial Intelligence (Amherst, N.H.: Graeme Publishing, published quarterly).

AI is growing too fast to list all the vendors in a book that attempts to do anything else. This directory describes the AI activities of several hundred companies in America and Europe and sorts them by application and product. There are over 300 citations in the bibliography.

Catalog of Artificial Intelligence Tools, Alan Bundy, ed. (New York: Springer-Verlag, 1984).

The book contains a long list of AI software packages, most of which are available from universities at nominal charge. Getting software from universities is a way to give a project a quick start but may not be ideal if results are needed quickly. Free software is often worth what it costs.

A Dose of Realism

These books are less optimistic about AI than some.

The Cognitive Computer, by Roger C. Schank (Reading, Mass.: Addison-Wesley, 1984).

This book earned Schank considerable criticism from his academic colleagues. It seems to be dirty pool to write a book that nonacademics can understand and that admits there are flaws in some of the latest theories. This book is an extremely well-written introduction to where AI is with respect to offering intelligent computers and why AI is worth studying. It speculates on what kinds of societal changes might result when intelligent computers become widely available. There is essentially no technical content in the book. Schank starts from how people think and shows how little computers can do by comparison.

Artificial Intelligence: A Personal Commonsense Journey, by William R. Arnold and John S. Bowie (Englewood Cliffs, N.J.: Prentice-Hall, 1986).

This is a discussion of AI for people who are not computer experts. It gives some of the history of Lisp and early AI research, discusses current status of AI research, and suggests ways to use AI commercially. The book adopts a technical point of view and introduces Lisp and Prolog programming. This makes it useful for people who need at least some technical knowledge of how AI and AI projects work. There is more discussion of social implications than a pure technologist would want, but the issues raised may interest some readers.

Philosophy of Innovation

These references provide background about entrepreneurs and the cultural effects of innovation. Innovation is usually extremely disruptive. As Walter Bagehot put it, "One of the greatest pains to human nature is the pain of a new idea."

The Sources of Invention, by John Jewkes, David Sawers, and Richard Stillerman (New York: Norton Library, 1958).

People who do not believe what I said about AI culture and management should read this book. It gives histories of sixty major inventions. Case studies such as the Wankel engine, xerography, nylon, jet engines, the automatic transmission, power steering, ballpoint pens, and DDT show that most inventions are made at the wrong time by the wrong people working in the wrong organizations.

Even when inventions are credited to corporations, the authors trace the roots of innovation to one person or to a small team who sacrificed everything for the project. One quote should suffice: "Their success is that of an ill-equipped and fanatical horde storming positions before which nine-tenths of the attackers perish while the tenth that wins through is generally robbed of the fruits of victory. But it would be wrong to attribute the success of those who survive to pure chance, to the fact that numbers must triumph. The fanatical enthusiasm is the output of a creative drive, the success is the result of certain essential elements of character" (p. 71).

Introducing Production Innovation into an Organization, by Dorothy Leonard-Barton (Cambridge, Mass: Center for Information Systems Research, MIT, 1983).

This case study tracks the introduction of structured programming methods for software development in a large organization. The author models some of the cultural and organizational factors that affect the ways in which the innovation was adopted or not adopted in various parts of the organization.

Innovation and Entrepreneurship: Practice and Principles, by Peter F. Drucker (New York: Perennial Library, 1986).

Drucker believes that principles of sound business management can be applied to innovative projects as much as to other tasks. He shows how many inventive firms destroy themselves by neglecting lessons from management and argues that management can be applied to the process of innovation itself. This view is contradicted by the book *Breakthroughs!*.

Breakthroughs! by P. R. Nyak and John Ketteringham (New York: Rawson, 1987).

The authors argue that there are no rules for successful business innovation, in contrast to Dr. Drucker. The book fails to find a common factor in a number of successful innovations ranging from 3M's Post-it notes to Federal Express to Toyota's just in time inventory management system.

Intrapreneuring, by Gifford Pinchot, III (New York: Perennial Library, 1987).

Written for the potential intrapreneur, it explains how to conduct entrepreneurial projects from inside a large organization. The basic thesis is that it is not necessary for an innovative person to leave a large corporation in order to be permitted to do something new. The failure rate of new firms is high. It is safer but less lucrative to innovate from inside an existing organization if possible.

Philosophy of Artificial Intelligence

These references provide general background on genuine intelligence. They are written from the viewpoint that AI should emulate human intelligence, and since computers do not do that, AI is essentially a failure. Whether you accept that view or not, knowing a bit about how the mind seems to work may be helpful, particularly if you ever have to defend a project against detractors who claim, "That isn't AI."

The Sciences of the Artificial, H. A. Simon (Cambridge, Mass.: MIT Press, 1969).

Simon explores genuine intelligence in an effort to scope the task of emulating it, reviews what is known of how the mind functions, and describes some of the experiments that tell us what we think we know. Although this book falls within the popular definition of AI, I think of it as a primer on cognitive science. For further thoughts on how the human mind works, see also "Expert and Novice Performance in Solving Problems in Physics," *Science* (1980) 208:1335-1342.

The Architecture of Cognition, by John Anderson (Cambridge, Mass.: Harvard University Press, 1983).

Anderson presents a unified theory of human cognition, and discusses knowledge representation, memory, learning, control of thought, and language acquisition among other topics. *Sciences of the Artificial* is a cognitive science primer; this is a more advanced text.

The Amazing Brain, by R Ornstein and R. Thompson (Boston, Mass.: Houghton-Mifflin, 1984).

This is a superb, lavishly illustrated explanation of what is known or theorized about how the brain works. The explanations are easy to understand, and the pictures show how the different parts of the brain are related to one another. The diagram showing how human vision works is worth the price by itself.

Academic Artificial Intelligence

These books go more deeply into some of the programming techniques developed by AI research than would fit in the book.

The Thinking Computer: Mind inside Matter, by Bertram Raphael (San Fransisco, Calif.: Freeman, 1976).

Raphael makes up in clarity what he lacks in currency. Not much has happened in AI ideas since 1976 except that expert systems are better known. If you read only one other AI book, read this—it is easy and short.

Artificial Intelligence, by P. H. Winston (Reading, Mass.: Addison-Wesley, 1979).

This book is a first class introduction to AI ideas and to the Lisp programs that go with them. It discusses common myths about AI. The first half has no programming and introduces natural language, vision, expert systems, commonsense reasoning, symbolic constraints, and search. The second half develops AI ideas through Lisp code. This is a lucid way to meet AI and Lisp at the same time. It is a technical book, but anyone with a mind for logic can grasp it, especially the first half.

Artificial Intelligence: An MIT Perspective, 2 volumes, edited by P.H. Winston and R.H. Brown (Cambridge, Mass.: MIT Press, 1979).

These volumes are a collection of papers about work at MIT AI Lab. Most of the work was sponsored by DARPA. The papers are considerably abridged. As the editors say, "The selections describe what can be done, but not much about how." Volume 1 discusses expert problem solving, natural language, intelligent computer coaches, representation, and learning. Volume II covers vision, robot manipulation, computer design, and symbol manipulation.

Computer Power and Human Reason: From Judgement to Calculation, by Joseph Weizenbaum, (New York: Freeman, 1976).

Weizenbaum tells what computers can do and what they cannot yet do. He covers natural language and expert systems. There are no charts or programs and minimal computerese.

Artificial Intelligence: Promise and Performance, by Alain Bonnet (Englewood Cliffs, N.J.: Prentice Hall, 1985).

Bonnet teaches at l'Ecole Nationale Superieure des Telecommunications in Paris. His European perspective gives him a different point of view from American authors. The main sections of the book describe natural language and speech understanding projects followed by a discussion of various ways of representing knowledge in a computer. The last sections deal with expert systems and speculations about the future. There is minimal computerese, so it is hard to figure out how the language-understanding programs or knowledge-representation methods described in the book could be implemented in a real project. The book discusses many past natural language and expert system projects.

Problem Solving Methods in Artificial Intelligence, by Nils J. Nilsson (New York: McGraw-Hill, 1971).

This is a somewhat dated compendium of methods worked out in prior years by AI researchers. Nilsson gives some of the mathematical background behind rule interpreters in expert systems.

Inside Computer Understanding, by Roger C. Schank and Christopher K. Riesbeck (Hillsdale, N.J.: Erlbaum, 1981).

Schank and Riesbeck describe five different programs that deal with different aspects of natural language understanding. Documented code is included, along with an introduction to the Lisp dialect used in the programs. The book is an interesting illustration of various approaches to natural language. Working through the programs will benefit people who are interested in natural language, but the programs deal with relatively limited domains and vocabularies.

Conceptual Structures: Information Processing in Mind and Machine, by J. F. Sowa (Reading, Mass.: Addison-Wesley, 1984).

This book starts out reviewing what is known of cognitive science and then applies cognitive theory to linguistics and knowledge engineering.

NETL: A System for Representing and Using Real-World Knowledge, by Scott Fahlman (Cambridge, Mass.: MIT Press, 1979).

Fahlman describes a method for representing ideas in terms of networks of concepts. He draws analogies between the network language and what is known of how the human mind works and gives implementation details of hardware that might be able to associate facts and meanings. NETL bears no resemblance to Lisp or to conventional programming languages and is a good source of things to think about.

Commercial Artificial Intelligence

These books discuss AI from the commercial perspective.

Artificial Intelligence in Business, Science, and Industry, 2 volumes, by Wendy Rauch-Hindin (Englewood Cliffs, N.J.: Prentice-Hall, 1986).

This two-volume series is a comprehensive treatment of many commercial uses of AI but is expensive and superficial. Volume 1 introduces AI, discusses expert systems, expert system development tools, and natural language understanding. Volume 2 discusses the use of expert systems in industry, finance, and medicine and introduces computer vision. That is too much for only 600 pages, which is why the books are superficial.

Artificial Intelligence Enters the Marketplace, by Larry Harris and D. B. Davis (New York: Bantam Books, 1986).

This book is a quick overview of the commercial possibilities of AI as seen by the founder of Artificial Intelligence Corp. Because Larry Harris was one of the first entrepreneurs to actually make a profit on AI, his viewpoint must be respected. See also *Expert Systems* by P. Harmon and D. King in the section on expert systems.

Getting Started in Lisp

Anyone with a technical background or serious interest in Lisp should start with Winston's AI book to get a running start before studying *Lisp*, by P. Winston and B. Horn. Less technical people should start with Greenburg's notes or Touretzky's book. Experienced technocrats who need to use Lisp for AI projects *could* go directly to Charniac, Allen, or Abelson and Sussman, but that would be jumping off the deep end.

No computer professional's education is complete without absorbing Abelson and Sussman. It would be reasonable to start there and retreat to the other books only if necessary.

Notes on the Programming Language Lisp, by B. Greenburg (Cambridge, Mass.: Student Information Processing Board, MIT, 1986).

This is the notes for a quick Lisp course taught at MIT between academic terms. The notes take an extremely pragmatic view of Lisp. They make an effective introduction or supplement to other books. Write SIPB at MIT for the notes. SIPB is staffed by volunteers, so be patient.

Lisp: A Gentle Introduction, by D. Touretzky (New York: Harper & Row, 1984).

This is an excellent slow introduction to Lisp. It makes minimal demands on the IQ, and the diagrams clarified details that had given me trouble. As always, we get no more than we pay for. The book is so gentle that absorbing it will not equip anyone to do serious Lisp programming. I recommend it as an easy head start before tackling another book.

LISP, by P. Winston and B. Horn (Reading, Mass.: Addison-Wesley, 1981).

This book reads like an expanded version of the second half of Winston's AI book. It is about programming instead of AI and goes deeply into detail. The second half is rich in examples, some of which draw on elementary AI ideas. The answers to problems are included, making it good for self-study. It tells how to implement a simple object-oriented programming system.

Common Lisp Reference Manual, by Guy L. Steele, Jr. (Bedford, Mass.: Digital Press, 1984). Shipped with Gold Hill Common Lisp.

Guy Steele was the major driving force behind the Common Lisp standard. Common Lisp is a successor to ZetaLisp, which grew out of MacLisp. The standard has been endorsed by the Defense Department, which concedes that they may have to accept programs written in Common Lisp when Ada will not do. The book is not a tutorial but is unusually rich in examples— Steele explained most of the important design decisions.

Introduction to Artificial Intelligence, by E. Charniac and D. McDermott (Reading, Mass.: Addison-Wesley, 1986).

This book teaches hard-core AI and Lisp programming in one step. Engineers should understand this material before spending too much money on AI, but the pace is heavy for people coming on AI and Lisp at the same time. I recommend going through *LISP* before tackling this, and preferably both Winston's AI book and *LISP*. Do not neglect Charniac; it contains working code, and some of the code is extremely clever. You may suffer a bit but will be a better person for it. Charniac has many exercises, but answers are not given.

Anatomy of Lisp, by John Allen (New York: McGraw Hill, 1978).

Allen teaches Lisp by explaining how Lisp works. The book tells how Lisp evaluates functions and discusses Lisp editors, debuggers, and compilers. Vendors offering Lisp or applications written in Lisp will want to understand this book. For people who just want to write code, the others will suffice. I think knowing how things work helps engineers use them better, but *de gustibus non disputandum est*. Unfortunately, Allen used a typesetter with many different fonts. The book is notation happy, which made it a bit confusing.

Structure and Interpretation of Computer Programs, by H. Abelson and G. J. Sussman (Cambridge, Mass.: MIT Press, 1984).

This is an indescribably fine book. It grew out of the notes for the introductory computer science course at MIT. The thrust is not directly at AI because the course imparts the accumulated wisdom of twenty years' experience developing large software systems. The book teaches Scheme, which is a dialect of Lisp. One of the exercises is a rule interpreter, which is the core of an expert system. No computernik's education is complete without this book.

Expert Systems

Expert systems are so old that there are beginning to be lucid books on the subject.

The Mythical Man-Month: Essays in Software Engineering, by F. P. Brooks (Reading, Mass.: Addison-Wesley, 1975).

Brooks describes many of the pitfalls in developing large software projects. Expert systems are large software projects, and managers should read this book before doing anything with expert systems.

Expert Systems, by Paul Harmon and Dave King (New York: Wiley, 1985).

Limited but broad and clear coverage of building and using expert systems. This is a good place to acquire a management overview. There are many diagrams that explain a number of issues that must be confronted in building a successful expert system. The authors discuss many different sets of expert system development tools. Implementers are probably better off with *Programming Expert Systems in OPS5* because it goes into more detail but should probably start with this book.

An Overview of Expert Systems, NBSIR 82-2525 (Gaithersburg, Md.: National Bureau of Standards, 1983).

This pamphlet is exactly what it claims to be. For those who are not sure they want an expert system, this book collects page after page of lists of expert systems, tells who did them, and what they were designed to do. The introduction tells how expert systems work.

Building Expert Systems, by F. Hayes-Roth, D. Waterman, and D. Lenat (Reading, Mass.: Addison-Wesley, 1983).

This is a neat book that tells what expert systems are, tells how to build one, tells how to evaluate an expert system once it is running, and compares different languages and tools which have been used for expert systems. The hints for keeping experts happy while computer types debrief them are very good.

Knowledge Based Systems in Artificial Intelligence, by R. Davis and D. Lenat (New York: McGraw-Hill, 1982).

The first half of this book discusses a program that hunts for new mathematical facts. The second section tells how to make an expert system user friendly. Davis gives specific ways to make it easy for experts to add rules themselves. The book is extremely well written. As an aside, Davis wins prizes for well-written papers. I read anything by Davis that I run across.

Programming Expert Systems in OPS5, by L. Brownston, R. Farrell, E. Kant, and N. Martin (Reading, Mass.: Addison-Wesley 1985).

OPS5 is a forward-chaining expert system language that was used to write R1, an expert system that configures DEC VAXes. This book is meatier than most introductions to expert systems because it includes code and explains how the code works. It has short reviews of fourteen expert system languages, some of which are available commercially. It is probably a good idea to read that section before buying an expert system development package.

The Emycin Manual, by W. Van Melle, A. Scott, J. Bennett, and M. Peairs, Report STAN-CS-81-885 (Stanford, Calif.: Department of Computer Science, Stanford University, 1981).

Mycin was one of the first medical expert systems. Emycin, which stands for Essential Mycin, is Mycin with the medical rules stripped out. Although Emycin runs only on PDP-10's, reading the user's manual tells a lot about how it works. Source code is also available, which is a good source of ideas. Texas Instruments sells an expert system shell called "Personal Consultant" which was based on Emycin.

The Rosie Language Reference Manual, Report N-1647-ARPA, (Santa Monica, Calif.: Rand Corporation, 1981).

Rosie is a language for writing expert systems. The Rosie syntax is designed to resemble English as much as possible. There are two other Rosie reports to order at the same time: *Programming in Rosie* (N-1646-ARPA) and *Rationale and Motivation for Rosie* (N-1648-ARPA). Rosie is written in InterLisp, which runs on VAXes and on Xerox Lisp machines, and is available from the Rand Corporation.

OPS5 User's Manual (Pittsburgh, Penn.: Computer Science Department, Carnegie-Mellon University).

R1, the expert system that configures VAXes for Digital Equipment Corporation, was written in OPS5. The program and documentation are available from Carnegie-Mellon University. OPS5 is offered commercially by Computer*Thought Corp. of Plano, Texas.

A Characterization of Expert System Development Tools for Industrial Applications, (College Station, Texas: Knowledge Based Systems Laboratory, Department of Industrial Engineering, Texas A&M University, 1986).

This report describes a study of expert system shells from the point of view of assessing their suitability for industrial applications. The first half of the report discusses criteria by which expert system development tools should be evaluated. The rest is a detailed evaluation of eight commercial shells according to the criteria described in the first half.

Prolog

Prolog is the base language for the Japanese Fifth Generation Computer Project and is easier to learn than Lisp. The problem is that Prolog supports only backward chaining, which figures out how to achieve goals. In expert systems of any real size, programmers need forward chaining to look at facts and figure out what goal to achieve first. Although it is possible to express forward-chaining rules in backward notation, it is inconvenient. It is likely that future expert system languages will support both.

Programming in Prolog, by W. Clocksin and C. Mellish (New York: Springer-Verlag, 1984).

This is a good introduction to programming in Prolog, with a number of examples. The Prolog syntax described in this book has become an unofficial language standard.

micro-Prolog: Programming in Logic, by K. Clark and E. McCabe (Englewood Cliffs, N.J.: Prentice-Hall, 1984).

micro-Prolog is a Prolog dialect intended for small computers. It is available for the Z80 under CP/M80, for the IBM PC under MS DOS, and for computers that run UNIX. There are many exercises, and answers are given. The book starts with simple exercises to introduce the concept of logic programming and works through more complicated examples at the end. Because so much of the book is devoted to doing things with Prolog, the book *Programming in Prolog* might also be useful, as it spends more time on the language itself.

The Art of Prolog, by L Sterling and E. Shapiro (Cambridge, Mass.: MIT Press, 1986).

This book is an advanced introduction to Prolog and its programming techniques. It explains both the basics and the novel programming methods Prolog makes possible.

Object-Oriented Programming

Smalltalk-80: The Language and Its Implementation, by Adele Goldberg and David Robson (Reading, Mass.: Addison-Wesley, 1983).

Goldberg and Robson explain the vision behind the creation of the Smalltalk object-oriented programming language. This book explains the language and tells how it was implemented.

Smalltalk 80: The Interactive Programming Environment, by Adele Goldberg (Reading, Mass.: Addison-Wesley, 1983).

Smalltalk 80: Bits of History, Words of Advice, by Glen Krasner (Reading, Mass.: Addison-Wesley, 1983).

Smalltalk V: Object-Oriented Programming System, (Los Angeles, Calif.: Digitalk Inc, 1986).

This is the user's manual for an excellent Smalltalk system for the IBM PC.

Japan

Shadows of the Rising Sun: A Critical View of the Japanese Miracle, by Jared Taylor (New York: Morrow, 1983).

Americans share a world with the Japanese and need to know what makes them run. Taylor explains what is really driving the Japanese when they come after your markets. He describes the cultural mechanism and human cost behind Japanese success. Americans may have to adopt some Japanese methods, but there are many aspects of Japanese culture we should not copy. Japan is more like a termite colony than a society of individuals. Chapters on hierarchy, conformity, groups, and corporations help you cooperate with the Japanese where you can and compete with them when you must. One reader said, "This book would have saved me a lot of money in my dealings with the Japanese. Wish I'd had it years ago."

The Mind of the Strategist, by Kenichi Ohmae (New York: McGraw-Hill, 1982).

Ohmae is the managing director of McKinsey & Co. in Tokyo. He presents some of the mental processes behind business decisions made by major Japanese companies.

Research Report on Fifth Generation Computer Systems Project, available from Institute for New Generation Computer Technology (ICOT), Mita Kokusai Bldg., 21st Floor, 4-28 Mita, 1-Chome, Minato Ku, Tokyo 108, Japan.

This report describes the goals, organization, and progress of the Fifth Generation project as of March 1983. There is relatively little technical detail, but the report lists the heads of committees dealing with various parts of the project and talks about publications that resulted from the work. The report gives an overview of the project and its future plans.

A Perspective on the Japanese FGCS Project, by Toshio Yokoi, Technical Memorandum TM-0026 (Tokyo: ICOT, 1983).

This report breaks down the various ICOT tasks and tells what they are trying to accomplish. The Fifth Generation Computer System (FGCS) project is intended to research and develop the technology to build computer systems equipment with knowledge processing capabilities, which ICOT expects to come into wide use in the 1990s. FGCS is working on only part of the technologies that will be needed for the coming revolution in computer use. FGCS covers networking to share data more effectively among computers. This work is being done mainly by Nippon Telegraph and Telephone Public Corporation (NTT).

ICOT is also working on man-machine interfaces with the goal of holding conversations between humans and computers. They are also working on methods of encoding broad areas of knowledge in a form in which it can be processed by a computer. ICOT is trying to extend the ideas of data processing and database management to process knowledge as well. They do not intend to restrict this capability to any single area of knowledge but want to cover knowledge in general. The Japanese are also interested in automatic programming because they feel that they are not able to program well.

FGCS is augmenting the Prolog language so that it can be processed by parallel hardware. This holds the potential of breaking through the technical limitations on computer speed. I hear rumors that they have added enough functions to Prolog to implement an operating system, and that it now looks like Lisp, but those stories may turn out to be as valid as the prewar rumors that the Japanese could not pilot fighter aircraft because their legs were too short to reach the pedals.

Inference Machine: From Sequential to Parallel, by Shunichi Uchida, Memo TR0011 (Tokyo: ICOT, May 1983).

This report describes progress in modifying Prolog so that it can be processed with parallel hardware architecture.

The Fifth Generation: Artificial Intelligence and Japan's Computer Challenge to the World, by Edward Feigenbaum and Pamela McCorduck (Reading, Mass.: Addison-Wesley, 1983).

The subtitle is more accurate than the title. Only section 4 deals with Japan. The other six sections are a general introduction to AI without enough detail to tell what to do. Other sections tell what England and France are doing, what the United States should do, and why AI is important to the future of humanity.

Other References

Agha, G. 1987. *Actors: A Model of Concurrent Computation in Distributed Systems*. Cambridge, Mass.: MIT Press.

Aho, A.V., and J.D. Ullman, 1972. *The Theory of Parsing, Translation, and Compiling*. Englewood Cliffs, N.J.: Prentice Hall.

Aho, A.V., R. Sethi, and J.D. Ullman, 1986. *Compilers, Principles, Techniques, and Tools*. Reading, Mass.: Addison-Wesley.

Aleksander, I. 1978. *The Human Machine: A View of Intelligent Mechanisms.* St. Saphorin, Switzerland: Georgi.

Brady, J. M., ed. 1981. *Computer Vision.* Amsterdam: North-Holland.

Edelman, G.M. 1978. *The Mindful Brain.* Cambridge, Mass.: MIT Press.

Grimson, W., and R. Patil, eds. 1987. *AI in the 1980's and Beyond: An MIT Survey.* Cambridge Mass.: MIT Press.

Horn, B.K.P. 1971. *The Binford-Horn Line Finder.* AIM-285. Cambridge, Mass.: The Artificial Intelligence Laboratory, MIT.

Marcus, M.P. 1980. *A Theory of Syntactic Recognition for Natural Language.* Cambridge, Mass.: MIT Press.

Marr, D. 1975. *Early Processing of Visual Information.* AIM-340. Cambridge, Mass.: The Artificial Intelligence Laboratory, MIT.

Michie, D., ed. 1982. *Introductory Readings in Expert Systems.* New York: Gordon & Breach.

Mishkoff, H. 1985. *Understanding Artificial Intelligence.* Dallas, Texas: Texas Instruments.

Nilsson, N.J. 1971. *Problem Solving Methods in Artificial Intelligence.* New York: McGraw-Hill.

O'Shea, T., and M. Eisenstadt, eds. 1984. *Artificial Intelligence: Tools, Applications, and Techniques.* New York: Harper & Row.

Popek, G., and B. Walker. 1985. *The Locus Distributed System Architecture.* Cambridge, Mass.: MIT Press.

Rich, E. 1983. *Artificial Intelligence.* New York: McGraw-Hill.

Schank, R. 1977. "Representation and Understanding of Text." Machine Intelligence 8:575-619.

Scown, S.J. 1985. *The Artificial Intelligence Experience: An Introduction.* Bedford, Mass.: Digital Press.

Sugihara, K. 1987. *Machine Interpretation of Line Drawings.* Cambridge, Mass.: MIT Press.

Sussman, G.J. 1975. *A Computer Model of Skill Acquisition.* New York: American Elsevier.

Tennant, H. 1981. *Natural Language Processing.* New York: Petrocelli Books, Inc.

Ullman, S. 1979. *The Interpretation of Visual Motion.* Cambridge, Mass.: MIT Press.

Weizenbaum, J. 1976. *Computer Power and Human Reason: From Judgement to Calculation.* San Francisco, Calif.: Freeman.

Winograd, T. 1976. *Understanding Natural Language.* New York: Academic Press.

Winograd, T. 1983. *Language as a Cognitive Process, Volume I: Syntax.* Reading, Mass.: Addison-Wesley.

Winston, P., ed. 1975. *The Psychology of Computer Vision.* New York: McGraw-Hill.

Winston, P., and K. Pendergasst, eds. 1986. *The AI Business.* Cambridge, Mass.: MIT Press.

Index